A History of
Elementary Social Studies

HISTORY OF SCHOOLS & SCHOOLING

Alan R. Sadovnik and Susan F. Semel
General Editors

Vol. 53

The History of Schools and Schooling series
is part of the Peter Lang Education list.
Every volume is peer reviewed and meets
the highest quality standards for content and production.

PETER LANG
New York • Washington, D.C./Baltimore • Bern
Frankfurt • Berlin • Brussels • Vienna • Oxford

Anne-Lise Halvorsen

A History of Elementary Social Studies

Romance and Reality

PETER LANG
New York • Washington, D.C./Baltimore • Bern
Frankfurt • Berlin • Brussels • Vienna • Oxford

KH

Library of Congress Cataloging-in-Publication Data

Halvorsen, Anne-Lise.
A history of elementary social studies: romance and reality /
Anne-Lise Halvorsen.
pages cm. — (History of schools and schooling; v. 53)
Includes bibliographical references and index.
1. Social sciences—Study and teaching (Elementary)
2. Social sciences—Study and teaching—History. I. Title.
LB1584.H25 372.83—dc23 2012039905
ISBN 978-1-4331-2286-6 (hardcover)
ISBN 978-1-4331-0647-7 (paperback)
ISBN 978-1-4539-0921-8 (e-book)
ISSN 1089-0678

Bibliographic information published by **Die Deutsche Nationalbibliothek.**
Die Deutsche Nationalbibliothek lists this publication in the "Deutsche
Nationalbibliografie"; detailed bibliographic data is available
on the Internet at http://dnb.d-nb.de/.

Cover photos: Detroit Schools, Upper and Lower Elementary
Classrooms ca. 1930s. Reprinted courtesy of the Walter P. Reuther
Library, Wayne State University.

The paper in this book meets the guidelines for permanence and durability
of the Committee on Production Guidelines for Book Longevity
of the Council of Library Resources.

Printed in the United States of America

10/6/14

Dedication

For Bil, Spencer, and Toby

Contents

Acknowledgments

In various ways, researching and writing this book pattern its subject, the origins and development of elementary social studies education. Both processes have been long, often complex, journeys, guided by passion, commitment, and good intentions. Although no book can fully describe the rich history of elementary social studies, the attempt here is to tell as complete and balanced a story as possible. Although many people have guided me on this journey, I am responsible for my conclusions and any errors.

The book has its roots in my doctoral studies and my dissertation. Throughout the process of writing both the dissertation and the book, many organizations, colleagues, students, friends, and family members have supported me. I am grateful to the Spencer Foundation, the University of Michigan School of Education, and the Michigan State University College of Education for funding my data collection and analysis. I thank the archivists and librarians at the Dolph Briscoe Center for American History (University of Texas, Austin), the Hoover Institution on War, Revolution, and Peace (Stanford University), the Library of Congress, and Teachers College (Columbia University): all have been extremely helpful. I am grateful to Susan Semel and Alan Sadovnik who accepted my book proposal and provided support throughout the writing process. I thank Peter Lang and its encouraging and patient staff, especially Sophie Appel and Chris Myers.

Many scholars in social studies education, the history of education, and beyond have given me valuable feedback on drafts of this book or have assisted in other ways. I am grateful to the members of my dissertation committee: Jeff Mirel (my advisor), Bob Bain, Annemarie Palincsar, and Maris Vinovskis, all of whom challenged me to reframe and clarify my arguments and ultimately to write a better dissertation. Keith Barton, Chara Bohan, Jere Brophy, Lauren McArthur Harris, Mark Helmsing, Stephanie Serriere, Kathy Swan, Suzanne Wilson, and

Joe Watras read sections of the book and offered critical and helpful feedback. In addition to providing commentary on Chapter 4, Jared Stallones generously shared resources on Paul Hanna. Jan Alleman, who, in many ways, has played a key role in the history of elementary social studies, read and commented helpfully on several chapters. Ron Evans, who read the book in draft, provided astute criticism and good ideas that improved the book greatly. Jeff Mirel, who read numerous drafts, offered insightful suggestions, many of them humorous, with each reading. All these friends and colleagues encouraged me to do justice to the story of elementary social studies education.

Stimulating discussions with my former and current students— undergraduate teacher candidates, master's students, and doctoral students—have kept me focused on the purpose of the book as well as reminded me of social studies in the "real world" of elementary schools. Their observations and questions about the goals and content of social studies education have influenced many of the book's arguments. In the kindergarten classes I taught, I learned in practice how ideas in social studies stimulate and challenge young minds.

Many good friends have contributed, directly and indirectly, to this book. David Harris, Marcia Harris, and Virginia Walden sparked my interest and eventual passion for social studies education for young students. I wish every student had the opportunity to learn from them. My interest in social studies education and the history of education developed among a lively group of fellow students at the University of Michigan School of Education. In particular, Tim Cain has been an excellent, all-around resource for me during my writing process. Francesca Forzani has provided invaluable intellectual and personal support. I am also grateful to many wonderful colleagues and friends at Michigan State University who are deeply committed to teacher education and K-12 education. In so many ways, Suzanne Wilson, my good friend and my department chair at Michigan State University, has supported this endeavor with her genuine interest in the topic and her probing questions. I am especially grateful to Jeff and Barbara Mirel who helped me in every stage of my dissertation and book, nourishing me with good food and wine, surpassed only by their conversation.

It surely took a family to complete this book. I am inspired by the dedication of the many public school educators in my family: my mother, my sister, and members of my family-in-law. My sister, Karin Halvorsen, and her husband, Jes Buehler, as well the entire Lusa clan have patiently endured hearing about this book and have also taken care of our children many times so that I could work on it. My parents, Marcia and Bill Halvorsen, helped greatly with the editing and formatting of the book. They also instilled in me the values of hard work, education, and civic commitment—all essential values needed for writing this book.

I dedicate this book to my husband, Bil Lusa, and our two children, Spencer and Toby. With humor, kindness, and love, they have provided support that made writing this book possible. As a committed, knowledgeable, and active citizen, Bil is a model of the future citizen that social studies educators strive for. It is my hope this book inspires them to continue working to preserve social studies in the elementary school—for Spencer, Toby, and all our youngest citizens.

Portions of Chapter 1, used with permission, are from Anne-Lise Halvorsen, "Back to the Future: The Expanding Communities Curriculum in Geography Education," *The Social Studies* 100, no. 3 (2009): 115–20. Copyright 2009 by Heldref Publications.

Introduction

Challenges for Elementary Social Studies

SOCIAL STUDIES, the multidisciplinary field of history and social science disciplines, first appeared as a school subject in the early twentieth century. Its creation was inspired by the desire among education practitioners and theorists to revitalize and restructure history and social science education. Its mission has never changed: to teach the principles of democratic citizenship and the core values of social responsibility. To that end, it draws upon the disciplines of economics, geography, history, and political science, among other social sciences, to engage students in the study of the human condition. Throughout the twentieth century, educators have developed innovative social studies programs to teach students how people live and work, how communities are governed, how institutions affect human life, and how the past shapes the present and future. Social studies teachers engage students in analysis of issues, in interpretation of evidence, and in reasoned study of traditions and cultures.

Since the introduction of the field, educators have argued that elementary school students (kindergarten through fifth grade) are capable of rigorous, active learning in social studies. Even before social studies replaced individual lessons in history and the social sciences, educators thought children could apply critical thinking to these subjects, as evidenced by a statement from the Detroit Board of Education in 1920: elementary education should give children "...not a head full of facts, but a head full of ideas; not rules of conduct learned, but the ability to conduct one's self properly; not a pupil knowing civics, but one who can think over civic questions...."[1] Using a variety of active instructional approaches intended to engage and challenge students, elementary social studies is the study of families, peers, cultures, institutions, and, not least, the students themselves.

Despite the constancy of its mission and the creativity of its programs, social studies now faces serious challenges in the elementary curriculum. Does social studies accomplish what it intends? Are the content and pedagogy of social studies relevant to students' lives? Does social studies challenge students intellectually? Does social studies motivate students to become committed citizens? Will social studies even survive? These are not new challenges for social studies, which has never had as much instructional time in the elementary school day as the language arts and mathematics. However, in the twenty-first century, in part the result of the force of the standards and accountability movements, the crisis in elementary social studies has intensified.

There is ample evidence of the declining position of social studies in the elementary school curriculum. We need only read the No Child Left Behind Act of 2001 (NCLB), the most important federal education legislation in recent years, which largely ignores social studies (at both elementary and secondary levels) in its recommendations for improving public education.[2] The 2008 Center on Education Policy's study of 229 school districts across the country found subjects not tested under NCLB were increasingly de-emphasized.[3] Of the four main academic areas, social studies has the least funding (for research and professional development) and the least instruction time in elementary schools.[4] This minimal amount of instruction time for social studies is particularly acute at the lower elementary level (grades K–2) although the situation at the upper elementary level (grades 3–5) is also a concern.

The fierce, often ideological, controversies about the goals, content, and methods of elementary social studies, which fragment educators and scholars, have weakened its support. Since social studies was first taught as a separate subject, there has been disagreement about what children should be expected to know and be able to do, as well as willing to do, as a result of their social studies lessons. These controversies, as never before, have created confusion, stubborn resistance, and even anger about the nature of social studies.

Another concern, raised by critics past and present, is that elementary social studies lacks sufficient disciplinary rigor.[5] Their main criticism is directed toward the expanding communities approach, long the dominant pedagogical approach in social studies education. The approach is best described as a series of ever-expanding, concentric circles in which kindergarteners study themselves, first graders study their home and school, second graders study their neighborhood or local community, third graders study their city or region, fourth graders study their state, and fifth graders study their country (variations of the approach exist). The main objection to the approach is that its emphasis on children's everyday lives and experiences, especially for the lower elementary grades, means less study of content and skills in history and the social sciences, as well as less study of diverse peoples and places. Students' evaluations of social studies are offered as support for this criticism: typically, elementary school children report disliking social studies because it is "boring" and "useless."[6]

Educators who are dissatisfied with the expanding communities approach have proposed various alternatives. For example, Jere Brophy and Janet Alleman have created an approach based on the study of "cultural universals": the enduring fundamentals of human life such as food, clothing, communication, transportation, and government.[7] Others favor an approach that highlights history and geography. For example, E. D. Hirsch Jr.'s Core Knowledge Sequence, a cultural literacy curriculum, uses story, drama, art, music, and discussion to teach significant people, places, and events.[8] Still others have proposed the social justice approach to social studies in which students study democratic values, evaluate historical narratives, and are taught to censure injustice and prejudice.[9] None of these approaches, however, despite reports of positive results in their limited usage, has displaced the expanding communities approach.

Despite its widespread use in U.S. public school education (as well as in U.S. private school education and in school systems around the world), not all social studies advocates support the expanding communities approach. Nevertheless, they have accepted the approach as the de facto curriculum[10] and approve its promotion, in John Dewey's terms, of the psychological over the logical (i.e., the importance of personal experience over subject matter learning).[11] The orderly, progressive steps of the expanding communities approach structure the curriculum into social units that increase in complexity, year after year.[12] Although we lack empirical evidence on the effectiveness of the approach, teachers' anecdotal comments reveal they find the approach a useful way to organize and teach elementary social studies. According to many teachers, children are very interested in exploring their surroundings, a key feature of the approach.

These challenges in elementary social studies—its diminishing place in the curriculum and the content and process controversy it provokes—call for thoughtful consideration. The citizenship and social responsibility mission of social studies education in the twenty-first century is no less important than it was when social studies first entered elementary schools. To the early twentieth-century list of threats to humanity, such as famine, human migration, and war, we have now added the existential threats of terrorism, climate change, nuclear warfare, and environmental devastation. And despite the progress made by individuals and organizations, we still struggle with corrosive and divisive economic, political, religious, and racial discord. Therefore, teaching children to be responsible national and world citizens remains a worthy goal in social studies education.

How did social studies reach this troubled and uncertain state? Why has social studies been marginalized in the elementary school day? To answer these questions, this book recounts the history of elementary social studies in the United States, beginning with its mid-nineteenth-century antecedents. This is the history of pedagogical assumptions and learning theories, of distinguished social studies scholars and educators, of powerful national organizations, of local educators and their curricula, and of ideological conflicts over the content and purpose of social studies. Moreover, the book reflects on the global and national issues that influenced the origins and development of elementary social studies. This history, which is often one of confused goals, cross-purposes, and deep divisions among theorists and practitioners, identifies the sources of many problems in contemporary social studies education. It explains why one particular approach has thrived in elementary social studies. It also highlights imaginative, rigorous alternative pedagogical approaches that may offer direction for reformers of social studies education.

Goals of the Book

The book is foremost a chronology of elementary social studies education, from its origins in nineteenth-century history and geography lessons to its current position in the curriculum as a stand-alone subject. This chronology provides the framework for the book's goals. One goal is to raise awareness of the endangered position of social studies in U.S. elementary schools. Despite the general consensus that elementary school children should learn the principles of democracy and the responsibilities of citizenship, social studies has not always succeeded in this mission. Much of the problem stems from the field's low status (and limited instructional time). This examination of how elementary social studies education evolved can illuminate not only its successes and its struggles but also help guide its revitalization.

A second goal of the book is to place social studies education, the most comprehensive and long-lasting reform effort of the Progressive Era, in its historical context. Much of elementary social studies education has not changed since it was introduced in the 1920s and 1930s. This is particularly true of the expanding communities approach to teaching social studies. Popularized in the 1930s by Paul Robert Hanna's textbooks, this approach has influenced local, state, and national recommendations for social studies ever since. It is one of the most enduring and important examples of progressive educational pedagogy in the history of U.S. education. While alternative approaches have been proposed, and some schools use them, none has had the same success or influence. This account of the expanding communities approach, which addresses the reasons for its longevity, helps us understand why pedagogical reforms survive.

A third goal of the book is to call attention to the gap between theory and practice in elementary social studies education. Survival is only one definition of success. As the book recounts, even with worthy intentions and well-thought-out assumptions, elementary social studies programs and methods have often not fulfilled their promise. Progressive Era education theorists intended school study to be lively, engaging, and relevant, but all too often the instruction they introduced (including social studies instruction) was, and is, none of these. With elementary social studies as the example, this book discusses this complex relationship between educational theory and practice and explores the difficulty in harmonizing social studies topics and discipline-based content.

Methodology of the Book

The book is a response to the 1981 call by O. L. Davis Jr. for "significant interpretive histories" that follow an interpretive framework used cautiously and reflectively to "understand" the field of social studies.[13] Since 1981, many education historians have written about social studies education, particularly secondary social studies education. The focus of the book is elementary social studies education with its various movements, influential institutions, leading figures, and historical turning points. The book may inspire others to write about the history of elementary social studies. Such histories will tell us more about how elementary social studies developed and may help guide its future direction.[14]

The book also responds to the recommendation by Christine Woyshner that histories of social studies should look beyond national reports in order to describe how social studies was taught in local settings.[15] While the book's underlying narrative structure is social studies at the national level, there are also data from local school districts that reflect the influence of national trends. These data are used to reconstruct, within the limitations of the available information, representative local social studies curricula "in practice." The primary sources for the national data are the American Historical Association Records, the National Council for the Social Studies Records, and the Paul Robert Hanna Papers. The primary sources for the local data are the curricular documents and superintendents' reports from several urban public school districts, including districts in Chicago, Cleveland, Detroit, and Grand Rapids. In addition, many accounts of curriculum history and the history of social studies inform this study, in particular books by Ronald Evans and Jared Stallones.[16]

Chapter Organization

Chapter 1 describes the elementary school curriculum in the nineteenth century. That curriculum was mostly "the three Rs" with a smattering of history and geography. History education in these years was the study of American heroes, patriotism, and good citizenship. In geography, children read maps and studied their local environment. While instruction was mostly memorization and recitation, there were glimpses of the child-centered education that the Progressive Era later promoted. The founding of the American Historical Association in the late nineteenth century was an important event in the chronology of social studies; it was the first professional organization to influence history education as well as social studies education.

Chapter 2 narrates the rise of social studies in the early twentieth century as this multidisciplinary subject began to replace history and geography lessons at the elementary level. These were the years in which urbanization, immigration, and social reforms provided the context for this complicated, new subject area whose main goal was to promote good citizenship. The Progressive Era introduced new pedagogical approaches that challenged traditional approaches, such as those featured in the new history and the child-centered education movements. The philosophies and approaches of these movements resonated with social studies advocates who sought to develop a field of study that would be relevant and engaging to children.

Chapter 3 focuses on the development of the social studies curriculum in the inter-war years of the mid-twentieth century. The National Council for the Social Studies, founded in 1921, assumed its role as the foremost advocate of social studies education. The American Historical Association, which had been closely involved in making recommendations for history instruction, began its retreat from elementary education. By the early 1940s, social studies had replaced history and geography lessons in elementary schools.

Chapter 4 describes Paul Robert Hanna's contribution to social studies education. More than any other educator, Hanna influenced the content and approach of elementary social studies with his curriculum work and his numerous articles and speeches on social studies and progressive education. One of his most famous articles addressed the dualism of "romance or reality" in progressive education.[17] According to Hanna, those who favored the romance, the "romantics," thought children should read legends, myths, and narratives from history; those who favored the reality, the "realists," thought children should study contemporary problems and issues. This dualism has troubled social studies education ever since.

Hanna also wrote social studies textbooks that popularized the expanding communities approach so successfully that their topics-based scope and their structured sequence became, and have remained, the standard in elementary social studies education. However, these textbooks, often criticized for their superficial coverage of topics, did not address the larger themes of social reconstruction that Hanna promoted in his scholarly writings.

Chapter 5 traces elementary social studies education from the 1940s to the 1970s. Despite the many social and political changes in the country, of the kind social studies would be expected to address, elementary social studies was essentially static. While there were a few experiments with new approaches that recognized these changes (e.g., intercultural education, Man: A Course of Study, issues-centered social studies, and ethnic studies) and some textbooks began to address cultural and social issues, most of these new approaches were short-lived. None replaced the expanding communities approach. The most significant event in social studies education in these years was its steadily diminishing place in the school day.

Chapter 6 presents the history of elementary social studies from the late twentieth century to the present. This is the period, often referred to as the Eras of Educational Excellence and Accountability, when educators and others, notably politicians, called for performance standards in all school subjects and greater teacher and school accountability. Disciplinary scholars wrote voluntary national content standards in civics and government, economics, geography, and history. The states wrote their own content standards that were usually aligned with their standardized assessments. The chapter describes the continuing decline of elementary social studies, particularly after the enactment of NCLB, which called for new education standards and assessments for English language arts and mathematics but made no reference to social studies.

The Conclusion presents opportunities for those educators and scholars who wish to strengthen and preserve the place of social studies in the elementary curriculum. These opportunities derive from this account of the origins and development of social studies. They include more interdisciplinary cooperation, more commitment of intellectual and financial resources, more innovation in textbook selection, more experimentation with non-traditional pedagogical approaches, and more cross-disciplinary integration.

The book makes few detailed recommendations for social studies education. A historical study does not lead to prescriptions. Readers must look elsewhere for specific recommendations on learning outcomes (e.g., standards, content expectations, and learning objectives), the curricular content of elementary social studies, and social education beyond the official curriculum (e.g., out-of-school learning opportunities, the implicit curriculum, and the hidden curriculum). However, the book does charge reform-minded policymakers and educators with the tasks of developing research-tested curricular materials for social studies and of creating assessments that measure student achievement in social studies.

The history of elementary social studies is not simply accounts of winners and losers, of opportunities seized or lost, of infighting among educators and scholars, or of ideological wars among politicians, the media, and the public—all of which this book describes. Those are only episodes in the broader narrative of a subject area that has never abandoned the noble intentions it began with. It is still the task of elementary teachers to teach children the knowledge, skills, and values of civic competency and social responsibility in active, engaging, and thoughtful ways. Yet social studies educators and theorists, school administrators, politicians, and concerned citizens have struggled to find a way for social studies to fulfill these noble intentions. This book narrates that struggle between romance and reality in the history of elementary social studies.

Chapter 1

Before Social Studies: Nineteenth-Century History and Geography Education

IN THE NINETEENTH CENTURY, children did not have social studies lessons. In fact, social studies was not taught as a school subject until the early twentieth century. Children in the nineteenth century learned good citizenship and moral behavior (the same focus social studies eventually took) in all their lessons, especially in their readers and their history and geography study. Although history and geography were not a major part of that curriculum, it was in those lessons that children also learned about their country. For these reasons, it is important to look at the nineteenth-century history and geography curriculum, which was the predecessor of social studies education. This chapter, which draws in part on textbooks, readers, and curricular documents from the Michigan public schools in Detroit and Grand Rapids, demonstrates that despite many historians' claim that the nineteenth-century curriculum was dull as well as irrelevant to students' lives, there is some evidence to the contrary. Even before the Progressive Era, as the descriptions of the school materials suggest, a few educators were attempting to add some spark to the curriculum while still emphasizing subject content. Although these materials do not necessarily tell us what teachers taught, teachers used them (and almost exclusively) for classroom instruction. Therefore, they are our best sources for understanding how geography and history were taught in the nineteenth century.

The chapter begins with a general description of nineteenth-century schooling and of the elementary curriculum (particularly, geography and history). Then the chapter deals with new developments in pedagogy that influenced elementary teaching and introduces the American Historical Association, the first national organization to make recommendations for history education. This analysis of the nineteenth-century elementary curriculum is background for the following chapters' analysis of twentieth-century elementary social studies.

Elementary Schooling and Curriculum in the Nineteenth Century

There was a wave of social reforms in the years between 1830 and 1860 in the United States. These reforms included the abolition of slavery, the temperance movement, and the founding of orphanages, prisons, and hospitals.[1] Many nineteenth-century reformers thought public education was the best hope for convincing citizens that these reforms were needed (although there was much controversy over how to build a coherent school system).[2] The most famous of the nineteenth-century education reformers was probably Horace Mann, the Secretary of the Massachusetts State Board of Education from 1837 to 1848. Mann, who championed public education for all children, laid the foundation for the country's public school system, known at the time as the common schools. In a series of twelve annual reports, he described the need for a good public education system. In the last of these reports, he famously described the common schools as "the great equalizer of the conditions of men—the balance wheel of the social machinery."[3]

These schools were called common schools because they were commonly available to all White children: tax-supported and free.[4] However, common schools across the country were anything but common in structure. They were found in the Northeast and Midwest but rarely in the South.[5] Even in the Northeast and Midwest, common schools differed. Some were small schools with only five to ten students, all family-related, and others were large, overcrowded schools with children from different families and different backgrounds. School settings could be barns, living rooms, one-room schoolhouses, or churches.[6] Teachers were usually young, unmarried women. Women could be paid much less than men and were thought better teachers for young children.[7] Moreover, there were few other occupations open to single women in the nineteenth century. Republicanism, Protestantism, and capitalism were the dominant ideologies in the country and in education. The most important goal of the common schools was to develop children's character, both personal and civic.[8]

Children in the common schools learned from the readers their families sent to school. Publishers produced readers directed at a range of skills so that children, at various levels, could use them year after year as they progressed through the grades. Children read at their desks and occasionally approached the teacher to recite memorized passages. Of course, there was little consistency in the selection of readers used in classrooms.[9] Nineteenth-century educators depended on the readers, however, since teachers generally could teach only a few school subjects.[10] While there may have been the occasional exception, teachers in general did not have the expertise or the time to teach these texts in pedagogically innovative or engaging ways. By the 1840s, state legislatures, particularly those in Eastern states such as Massachusetts, passed laws that required schools to use specific textbooks.[11] The intention was to ensure that school children had the same (and proper) books. When enacted, and followed, these laws probably brought some uniformity to the curriculum.

Gradually, support for the common schools grew in the years before the Civil War, virtually silencing the opposition to them. The goals of the common schools (i.e., tax-supported, uniform, nonsectarian, open to all White children, and with professionally trained teachers) were not yet fully achieved (especially in the South), but progress was steady, helped by the compulsory schooling laws.[12] Graded schooling, in which children were grouped in separate classrooms according to their accomplishments (rather than their ages), began to replace the one-room schoolhouse, especially in urban areas.[13] Normal schools, which trained many of the nation's teachers, were founded, and professional standards for teachers were established.[14]

During these years, challenges to the traditional pedagogy in schools increased. Two Europeans were particularly critical of this pedagogy: the Swiss educator, Johann Pestalozzi, and his follower, the German pedagogue, Friedrich Wilhelm August Froebel. They recommended approaches that were quite different from traditional pedagogy. In their approach to teaching, the emphasis was on learning through activities and physical contact with the world, which often meant abandoning the textbook for experiential learning.[15]

Some historians argue that in the nineteenth century, particularly after 1860, Pestalozzi's theories dominated elementary school reform.[16] Pestalozzi, inspired by the philosopher, Jean-Jacques Rousseau, encouraged children to experience natural objects rather than to study words and abstract concepts they did not understand. The Pestalozzian notion of "sense perception," the idea that people learn through their senses, was the basis for the object method of instruction. The method recommended that children should see and touch objects, not just read about them or listen to the teacher describe them. Such an instructional method had new implications for education since it favored direct student involvement with objects over textbook study; this became an education theme in the Progressive Era in the twentieth century.

Froebel, best known as the founder of the kindergarten movement, argued that children have certain natural impulses and desires—the need to play, the need for real-life experiences, and the need to handle objects and materials. School should recognize these needs and adapt instruction to meet them. At the time, these were radical ideas about teaching.[17] Yet today, some of Froebel's methods are still used in kindergartens. He also inspired generations of followers, the Froebelians, who, variously interpreting his work, determined to change how children experienced schooling. They had more influence on geography study than history study, perhaps because there are more opportunities in geography lessons to handle objects (e.g., maps, globes, and plants) and to visit places (e.g., local landforms and bodies of water).

Although neither geography nor history held the valued place in the elementary school that reading, writing, spelling, and arithmetic did, teachers devoted *some* attention to these two subjects.[18] Four themes emerge that describe how geography and history were taught in the nineteenth century. First, by the mid-nineteenth century, geography was more often taught as a separate course of study than history.[19] Second, history usually appeared in the curriculum in the reading "primers" and in the geography lessons. Third, teachers used the study of history to teach patriotism. Fourth, some educators tried to make both geography and history interactive and engaging.

Nineteenth-Century Geography Education

At the beginning of the nineteenth century, geography was not an individual discipline, even in colleges where it was collapsed into mathematics and astronomy.[20] At the elementary level, where "the three Rs" dominated the curriculum, geography was usually taught in association with other subjects. Yet, as the population west of the Mississippi grew, with the Louisiana Purchase and westward migration, citizens realized they needed to know the geography of their own country. Business interests and other practical pursuits pushed geography into the schools.[21] In addition, Lewis and Clark's account of their Corps of Discovery Expedition to the West Coast from 1804 to 1806 fascinated the public. Not only did citizens need to know the geography of their country, now they wanted to know it.

This interest in geography was also evident at the elementary school level.[22] In 1804, there were only six geography textbooks in print; by 1832, there were thirty-nine.[23] The pedagogy of these texts was traditional: memorization and sometimes question-and-answer activities. For example, an 1814 geography text condensed information from texts for older students into simple, digestible chunks that younger students could memorize and repeat to their teachers.[24]

By the mid-nineteenth century, geography study was becoming more "scientific." Two German geographers, Carl Ritter and Alexander von Humboldt, remembered as the founders of modern geography, traveled widely and wrote prolifically about their travels. They brought a new perspective to geography study with their rejection of "old geography" as a mere collection of facts. Instead, they proposed a new, scientific geography based in inductive reasoning: observing phenomena repeatedly until general laws can be derived. Although Ritter and von Humboldt had no direct influence on elementary instruction in U.S. schools, their ideas influenced American geographers and the geography textbooks they wrote. This was the beginning of a new direction and a new emphasis in geography study.

This new trend in geography scholarship inspired W. C. Woodbridge, the American textbook author.[25] In the textbooks he wrote following his travels and studies in Europe, he conceived of geography study as the study of the earth's topography. The core of the discipline was locating objects and places on maps. Woodbridge advocated, "Let the student next draw simple maps, beginning with a plan of his table, or the room in which he is. Proceeding to delineate successively a plan of the house, garden, neighborhood, and town...."[26] Woodbridge thought that children needed firsthand experience with objects and materials before they studied abstract concepts like longitude and latitude.

This approach, as proposed by Woodbridge, appeared in many other geography texts. For example, another educator recommended geography study that involved "taking the child about his home locality first, then on journeys farther and farther from home."[27] Called "local geography," the approach had emerged in part from the inductive method of studying what is near at hand and then making generalizations from these observations. As a reflection of educators' view of people's natural social development, local geography foreshadowed the sequencing approach known later as the expanding communities approach.[28]

Toward the end of the nineteenth century, geography study became more the study of places and peoples, including the human races. Textbooks compared the customs, habits, and achievements of peoples around the world. In some instances, the comparisons were xenophobic and racist. In her analysis of geography textbooks used in nineteenth-century South Carolina public schools, Mindy Spearman shows that Africans, Indians, Arabs, and Aboriginal Australians were portrayed as odd, uncivilized, savage, and barbarous.[29] Other geography textbooks claimed the Caucasian race was superior to other races and that the United States had a unique place in the world (the American exceptionalism that Frederick Jackson Turner had promoted).[30]

Nineteenth-Century History Education

Elementary school children in the early nineteenth century learned history mostly from their readers although sometimes also from their geography lessons.[31] It was not until the mid-nineteenth century that history became a separate subject in the curriculum in some elementary schools in the East.[32] The most popular readers were by Reverend William Holmes McGuffey (the McGuffey readers) although many other readers were also used.[33] According to Henry H. Vail, the aims of the McGuffey readers were to teach the art of reading, the love of literature, and "true patriotism, integrity, honesty, industry, temperance, courage, politeness, and all other moral and intellectual virtues." The readers quoted the "greats," such as poets, orators, preachers, and historians, and featured significant historic events.[34] George H. Callcott found that history lessons accounted for about 10 percent of *McGuffey's Newly Revised Third Reader* (1848).[35]

History lessons in the nineteenth century, which often glorified American heroes, above all aimed at teaching patriotism and developing moral character.[36] Like geography study, history study was the study of American exceptionalism.[37] For example, Noah Webster, the publisher of the first American dictionary and the author of grammar and spelling texts, wrote of the child, "As soon as he opens his lips, he should rehearse the history of his own country; he should lisp the praise of liberty and of those illustrious heroes and statesmen who have wrought a revolution in her favor."[38] Webster continued, "A love of our country, and an acquaintance with its true state, are indispensable—they should be acquired in early life."[39] Many other American educators and writers in these years concluded that the study of U.S. history could unify the country's diverse groups of people by developing a common historical consciousness among them.[40]

An important consequence of this emphasis on patriotism and citizenship in history study was that textbooks generally avoided controversial topics such as slavery and tariffs. Instead, they focused on unifying national symbols and ideals.[41] Textbooks praised Christianity, market economies, and democratic principles as the bedrock of modern civilization.[42] Teachers should indoctrinate students with lessons in patriotism, morality, and good citizenship. Students were not expected to question, interpret, or evaluate.

There is a common perception that most history instruction in the nineteenth century was general and universal rather than particular and local. It is also thought that the main teaching strategy was "mindless verbatim recitation."[43] The first claim appears well-founded; nineteenth-century history textbooks were mostly general-ized narratives rather than local histories. It is probable that the national textbook market explained this focus. The few textbooks in print were sold throughout the country to readers whose main commonality was their citizenship.

As for the second claim, very likely nineteenth-century history study was generally uninspiring, at least in terms of twentieth- and twenty-first-century ideas about teaching. In most nineteenth-century classrooms, children studied independently (and quietly) as they memorized dates, names, and places. As Barbara Finkelstein found in her study of elementary classrooms from 1820 to 1880, teachers talked, and if children ever spoke, it was only to recite.[44] Children sat at their desks and only stood to recite the passages they had memo-rized. The curriculum was as rigid as their bolt-down desks.[45]

Various other sources confirm this observation that nineteenth-century history study was largely memorization and recitation. For example, histories of curriculum and pedagogy in the Detroit Public Schools reveal that history and geography instruction was mostly dry as bone. One study stated, "[these] early textbooks were unsuited to the interests and experience of children...geographies and histories were purely factual. All the books had fine print and dull covers. Few had pictures."[46] However, many educators recognized the deficiencies of such an approach to history that set aside the analysis of cause and effect. One Chicago educator commented on the nineteenth-century curriculum: "The main discipline was that of the memory, reinforced by the rod. Little appeal was made to the interest, and the availability of the immediate environment as a source of knowledge and power was not dreamed of."[47]

Yet there are challenges to this assessment of nineteenth-century history study. In his examination of history textbooks from these years, Callcott argued that history "led the way" in pedagogical reform. Callcott found that, by the 1830s, history textbook authors were pleading with teachers to emphasize the relevancy of social history (e.g., daily life in the past). According to Callcott, some nineteenth-century textbook authors, in turning away from the march of dates and events, even encouraged teachers to rely less on text-books and more on lecture, classroom discussion, and projects.[48]

It is possible to find evidence for this claim in some nineteenth-century history textbooks. One such book is Peter Parley's *Universal History on the Basis of Geography*.[49] In its preface, Parley rejected the memorization of dates and facts as the way to teach history. He wrote:

> Abridgments of history...are little more than dry lists of dates, presenting no pictures to the imagination, exciting no sympathies in the heart, and imparting few ideas to the understanding. If, by dint of labour, a meager chronological table is extracted by the reader, and fixed in the memory, it is of no practical use. It is but a skeleton, without flesh, sinews, or soul; a mass of words, to which the mind can assign no clear definitions.[50]

Parley began his narrative with local stories and events before working through U.S. history chronologically. The book is lively and engaging, with many pictures and maps. After each chapter, Parley listed questions, some of which invited open-ended responses. A typical question was: "Suppose we should meet with some old building, what should we desire to know?"[51] This is a question that encourages the student to think about the building's history and purpose rather than just memorize its architectural features. Parley's book provides evidence for Callcott's finding that history made its way into the curriculum as "a pleasant and exciting subject of stirring narrative and intellectual adventure."[52]

In the nineteenth century, the expanding communities approach, as it is now known, was more evident in geography study than in history study. However, there were history textbook reviewers who favored a similar approach for teaching history. As one critic explained, "The study of history must be made to begin at the residence of the pupil, and the sphere of historical knowledge be gradually widened, as formerly mentioned."[53] Thus, there were traces of the expanding communities approach in the conversation in this period even if the history textbooks did not use it.[54]

In summary, for most of the nineteenth century, geography and history study, like lessons in other subjects, had little resemblance to the active, child-centered learning approach popularized in the Progressive Era. The schoolroom was a place for silent reading, memorization, and recitation. There was little, if any, "hands-on" learning. However, nineteenth-century geography and history education was more progressive than is often assumed. There were hints that book learning should have relevancy for children's lives. An embryonic form of the expanding communities approach was developing. And educators were raising concerns about the dullness of a pedagogy that emphasized names, dates, and events. In the twentieth century, these ideas would acquire force and support.

New Developments in Pedagogy in the Nineteenth Century

Toward the end of the nineteenth century, elementary studies in general began changing as a result of new developments in the field of psychology. Similar to the trend in geography, psychology began to take a more scientific approach as psychologists tried to understand the cognitive development of young children. This effort was led in part by the Herbartians, a group of scholars inspired by the German philosopher, Johann Friedrich Herbart. Herbartian theory exerted a strong influence on elementary education until the early twentieth century; thereafter, John Dewey's ideas about education were far more influential. According to Herbartian theory, teachers should relate new content to prior knowledge and should use tangible objects and concrete experiences.[55]

Charles A. McMurry, Superintendent of Schools in DeKalb, Illinois, and a professor at Northern Illinois State Normal School, introduced the Herbartian approach to elementary education in the United States.[56] McMurry wrote numerous pedagogical texts and children's textbooks based in Herbartian theory.[57] Like other Herbartians, McMurry thought the literary classics belonged in the curriculum: fairy tales in the first grade, *Robinson Crusoe* in the second grade, mythology in the third grade, and pioneer history stories in the fourth grade. In McMurry's plan, children would study history more formally in the sixth, seventh, and eighth grades.[58]

McMurry thought young students learned virtuous behavior by studying the lives of exemplary people in fiction and history. Such stories and biographies (in which obedience and good behavior are always rewarded, and disobedience and bad behavior are always punished) could shape character, inspire imagination and creativity, evoke sympathy and love for the oppressed or abandoned, and foster a sense of justice. McMurry also argued for the linkage between fairy tales and myths and language studies, history, and science.[59] In studying such tales and myths, children learned the history and geography of Europe. Pioneer stories (usually biographies of heroes) prepared elementary children for history lessons in the upper grades. In all these curriculum recommendations, McMurry emphasized speaking to the "heart" of the child and to "awakening his interest."[60]

McMurry and the other Herbartians strongly supported teaching children the connection between the universal themes in stories and their own lives. To help them make this connection, McMurry created a school sequence for elementary students that resembled the expanding communities approach of later years—from fairy tales to stories of the home, the neighborhood, the state, and the country.[61] McMurry repeatedly stressed the importance of school-life connections: "At every step the sympathy and life experiences from [outside] the school should be intertwined with school acquisitions."[62]

Other educators also encouraged elementary schools to add these classic tales to their curricula. For example, Charles Eliot, Harvard University President, recommended the study of literature in the elementary schools. He rejected readers that were, in his words, "ineffable trash" and that taught children nothing of "the ideals of the human race."[63] He observed approvingly that the Greek and Roman myths and the European and English literary classics gave children the opportunity to read about other histories and cultures.

About the same time that the Herbartians introduced their pedagogical ideas, another group of scholars began to make their mark on education. These scholars, including Herbert Spencer and G. Stanley Hall, belonged to the "developmentalist" group, as Herbert Kliebard has categorized them.[64] They believed the natural development of children—learning that relates to reality, discovered through scientific study—should inspire the curriculum and instruction.[65]

Hall, the first president of the American Psychological Association, was especially influential in the evolution of elementary pedagogy. In his recommendations for teaching history, he disparaged the "purely colorless presentation of facts" and encouraged instruction in investigative skills.[66] However, Hall is more remembered for his ideas on cultural epochs and child study.[67] Hall developed his cultural epochs theory from Ernst Haeckel's biological theory of recapitulation, or "ontogeny recapitulates phylogeny," the idea that the stages in each person's development resemble or follow the pattern of the stages of adult evolutionary history. Applied to education, the cultural epochs theory assumes children progress through stages (i.e., epochs) that repeat the developmental stages of the human race.[68] In practice, this theory supported the chronological approach to historical study: children learned about their ancestors and then traced human development, over time, to the present.[69]

Hall's other notion, child study, placed the interests of the child at the center of the curriculum. For Hall, child study, which was "partly psychology, partly anthropology, partly medico-hygiene," grew out of his concern for the child's psychological and physical well-being.[70] Child study was a reaction to practices in education that prioritized curriculum content. Hall wrote that children's "reason is still very undeveloped...[therefore]...show, demonstrate, and envisage should be our watchwords, not explain."[71] For the practical implementation of child study, intensive observation of children was needed.[72] Intensive observation meant gathering data on the "contents of children's minds" by asking them about nature, body parts, geometric shapes, and human behavior.[73] If educators used this evidence, Hall thought they could design appropriate instruction. Child study, in short, "fit the school to the child, rather than the child to the school."[74] However, Hall lost influence when critics charged that his ideas were based on "pseudoscientific" research. Biologists at the time firmly rejected his cultural epochs theory.[75] Nevertheless, in the following years, progressive educators used Hall's child study idea to develop the project method teaching practice and to promote the whole child movement.

Recommendations for History and
Geography Education: National Reports

Education leaders in the late nineteenth century increasingly worried that schooling in the United States, including elementary schooling, was too unsystematic. Three national committees of educators were formed in the last decade of the nineteenth century to address these concerns: two were National Education Association (NEA) committees and one was an American Historical Association (AHA) committee. The reports from these committees addressed the content and structure of history education and made various recommendations for what and how students should be taught. Some reports were more influential than others, but all are of interest in tracing the origins and development of elementary social studies. Besides the NEA, the organization most involved in this effort was the AHA. In its formative years, the AHA focused on secondary and college-level history education, but it also made recommendations for common school (elementary) history education. The role of the AHA in shaping the history curriculum is an essential part of the story of elementary history and social studies education.

The AHA, founded in 1884 as an offshoot of the American Social Science Association, was dedicated to the study of history as well as to the study of economics, political science, and other social sciences.[76] At the time, history was a new discipline in colleges and universities, employing only twenty history professors nationwide.[77] Forty people responded to the call to form an organization devoted exclusively to the study of history. Membership in the AHA grew rapidly: by 1890, there were 620 members. In 1889, the U.S. Congress incorporated the AHA, which had as its mission "the promotion of historical studies, the collection and preservation of historical manuscripts and for kindred purposes in the interest of American history and of history in America."[78] During the AHA's first thirty years, only 25 percent of its members were academics; the rest were wealthy amateurs interested in history.[79]

The motivations for the founding of the AHA were the nineteenth-century historians' increasing respect for science and objectivity in their work (as influenced by German historical scholarship) and their desire to achieve "professional" recognition.[80] To promote their scholarship and to achieve this status, the historians knew they had to publish a journal, offer skills training, and establish licensure requirements. Founding a professional organization was the first step. Some ten years after its founding, in an intellectual climate in which history scholarship and ideas about child development were in flux, the AHA began to address curriculum development. The reason for this change in its focus was the NEA's invitation to historians to contribute to a study that would be known as the Committee of Ten report. This report, published in 1893, was one of the most important events in American curricular history.[81]

The Committee of Ten consisted of a group of prominent educators chaired by Charles Eliot.[82] For its final report, the Committee asked the nine "subject-specific" conferences, each consisting of ten members, to make curricular recommendations.[83] The history conference (hereafter the History Ten) dealt with history, civil government, and political economy. The geography conference (hereafter the Geography Ten) dealt with physical geography, geology, and meteorology.[84] The Committee of Ten report established history as a separate discipline in the schools.[85] In general, the report conservatively recommended continuing the current curriculum but radically rejected current methods of instruction. The report called for instruction methods that included student presentations, the use of original sources, individualized work, "rambling excursions" (field trips), debate, and graphic aids.[86]

The History Ten recommended oral instruction, simple biographies, and myths for fifth and sixth grades. It recommended the study of American history, civil government, and Greek and Roman history for seventh and eighth grades.[87] The History Ten advised that some information should be memorized (e.g., dates of significant events) as background information necessary for understanding cause and effect.[88] To learn civil government, the History Ten recommended students take trips to see "their own local and state government in operation."[89] Although there were indications of the History Ten's concern with how children learned, the emphasis was on mastering history content.

The Geography Ten enlarged the subject of geography to include geology, meteorology, zoology, botany, history, and political science.[90] For all grades, the Geography Ten emphasized the importance of "observational geography": the study of natural features such as landforms, waterways, temperature and weather, and plant and animal life.[91] The Geography Ten advised, "The exercise of the imagination of remote objects should always be preceded, if possible, by the exercise of the observation of similar facts near at home."[92] Direct experience with the natural world was important for abstract learning.

In its specific pedagogical recommendations, the Geography Ten promoted a learning procedure that prefigures the expanding communities approach of the twentieth century. For example, for map study the Geography Ten recommended students first draw the schoolroom, using symbols for doors, windows, and desks. Then they should draw the schoolyard, local streets and roads, states, and the country. The Geography Ten explained that in this progression, students would cultivate "good intellectual habits" that were useful for making "correct observation and accurate statement of simple facts" as they studied foreign places.[93]

A second NEA-sponsored committee, the Committee of Fifteen, issued its report in 1895. The Committee consisted of three subcommittees, one of which was "On the Correlation of Studies in Elementary Education." Although the Committee of Fifteen report was not as influential as the Committee of Ten report, it is of interest because of its specific ideas on elementary education.[94] The Committee of Fifteen report identified five subjects it called "windows of the soul": grammar, literature, mathematics, geography, and history. Notably, geography and history were identified as subjects equal in importance to "the three Rs" that elementary schools traditionally emphasized. The Committee of Fifteen report commented on geography: "The child commences with what is nearest to his interests, and proceeds gradually toward what is remote and to be studied for its own sake."[95] The report also claimed there was a direct relationship between geography and good citizenship. Good citizens knew about the world. Memorization of facts and figures was mere "sailor geography."[96]

However, according to the Committee of Fifteen report, history was more useful than geography for teaching good citizenship. Moreover, like geography instruction, the report described history study as a progression from the known to the unknown. The report stated: "[The pupil] should move outward from what he has already learned, by the study of a new concentric circle of grounds and reasons...."[97] Similarly, children should study the historical evolution of government in order to see how institutions adapt to "permit individual freedom, and the participation of all citizens in the administration of the government itself."[98]

The third national committee on education in the late nineteenth century was the AHA Committee of Seven that the NEA had asked the historians to form. The NEA gave the AHA a fourfold charge:

1) to study the current state of elementary and high school history instruction in the United States; 2) to research history instruction in Europe and Canada; 3) to make recommendations about the U.S. history curriculum; and 4) to prepare a plan of college entrance requirements for history.[99] In 1898, the Committee of Seven issued a report titled *The Study of History in Schools*.[100] This report was to have an important and lasting effect on the history curriculum in U.S. schools. More than a decade after the report's publication, J. Franklin Jameson, an AHA member, credited it with elevating history's sense of "importance and dignity," and Andrew C. McLaughlin, the Committee of Seven chairman, claimed it influenced history pedagogy "from one side of the continent to the other."[101]

Although the Committee of Seven report mainly focused on history instruction at the secondary level, one chapter, by Vassar College Professor of History Lucy Salmon, focused on history in "the grades" (those below high school).[102] Salmon was the first woman to serve on the AHA Executive Committee, and she was the only woman to serve on the Committee of Seven. Her chapter on the grades was highly critical of the current state of elementary history instruction. She wrote that such instruction left "much to be desired."[103] According to Salmon, such instruction, which focused too much on U.S. history and too little on world history, lacked uniformity and wrongly used history to teach patriotism.[104] Furthermore, because history was only taught formally in the last two years of elementary school, opportunities were lost for engaging younger students in the study of the past.

Turning from content to pedagogy, Salmon claimed history instruction was too dependent on textbooks, lacked innovative teaching techniques, and isolated history (from geography and literature) in the curriculum.[105] The ultimate goal of history instruction, she argued, was the search for truth, developed through "intelligent understanding of the past as well as of present political conditions."[106] For Salmon, an "objective" understanding of U.S. history meant understanding all aspects of the country's history, including its failures.[107]

To solve the problems she had identified in history instruction, Salmon recommended a detailed program of history instruction for elementary schools. Grade 3: Literature and Legends; Grade 4: Biography; Grade 5: Greek and Roman History; Grade 6: Medieval and

Modern Times; Grade 7: English History; and Grade 8: American History.[108] Three recommendations are striking in that they challenged the status quo of history education. First, eight- and nine-year-olds should study myths, fables, and legends from world cultures. Salmon recommended stories from *The Iliad, The Odyssey,* and *The Aeneid,* and the tales of King Arthur, Roland, and Hiawatha. She also recommended biographies of peoples from Europe and the Middle East.[109] Second, children should begin their formal study of history in the fifth grade rather than in high school. In fact, the history study she recommended for fifth through eighth grades mirrored the recommendations for ninth through twelfth grades made by the AHA Committee of Seven and the NEA Committee of Ten. Third, the study of history should proceed chronologically, from the distant past of ancient Greece to recent American history.

In recommending this chronological approach, Salmon opposed several popular approaches to geographical and historical study that recommended a quite different path (i.e., moving from the known to the unknown). She defended her recommendations for a chronological approach, stating, "…the demand that a study should proceed 'from the known to the unknown,' may involve a fallacy, that what lies nearest may sometimes be most obscure, and what is remote in time or place be most easily understood."[110] Salmon evidently thought young children would benefit from the same, if simplified, approach she used at Vassar College. She also encouraged teaching historical inquiry skills by emphasizing the importance of original sources, even at the elementary school level.[111]

Educators in later years would support many of the recommendations in the Committee of Seven report. They approved the report's recognition of the need to appeal to the interests of the child. Salmon, in particular, thought "story" could be used to present legends and events in ways that both taught and entertained the child.[112] They also agreed with the report's criticism of rote memorization and recitation and with its approval of critical thinking that linked the past to the present. The report stated, "We can fully understand the present only by a study of the past; and the past, on the other hand, is appreciated only by those who know the present."[113] Educators also liked the report's promotion of the "correlation" among subjects. For example, the report recommended that history and civil government should be taught "not as isolated, but as interrelated and interdependent subjects;" history without civil government was only "wars and rumors of wars."[114]

The Elementary Curriculum at the Local Level in the Nineteenth Century

Education in the United States is mostly a local undertaking. Historically, there has always been a gap between national recommendations and their local implementation.[115] To learn if and how administrators at the local level dealt with the national recommendations during the mid to late nineteenth century, the public school districts' annual reports (which often included a "course of study") are our best sources. Two Michigan school districts, the Detroit Public Schools (DPS) and the Grand Rapids Public Schools (GRPS), exemplify two different, although somewhat overlapping, local approaches to history and geography study. Their annual reports give us an idea of the influence that *some* AHA recommendations had at the local level.

With their extensive detail, the DPS and GRPS courses of study present a persuasive description of the reality of classroom instruction in these two districts. For example, the courses of study list titles of textbooks used, excursions taken, and particular skills taught, in addition to what appear to be firsthand accounts of superintendents' classroom visits. Because superintendents in general were probably unaware of everything that was taught in classrooms, the DPS and GRPS teachers may have taught different content than that described in the courses of study. However, at least one DPS superintendent was convinced that principals and teachers followed the recommended program. In one report he expressed his "appreciation of the loyal support and assistance of the principals and teachers, and their ready willingness to adopt and carry into effect all suggestions and direction given by me."[116]

Incorporated in 1824, Detroit was Michigan's oldest and most populous city in the late nineteenth century. In 1869, the state combined all the schools in the City of Detroit into a unified school district.[117] By 1900, the City had almost three hundred thousand inhabitants and thirty thousand school children.[118] In the nineteenth century, according to the courses of study, children in Detroit studied geography in grades two through seven. History not was taught separately until the eighth grade. However, we have few details about specific content or instruction methods. Perhaps the most illuminating description of nineteenth-century education in Detroit was the following: "The instruction in most schools was very rudimentary in character, while it cannot be said that there was much, if any, method in the manner in which it was given."[119]

In the 1890s, in addition to general information on the district, the DPS *Annual Reports of the Superintendent* began to give greater detail on content and instruction in the schools. These reports covered district finances, school construction, student enrollment, school personnel, and sometimes "courses of study" (including those for the elementary grades). This section of the chapter focuses mainly on the 1894 and 1895 DPS reports that provided extensive descriptions of content and sometimes of methods (the other reports from the 1890s do not describe courses of study). The courses of study identified reading, writing, and arithmetic as the key subject areas; history was not a separate course of study until eighth grade. However, geography was taught at all grade levels ("elementary geography" for grades one through three and "foreign geography" for grades four through eight). Geography and history often appeared in the curriculum as reading material (in "correlation," although the reports do not use that term).[120]

The 1894 and 1895 DPS reports described curricular content for each grade level. For example, in both first and second grades, history and geography, with other subjects, were correlated with oral language instruction. Evidently, educators in the DPS worried about school-age children's ability to speak and write English. The recommendation was that students repeat their history, geography, and literature lessons orally in the classrooms. Another recommendation was that children study history primarily in "story": biographies of famous people with emphasis on their childhoods. The 1895 DPS report explained, "Some prominent character, Benjamin Franklin, for instance, is selected, and the story of his life, more particularly his boyhood, because that is more interesting to and more easily understood by the children, is told by the teacher."[121] We may conclude also that such stories taught children about former customs, transportation modes, and occupations. The same report claimed, "Theoretically it might seem as if [history] were beyond the younger children, but the fact has been proven that they can not only understand it, but they are intensely interested in it when properly adapted and prescribed."[122]

According to the 1895 DPS report, geography education in the lower elementary grades taught children to observe their immediate environment. In the study of local bodies of water and landforms, such as the Detroit River and Belle Isle, they learned abstract concepts such as direction, distance, and location. For instance, students observed "the weather, together with the special study of the seasons, as they come and go, [which] furnish many ideas about climate, rainfall and the change of season."[123] The report also linked local geography to global geography:

> Their study of home animals, domestic and wild, together with that of our commerce, mineral productions, our people, our ways of traveling, our building, our occupations, our manufactured articles, our principal streets and public buildings open the eyes of our children and help them to much information which is valuable in itself, and more valuable to use as an aid to the study of the world which lies beyond them, and which cannot be studied through observation, but only through imagination.[124]

According to the 1894 DPS report, third-grade geography covered even more topics. In lessons on Detroit and Michigan, third graders studied climate, vegetation, animals, minerals, people (the various races in the community), "modes of life," and government. They also studied "structure": landforms and water bodies, Detroit and Wayne County maps, and Michigan's regions, boundaries, surface, drainage, coastline, climate, vegetation, occupations, cities, and railroads.[125] The report did not refer specifically to history lessons although it recommended that students read fables and folk stories and then retell them in writing. The report recommended teaching certain skills, such as recall, sequencing (narrating facts in logical order), and good use of language. It seems that the principal instructional method in the DPS elementary schools was recitation-based. There is little evidence of the active learning that Salmon, for example, had recommended.

The 1895 DPS report described fourth-grade geography. Fourth graders studied "foreign geography," including physical geography (e.g., climate, vegetation, landforms, and waterways) and political geography (e.g., population, government, religion, and occupations). The report called for study of the important concepts in geography — the "great essentials" instead of the "burdensome details."[126] These essentials included travel, mineral production, manufacturing, and the earth–human relationship (generally referred to today as human ecology). Fifth graders studied sociopolitical features of the United States (e.g., population, education, religion, government, and history) and began the study of South America and Europe.[127]

The 1895 DPS report explained that sixth and seventh graders studied more geography and history in their reading lessons than they had in the earlier grades. Geography study now covered Africa, Australia, and the Earth. The focus was on structure, drainage, outline, climate, vegetation, animals, minerals, and people. In political geography, seventh graders studied political divisions, religion, occupations, commerce, and state and national government, concluding with lessons on Great Britain, Germany, Russia, France, Turkey, India, China, Japan, Egypt, and Brazil.[128] The sixth and seventh graders in the DPS studied history by reading biographies (e.g., Benjamin Franklin and Abraham Lincoln).[129] History was correlated with the arts curriculum; children examined drawings of historic Greek, Moorish, and Gothic ornaments and then associated a story from history or a myth with the drawings.[130] In seventh grade, the reading curriculum featured texts and poetry with historic subjects and themes.[131] According to the 1895 DPS report, history was a separate area of study in the eighth grade. The focus was U.S. history and government through the American Revolution, although specific details of the course were not described. (The report used the word "formal" to describe this separate treatment of history in the curriculum.) Because of their previous history study in their readers, the report concluded eighth graders were prepared for and interested in the subject.[132]

The DPS courses of study are of pedagogical interest in several respects. First, they suggested innovative instructional methods were not unknown in the DPS. Although teaching and learning were largely drill and recitation, there were indications of more complex ideas about instruction, particularly in geography education. For example, the 1895 DPS report stated the purpose of geography study was "to train the children to observe, to see relations, to think for themselves, rather than to memorize the thoughts of others, to study geography in an intelligent way and get a method of learning rather than simply an accumulation of memorized facts without the power to learn new ones continually and independently."[133] To some extent, this statement reflected the rejection by the Committee of Ten and the Committee of Seven of memorization and recitation. Second, the DPS geography lessons took children from their local neighborhoods to ever-larger communities (the city, the county, the state, the nation, the continent, the world). This curricular structure suggested an early version of the expanding communities approach that appeared nationwide in the next century. Third, there was no separate history course in the DPS until the eighth grade. Children read stories, myths, fables, and legends in the early grades (as McMurry and his followers had recommended), but this was not the formal study of history recommended by the Committee of Ten and the Committee of Seven. The eighth-grade history course would have disappointed Lucy Salmon in any event since it emphasized U.S. history more than ancient or European history.

The City of Grand Rapids, which was incorporated in 1850, was Michigan's second largest city in the late nineteenth century. Its public school district was established in 1871. At the turn of the century, Grand Rapids had a population of about eighty thousand. There were about fifteen thousand children in school, mostly in the elementary schools.[134] Like the DPS, the GRPS issued annual reports on the school system, although the Board of Trustees issued the reports instead of the superintendents as in the DPS. The GRPS reports covered school finances, construction data, and often (perceptions of) the school curriculum.

The 1865–66 GRPS report included short sections on recommended teaching methods for the disciplines at the elementary level. Although history was not mentioned, geography was described for the third, fourth, and fifth grades. The report recommended children in these grades learn the cardinal directions by drawing a map of a table, using a book on the table as a reference (e.g., comparing lengths of the table's sides, distinguishing the North and South table ends, and locating the book on the table). The idea was that such simple map study would teach children how to draw maps of the school-room, the schoolyard, and their city: "They trace the principal streets, find their own homes and the post office and other public buildings, and measure distances."[135] After studying maps of their local neighborhoods and communities, children studied maps of their state, the country, and Europe. In this map study, the GRPS students were learning geography skills, linked to their immediate environments, directly and in engaging ways.

Reports from the GRPS two decades later, in the 1880s, also described the use of the local community in geography lessons. Students practiced using a compass, reading maps, and drawing maps. The 1889–90 GRPS report stated that the local and familiar were used to teach new concepts: "All new terms should be explained by reference to what is near and common before the pupils begin the study of the lessons."[136] Second graders studied direction and distance by making maps of their desks and classroom. Third graders mapped their ward and their city. By fourth and fifth grades, students were ready to study the physical and political geography of their country and the world, often using textbooks such as *Harper's School Geography.*[137] As in the DPS, there was no formal study of history in the GRPS until the eighth grade.[138]

In the 1884–85 GRPS report, the superintendent called for practical changes in the curriculum. He agreed with the criticism made in several magazine articles about current courses of study in the GRPS: "They [the courses of study] are founded too exclusively on the idea that some boy may become President of the United States rather than on the basis that nine boys out of every ten will become clerks, bookkeepers, carpenters, and machinists."[139] He also argued that the culture in a school community should determine its curriculum. As examples, he pointed to Ann Arbor and Ypsilanti, two Michigan cities with scholastic cultures, where schools appropriately focused on classical and scientific learning. However, in Grand Rapids, "a manufacturing community," the GRPS superintendent continued, schools should prepare children for "laboring" work. Thus, the GRPS children should study utilitarian subjects such as mental arithmetic, handwriting, spelling, and reading. He admitted GRPS children should know some history and geography of Michigan; however, they did not need to study the theoretical and complicated aspects of these disciplines.[140]

The superintendent's comments and the curricular recommendations in the 1892–93 GRPS report plainly emphasized the practical in education.[141] Superintendent W. W. Chalmers stated that "the new education," with its philosophical and utilitarian approach to learning, was not a fad; rather, it was a radical reorientation of former practices and methods that have failed in the past. This new approach, he claimed, would develop children's innate skills and talents through intellectual drill and imaginative teaching that was more "suggestive" than "didactic." Moreover, "the new education," which was strongly utilitarian, would develop the hands as well as the brain, and would give children respect for the tasks they learn in school.[142]

It is clear from reading this report that Chalmers thought teachers should adopt this new education. He portrayed himself as the instructional leader who was responsible for passing on new pedagogies to his staff. To that end, Chalmers provided the GRPS teachers with courses in reading, psychology, and pedagogy, and with additional instruction in science and in literature, among other subjects. However, assuming the teachers took these courses, there is no evidence in the reports of their effect, if any, on their teaching.

In the next year's GRPS report (1893–94), changes in the course of study appeared. The disciplines were still taught separately in the grades, but the topics were much more defined, especially science topics. The topics in the science curriculum, which in many ways overlapped later versions of the social studies curriculum, were organized by months and seasons. In October and November, children studied the length of the day and temperature changes; in January, they studied sunrise, sunset, and the points of the compass; and in May and June, they studied agriculture and weaving. Other occupations appeared throughout the year. In December, second graders studied holidays and American Indians; in February, they read about the poet, Henry Wadsworth Longfellow. Although other topics were based in the natural sciences, *some* geography and history lessons hinted at a thematic (or correlated) approach to curriculum.[143]

The 1893–94 report described a reading course of study with a broad range of stories, including Greek mythology in the second grade.[144]

Two features of the GRPS geography curriculum are especially noteworthy. First, rather than recommending children memorize geography terms and foreign places by rote, the reports recommended that children be actively and physically involved in learning. This "new education" approach, which departed from the "classical and didactic" approach, shifted education toward the "scientific and laboratory."[145] Second, the reports recommended a curricular structure in which children moved from their immediate environment outward: from their classroom, to their homes, to their local community, state, and country. This structure, like that in the DPS, was an early version of the expanding communities approach.

The GRPS and the DPS curricula of these years are alike in another respect. Neither paid much attention to history lessons in the elementary grades. Formal study of history began in both districts in the eighth grade. In the earlier grades, history, which appeared only in stories, myths, and fables and in geography lessons, was not taught separately. In both districts, however, geography had a much more independent position. In both the DPS and the GRPS, geography was a separate subject in the lower elementary grades.

Research cannot tell if teachers offered classroom instruction that emphasized both rigorous content and engaging, instructional approaches. At the local level, however, as the DPS and GRPS reports reveal, there was a preference for new pedagogical methods over discipline-based content. Educators in the DPS and the GRPS described an instructional method that was quite similar to the Pestalozzian emphasis on objects. They also proposed sequential learning in geography lessons that resembled the expanding communities approach of the twentieth century.

Predictably, there was criticism of such "new education." A common complaint, one that Lucy Salmon made, was that concepts and places in the child's immediate environment could be just as obscure, or more so, as those that were far away. At the end of the nineteenth century, as the new ideas and the new methods achieved greater recognition, even popularity, there was fierce disagreement about the future of elementary education, in particular how geography and history should be taught. In the twentieth century, supporters and detractors would refine their ideas and methods as social studies became a field of study.

Chapter 2

Social Studies Is Born: The Early Twentieth Century

SOCIAL STUDIES FIRST APPEARED in the early twentieth century. By the 1920s, some school districts had established social studies departments, and some elementary schools had added social studies lessons to the curriculum. This chapter describes the societal, political, and educational forces, including their associated rhetoric and theory, that helped transform the separately taught subjects of history, geography, and civics to the multidisciplinary subject of social studies. These forces included urbanization, migration, immigration, and political reform. They also included advances in academic professionalism, research in educational psychology, and various developments in pedagogy. Social studies advocates found support for their newly developing field in ideas promoted by groups such as the New Historians and the child-centered progressive educators. Before and during World War I, there were renewed demands to teach democracy and citizenship in schools. These demands also helped shape social studies.

At the turn of the century, America's agrarian society was becoming more urban and industrial. Cities grew rapidly with internal migration, mostly from the southern states, and massive immigration, mostly from southern and eastern Europe.[1] It was the age of the automotive assembly line, large-scale electrification, and heavy industry. In these years of enormous change, Americans sought predictability and stability. In Robert Wiebe's words, there was "a search for order."[2] It was also an age of government reforms, regulatory agencies, tenement housing, and child labor laws. Powerful social movements arose (e.g., anti-vice campaigns, de jure and de facto racial segregation, and immigration restrictions) that molded public opinion and transformed society.[3]

As American life became more urban, the population more diverse, and work more industrial, professional opportunities in medicine, law, journalism, social work, and education also increased. Professionalization gave occupations in these fields power and sometimes prestige. Physicians and attorneys founded associations and set licensure requirements.[4] Universities established hiring qualifications for professors. The National Education Association (NEA) increased its membership, and organizations such as the American Educational Research Association and the National Society for College Teachers of Education were founded.[5] The professionalization of teachers was underway, although it lagged behind the professionalization of other occupations by about a decade.[6]

The rapid increase in public school enrollment posed an enormous challenge for educators. Between 1890 and 1910, the number of teachers and students in the country's public schools increased more than fourfold.[7] Between 1900 and 1930, the number of students in kindergarten through eighth grade increased from 16,422,000 to 23,553,000, a jump of over 40 percent.[8] In the Detroit Public Schools, a large urban district, enrollment in kindergarten through sixth grade more than doubled between 1911 and 1921.[9]

The demographics of the national student population also changed as the schools, especially urban schools, became increasingly diverse, both racially and ethnically. In the cities, the families of school-age children came from more than sixty different countries. In thirty-seven American cities, 58 percent of the students' fathers were immigrants.[10] Northern city schools also enrolled many African American students following the Great Migration between 1900 and 1915 when one hundred thousand African Americans moved north.[11] The number of African Americans in Detroit, for example, increased by 600 percent between 1910 and 1920.[12]

At both policy and practice levels, educators struggled with the pedagogical problems posed by the differences in students' backgrounds and cultures, and by the non-English languages spoken in their homes. One popular policy decision was to Americanize students by teaching them Anglo-Saxon culture, middle-class values of thrift and hard work, and the American Creed.[13] Another policy decision was to adapt the curriculum for immigrant and African American children whom some educators believed were cognitively deficient.

The new social studies curriculum that would develop, at least in theory, reflected these multi-dimensional changes in the population. Yet change in education practice lagged change in society. An examination of curricula in several public school districts in these years, which concludes the chapter, reveals classroom instruction in social studies changed very slowly.

Educational Psychology and Social Studies

In the early twentieth century, research in educational psychology that used controlled experiments and quantitative measures provided empirical data on, and theoretical support for, teaching, learning, and assessments.[14] Gradually, psychologists began to influence educators' theories on how children learn and which teaching strategies best facilitate that learning. In various ways, this research helped transform history, geography, and civics into social studies education.

Two theoretical strands in educational psychology theory particularly influenced social studies education. Behaviorism as applied to education initially had a direct influence. The psychology of education content had an indirect influence.

The first theoretical strand, behaviorism, related to the gradual accumulation of knowledge and skills through the process of stimulus and response. An influential proponent was Edward L. Thorndike, Professor of Psychology at Teachers College, Columbia University (TC). Thorndike argued that school subject content should interest learners and help them function in social situations.[15] The behaviorists recommended parceling education out in small, digestible chunks of knowledge that related to daily life. This was a theory of learning custom-tailored to the new social studies education that promoted accessible and manageable learning in a range of disciplinary subjects, often presented in piecemeal fashion.

Thorndike and the other behaviorists concerned with education did not comment on the teaching methods best suited for history and the social sciences. Nor did they specify the content they thought important. However, when they discussed the discipline of history, they prioritized factual understandings, often using facts to exemplify what children should learn (e.g., Christopher Columbus's exploration in the Americas). Typically, they discussed content in general terms, always emphasizing the applicability of the content learned. This viewpoint was consistent with the behaviorists' belief that content should generate interest in the learner and should improve the learner's relationship with the physical world and social situations. For example, Thorndike emphasized the importance of knowledge of "the real" (as opposed to knowledge of "the non-existent," or make-believe), knowledge that had application and utility, and knowledge with the power of prediction (rather than knowledge of the past).[16] In another form, this was psychological theory endorsing the progressive idea of utilitarianism in school studies.

Not all educators agreed with the behaviorists' ideas about learning. Many educators considered behaviorism, when applied to education, authoritarian and insensitive to children's needs. To these critics, the behaviorists' ideas conflicted with traditional and commonsense views of child rearing and turned "natural" learning into overly prescribed and mechanical instruction. In opposing the behaviorists' conception of learning, John Dewey, for example, argued for a more holistic view of education. By the 1930s and 1940s, behaviorism had lost much of its direct influence on education. However, its indirect influence in weakening the rationale for traditional learning methodology was significant.

The second theoretical strand related to the psychology of education content. University of Chicago Professor Charles H. Judd, who was a key supporter of this theory, thought that students acquired special skills and habits in the disciplines or subjects, each of which had its own psychology and a set of principles, structures, and intellectual challenges. Judd explained:

> The highest powers of the mind are general, not particular, that mental development consists neither in storing the mind with items of knowledge nor in training the nervous system to perform with readiness particular habitual

acts, but rather in equipping the individual with the power to think abstractly and to form general ideas.[17]

However, Judd also thought there were particular skills and habits that could be acquired in each subject matter. He argued that each subject had its own psychology—that is, its own principles, structures, and sets of intellectual challenges. For example, the discipline of history addressed such challenges as presentism, the complicated nature of causal judgment, and the difficulties in using historical evidence.[18]

Of all the academic subjects, Judd thought history was the most complex and the broadest. Subjects like mathematics or Latin could be organized around a sequence of study that grew cumulatively more difficult from grade to grade. On the other hand, students generally studied history chronologically, from grade to grade, with no necessary increase in content difficulty. History's complexity, Judd argued, resulted from its multidisciplinary nature since all history study naturally included economics, constitutional law, legislation, finance, and strategy (presumably military and political strategy).[19] Judd therefore advocated the Herbartian notion of teaching history from a multidisciplinary perspective (as described in Chapter 1, the Herbartians were pioneers in the "correlation" of study). He also prescribed the historical thinking skills central to the study of history; these skills included chronological thinking, causal judgment, critical examination of historical evidence, and even training of the imagination (through reconstruction of events from the past).

Judd explained that each of these thinking skills, while fundamental, also posed challenges to children. For example, by dramatizing the past, children risked replacing the enacted drama with their personal versions of the past, based upon their individual readings of history.[20] Passing judgment on historical events was impossible without a thorough and objective understanding of the conditions surrounding the events.[21] Judd was remarkably prophetic in calling attention to such dilemmas posed by historical thinking skills (such as the difficulty of avoiding "ahistoricism" since presentism is our natural state). As Sam Wineberg concludes, these dilemmas still exist in historical study.[22]

Judd recognized that elementary students were probably not prepared for the challenge posed by the kind of historical analysis he proposed. He wrote that young students have "no more notion of periods of time than they have of great spatial areas."[23] Perhaps because of his concern that history and geography were badly taught and badly learned, Judd supported the new social studies curriculum. He found it more accessible and understandable than the separate disciplines curriculum.[24] This was a roundabout path to supporting social studies over the traditional disciplines.

Elementary Education Reform: Educational Progressivism

This fresh look at how and what children should learn resulted in a dramatic transformation in education in the United States in the early twentieth century. John Dewey was the most famous advocate of the new "educational progressivism." There is still no common agreement, however, on the meaning of progressivism in education, although many educators and historians have offered interpretations.[25] Probably because of its broad philosophical approach, many education reforms in the twentieth century descended in part from the goals and theories of educational progressivism.[26]

However it is interpreted, educational progressivism was a reform movement directed at society as well as at schooling. Lawrence Cremin identified four themes that are central to progressivism in education: an expansion of the school curriculum to include non-academic content, the introduction of new pedagogical techniques developed from research, increased attention to students' diverse backgrounds, and greater efficiency in school administration.[27] A fundamental principle of this reform movement was that education should promote democracy by giving children more educational opportunities and by teaching them citizenship skills. In addition, schools should value expert knowledge and specialized teaching, adopt more child-centered practices (e.g., dramatizations, building projects, teacher-pupil and pupil-pupil discussions, and other play-related activities), and broaden the study of traditional academic subjects. Despite the opposition of critics, progressive educators, as the subsequent history of social studies education shows, had an enduring influence on elementary education.[28]

The progressive educators generally objected to the traditional elementary curriculum of "the three Rs" that was slightly supplemented with history and geography lessons.[29] Progressive educators proposed broadening the curriculum to include "nature study, manual training, construction, domestic arts, literature and language work, and real instruction in the social and political institutions of our country."[30] These were the skills and topics they thought were relevant to children in their daily lives. Moreover, as the rhetoric about content changed, so did the rhetoric about method. For teaching these new subjects, progressive educators called for teachers to abandon memory tests and recitations and to reduce textbook reading; instead, teachers should use active learning activities in which children handled tools or took community field trips.[31] While progressive educators did not argue that schools should abandon textbooks, they did argue for reducing their exclusive use as guides to instruction. However, in these years, generally there was more policy talk than policy action about innovative teaching methods and new subjects.[32]

In an attempt to bring some order to this nebulous movement, with its assortment of theories and theorists, ideals and idealists, reforms and reformists, various historians and educators have separated the progressive educators into groups. For example, David Tyack and Larry Cuban distinguish between the "administrative progressives" and the "pedagogical progressives." The administrative progressives, in particular, had a lasting influence on schools. They classified students using objective measures, added multiple tracks in high schools, set standards for teachers, and instituted student record keeping.[33] According to David Labaree, the administrative progressives were more influential in changing education than the pedagogical progressives. The latter group focused more on "child-centered instruction, discovery learning, and learning how to learn."[34]

Herbert Kliebard separates the progressive education movement into administrative progressivism (supported by the advocates of social efficiency and social meliorism) and pedagogical progressivism (supported by the developmentalists). According to Kliebard, the goal of the social efficiency educators was specialized, differentiated curricula for students that would educate them for their role in society; the goal of the social meliorists was structure and efficiency in education that would reform and improve society. The anti-traditional developmentalists, with no interest in administrative reforms, wanted to replace a dull and outdated curriculum with subject matter they thought suitable for children's various developmental stages.[35]

There were even more splinter groups among the pedagogical progressives, especially among the social studies reformers. In his history of the groups who battled for control over the high school social studies curriculum, Ronald Evans identifies the traditional historians, the mandarins (who supported social studies as a social science), the social efficiency educators, the social meliorists, the social reconstructionists, and members of the consensus and eclectic camps.[36] These groups, all theoretically-based, some now obscure, a few still influential, give us a sense of the disparate, although sometimes overlapping, ideas on education in the early twentieth century. In this listing, there is yet room for the New Historians and the child-centered progressives, two groups who particularly help us understand how elementary social studies education developed.

The New Historians

The New Historians, a school of American historians who were active in the early and mid-twentieth century, included such respected historians as Frederick Jackson Turner, James Harvey Robinson, Carl Becker, and Charles Beard.[37] Despite some commentators' inclusion of many of these historians in the school, it was not a unified group. They were, as historian Ernst Breisach described them, "a loosely knit school of thought with a tolerably coherent web of explanatory themes."[38] While these historians did not march in lockstep, there was one important path all followed. All of them thought historical insights should inform the debate on current issues—that is, history education should be modern, functional, and relevant. They charged that traditional history instruction had failed to fulfill its primary purpose: teaching students to understand and solve society's problems. They also encouraged the use of progressive instructional methods.[39]

In 1912, the new history movement came to prominence with the publication of Robinson's *The New History*.[40] This collection of essays recommended that history instruction focus on recent history, the everyday life of ordinary people, and social, economic, and political change. History study that featured morality tales and ancient, historic events was behind the times.[41] The New Historians offered three recommendations on how history should be studied. First, history education should focus on finding solutions for current as well as future problems in society. As Robinson wrote, "The present has hitherto been the willing victim of the past; the time has now come when it should turn on the past and exploit it in the interests of the advance."[42] Second, they recommended adding new topics to the study of history, such as contemporary social phenomena and problems, and diminishing the traditional political and military focus. Third, they called for a broader conception of history study in order to bring in methods and ideas from economics, anthropology, psychology, and sociology. In essence, they were adding, as Peter Novick observes, "some new layers of brickwork to the political and constitutional edifice of historical knowledge."[43]

The first and second of these recommendations were particularly salient for elementary school education. As one proponent of the new history stated, "The object of teaching history is narrowly said to be to make good citizens—intelligent voters....The main object of teaching history is to make good men and women, cultivated and broad men and women."[44] If good citizenship and character development were now the responsibility of history instruction, clearly the history curriculum had to include other disciplines. In both content and method, the study of history had to change.

Some of the less well-known historians in this group addressed elementary education directly. For example, William H. Mace, Professor of History at Syracuse University, tried to make history study more accessible to the young learner. Mace identified the five great "social institutions" that children experience (the family, industry/occupation, church, government, and school) as the foundations of history study.[45] Firsthand experience with these institutions prepared children for conceptual study at school. Mace claimed, "This study of local and other institutions through observation goes right on through life—widening and deepening as the years go by."[46] It may be noted that Mace's approach to instruction was very similar to the expanding communities approach that was institutionalized nationwide in elementary schools a few decades later.

The New Historians had little direct involvement in elementary social studies education. However, indirectly, they influenced how history, in the new social studies curriculum, was taught. As noted, they favored social and economic history more than political and military history. They also thought that the study of history led to an understanding of the present. And, much more than other historians, they were willing to engage with the social scientists.[47] As a result, the New Historians influenced the theory and methodology of history study, which was (and to some, still is) the cornerstone of social studies education.

The Child-Centered Progressives

Child-centered progressive education was based on a set of fundamental principles: school should follow the child's natural interests, should relate to the child's world outside school, and should engage the child actively. These were principles that departed radically, at times, from most nineteenth-century ideas about schooling.[48] Many members in this broadly inclusive group could fit easily into other categories of the educational progressivism classification scheme. For example, John Dewey and Harold Rugg may be classified as social reconstructionists (reformers who thought schools should lead the effort to transform society) or social meliorists (reformers who thought schools should improve society). Yet, as child-centered progressives, Dewey and Rugg championed learning directed at the "whole child" and provided theoretical support as well as practical suggestions for transforming elementary history and geography study into social studies.

In addition to Dewey and Rugg, the child-centered progressives included Francis W. Parker, William Heard Kilpatrick, Lucy Sprague Mitchell, and Caroline Pratt. It is important to note that their thinking evolved as their curricular ideas about the child's interests and needs shifted. However, they disagreed as to how much these interests and needs should influence the curriculum. Dewey, for example, called for a balance between the child and the curriculum, while others, such as Kilpatrick, prioritized the child's interests and needs over the curriculum. However, all these educators fit comfortably into the child-centered progressive group because of the influential role they played, at various times, in the evolution of social studies education.

Dewey, the great philosopher of progressive education, called Parker "the father of progressive education."[49] In Chicago, both Parker and Dewey put their pedagogical ideas into practice: Dewey at the University of Chicago Laboratory School and Parker at the Frances W. Parker School. Because of their dissatisfaction with traditional schooling, which they claimed emphasized rote learning and neglected children's natural curiosity, both men experimented with informal classroom settings and innovative teaching methods. Their goal was to educate children for "democratic living."[50] This was the goal of social reconstructionism.[51] Parker called his approach "new education."[52] Although both Parker and Dewey influenced educational thought, the extent of their influence on practice is debatable. In any case, decades later their ideas still resonate with many proponents of social studies education.

Parker was the ideological heir of Jean-Jacques Rousseau, Johann Pestalozzi, and Freidrich Froebel. As such, he was well versed in the psychology of childhood.[53] He advocated learning that drew upon the child's natural interests, that attended to all aspects of the child's development, and that correlated the school subjects. The concept of correlation referred to the integration of subjects by which children learned about their world in an authentic way rather than by an artificial separation of the subjects.[54] In many respects, Parker's concept of correlation became the foundation of social studies that integrated history and the social sciences.

Like most of his ideas about education, Dewey's opinion of history education in elementary school was rather complex. He thought learning was relevant if based in the child's experiences with the natural world. However, he was also a supporter of disciplinary content. In his seminal essay, *The Child and the Curriculum*, Dewey rejected child-centered education that weakened subject matter instruction.[55] Yet, in an earlier essay, *The School and Society*, Dewey wrote, "If history be regarded as just the record of the past, it is hard to see any grounds for claiming that it should play any large role in the curriculum of elementary education. The past is the past, and the dead may be safely left to bury its dead."[56] Taken in isolation, this statement has sometimes been interpreted to mean Dewey rejected subject content entirely even though, in the same essay, he argued history study was useful for understanding contemporary social life.[57] Considering his work as a whole, it seems Dewey took a compromise position between the child-centered focus and the content-centered focus; for Dewey, the child and the curriculum needed to interact in a "dynamic" fashion. Just as he avoided dichotomies generally, Dewey avoided the dichotomy between the child and the curriculum.

Taking inspiration from Parker and Dewey, progressive educators tended to elevate the interests of the child over curriculum content— clearly in theory and often in practice. Probably the most famous advocate of child-centered education was William Heard Kilpatrick. Kilpatrick spent decades at TC as a student, lecturer, and professor. He was known as the "Million Dollar Professor" because of the tuition revenues he generated from the thirty-five thousand students he taught over his lifetime. On a nonpecuniary level, he is remembered for his pedagogical approach called the "project method" that reflected the fundamental, child-centered learning philosophy of the progressive education movement.[58] He proposed projects (pedagogical activities for elementary students) that patterned adult activities such as dress making, boat building, and letter writing. Kilpatrick valued teachers because he thought they could ground children's ideas in projects that encompassed "the wider social life of the older world."[59] These projects, which involved the children "wholeheartedly," were conducted in a social environment.[60] Probably the most important requirement of his projects was that they should be "purposeful": all should be driven by a clearly articulated purpose and should produce a real product (e.g., a dress, a school newspaper, a play). Individually or in groups, children could work on projects in any subject. Kilpatrick's project method was popular with many social studies educators. For example, in the 1920s, the *Detroit Journal of Education* published several articles on teaching social studies using the project approach.[61]

Harold Rugg, also a TC Professor, agreed with Kilpatrick that children should actively participate in school by "working" rather than simply by "listening." In their book, *The Child-Centered School*, Rugg and his co-author, Ann Shumaker, echoed Dewey's ideas on individual experience and free expression, recommended that teachers use group activities and projects in their lessons, and addressed the lack of structure or programmatic design in schools.[62] For Rugg, the child-centered curriculum was a tool of social reform.[63] Thus, he and Shumaker urged replacing subject content with "centers of interest" or "units of work" that focused on authentic topics or issues.[64] They approvingly quoted the educators at Columbia University's Lincoln School, a laboratory school known for putting progressive pedagogy into practice: "The unit of work must be selected from real-life situations and must be considered worthwhile by the child because he feels that he had helped select it and because he finds in it many opportunities to satisfy his needs."[65] This book, although a minor part of Rugg's lifework, departs in many ways from his textbook writing. Nevertheless, it offers an important insight into how an important educational reformer in this era saw the role of the child in school learning.[66]

Lucy Sprague Mitchell was another active member in this broadly defined group of child-centered progressive educators.[67] In addition to her work as an education theorist, teacher, and social reformer, Mitchell is also remembered as a children's author whose storybooks presented alternatives to fairy tales, folktales, and classical myths, all of which she found too remote from children's lives. This same viewpoint is evident in her support of a teaching approach similar to the expanding communities approach. She wrote, "The school gives the children the opportunity to explore first their own environment and gradually widens this environment for them along lines of their own inquiries...so stories must begin with the familiar and immediate."[68] She promoted a curriculum that centered on the "here and now" because she thought children were most interested in, and able to grasp, the things, places, and people they encountered daily. Beginning with these immediate experiences, children could then broaden their study of concepts and relationships.

Mitchell's stories in *The Here and Now Storybook,* which featured people such as the grocer and the farmer, and places such as the skyscraper and the subway, were child-centered and based in the everyday reality of many children's lives. She believed that such topics, as well as engines, boats, wagons, the milking machine, and so forth, interested children, especially when they were presented in story form rather than in an encyclopedic listing.[69] Mitchell's stories became the model for the realistic genre of children's books. The popular bedtime story, *Good Night, Moon* by Margaret Wise Brown (who studied with Mitchell), followed that model.[70] For upper elementary children, Mitchell thought geography deserved a prominent place in the curriculum because it helped students understand the world.[71] Geography taught children how people interact with their environment, how city and country life differ, and how to read and draw maps. Her geography books for children included activities (e.g., visits to places in the community) that could be used to teach geography concepts and skills.[72]

Mitchell's colleague, Caroline Pratt, put many of these ideas into practice at the City and Country School in New York City, which she founded in 1914.[73] This private school, which was originally housed in Pratt's Greenwich Village apartment, later moved to West 12th and 13th Streets in New York City, still its present location. Pratt's instructional approach reflected Dewey's ideas on the importance of inquiry and experimentation in education and on the development of a cooperative school community. Instead of studying traditional school subjects, young children (ages three to seven) constructed replicas of neighborhood buildings with wooden blocks. Older children (ages eight to twelve) ran the school store and helped print instructional materials. In these activities, social studies was, as Susan Semel describes it, "the core subject of the curriculum."[74] In block play, children learned about the community; in store play, they learned about money; in the printing activity, they learned cooperation and even a little history (e.g., the invention of the printing press).[75] This was multi-faceted education for the "whole child."

In summary, most child-centered progressive educators argued for the structural compatibility between the project method and social studies education. They also promoted curriculum linkages between children's experiences and life topics and story genres. For these educators, it was clear that social studies had greater educational value than traditional history and geography study. Next we look at history and geography education in the early twentieth century by examining key studies produced by academic organizations before the social studies curriculum entered the public schools.

The American History Association's
Committee of Eight Report

In 1909, more than a decade after the publication of its recommendations for high school history in the Committee of Seven report, the American History Association (AHA) wrote history recommendations for elementary schools in its Committee of Eight report called *The Study of History in the Elementary Schools.*[76] The report struck a balance between attention to academic content and child-centered learning strategies. This carefully constructed balance, which rarely appeared in later history and social studies curricula, was likely due to the composition of the Committee. It was an AHA committee, but its members were mostly K–12 educators.[77] In fact, the Committee wrote that "care was exercised to secure a majority who should be in actual touch with the work of the elementary schools" in order to avoid producing a document that was "the result of the working out of fine spun theories on the part of college men."[78]

The report declared that the primary aim of history lessons in every elementary grade was to relate the past to the present. The report's introduction stated categorically, "We believe that a leading aim in history teaching is to help the child to appreciate what his fellows are doing and to help him to intelligent voluntary action in agreement or disagreement with them."[79] Children could better understand contemporary social conditions from the study of history. Ruing the loss of "surprise and novelty" in history teaching, the report encouraged teachers to make their history lessons appealing to children's imaginations.[80]

The report proposed a model curriculum with recommended topics for each grade, one through eight. For example, instead of myths and legends in the lower elementary grades, the report recommended simple biographies of American heroes and the study of Indian life, holidays, and local events. In fourth and fifth grades, the recommendation was that students study U.S. history by reading biographies. Eighth graders should study the American Revolutionary War and the American Civil War rather than the histories of Greece, Rome, and the Middle Ages that the AHA had previously recommended (in the Committee of Seven report).[81] In her analysis of the report, Chara Bohan explains, "A critical manner of encouraging allegiance to the nation-state was through the school curriculum, and especially the history curriculum."[82] She describes the recommendations as "nationalistic" and argues that the nationalistic slant might prevent students from learning about other nations, cultures, and people.[83] Jeffrey Mirel has suggested that this greater attention to U.S. history may have been a response to the increase in the number of students from immigrant families.[84]

The report stated that children in grades one and two lacked the intellectual capacity for understanding causal relationships in history. Thus, the report recommended stories about heroes and adventure that taught children important facts, universal truths, and moral lessons. The report also stressed the importance of children's active engagement in course material at every grade level. The history teacher's role was to make "the past live again in the heart and head of the child."[85] By taking a biographical approach to the study of historical figures, the teacher could tell good stories that "captivated the attention of his youthful listeners."[86] Additionally, children should look at photographs, scrapbooks, and diaries, and engage in debates, games, and dramatization. This was active, participatory learning.

The report was credited with influencing elementary history instruction—at least in rhetoric. It was also praised soon after its publication. In a 1912 account, AHA member, J. Montgomery Gambrill, said the report "presents for the first time in this country, a complete and coordinated course of study in history for the elementary schools," and is "a standard for the great body of elementary schools to follow."[87] In a 1929 journal article, an associate superintendent of the Philadelphia Public Schools stated, "Few educational pronouncements have exerted a more profound influence upon the curriculum of the elementary schools of the nation." He concluded that the report "has furnished the basis for general practice throughout the country."[88] (However, he admitted he based his conclusion on more than twenty years of experience in the Philadelphia Public Schools rather than on a comprehensive survey or on scientific research.) In a 1935 account of social studies, Rolla Tryon, an AHA member, wrote, "Courses of study in history for the elementary school soon began to appear which were almost verbatim duplicates of [those proposed by the Committee of Eight]." Tryon also noted that the report had a "stabilizing influence" on elementary curriculum and was "very well-received."[89] According to Bohan, even contemporary social studies programs of today seem to reflect some of the report's recommendations.[90] However, there were criticisms of the report, such as the disorganization in the teacher training section and the cursory (and sometimes inaccurate) treatment of foreign countries.[91] Bohan also notes its overt nationalism.[92]

Today, historians of education recognize that the 1909 AHA Committee of Eight report had two major effects on elementary social studies. It proposed a structure for history study that was national, biographical, and social. More significantly, in terms of the progressive education movement, it gave authoritative approval to the idea that history study should be imaginatively linked with contemporary life and the interests of the child.

Social Studies Curricula at the
Local Level, 1905 to 1913

There is evidence that the progressive education movement, to some degree at least, influenced the elementary school curricula of the early twentieth century. Social studies had not yet replaced traditional instruction in geography and history in the classrooms, but at the policy level there were new ideas about how these subjects should be taught. Progressive educators had given administrative educators a theoretical toolbox they could use to build a new social studies curriculum. For example, the annual reports from the early twentieth century in the Detroit Public Schools (DPS) and the Grand Rapids Public Schools (GRPS) show that policy makers in urban Michigan encouraged imaginative history and geography teaching that used participatory activities, map making, and field trips. In this section we examine the influence of the new ideas in elementary social studies education in these two school districts.[93]

Until the mid-1910s, the DPS history curriculum listed European fables, myths, legends, and fairy tales for reading lessons in the lower elementary grades. History was a separate course in the upper elementary grades. According to the 1905 DPS curriculum, first graders studied American Indians, Eskimos, and the Japanese. Second graders studied the Greeks, the Romans, and the Dutch while third graders studied cave dwellers.[94] The 1902 GRPS curriculum listed as topics for study Hiawatha, the American Revolutionary War, and Julius Caesar; the 1904 GRPS curriculum listed the Vikings, King Arthur, and Aeneas.[95] With its curious mixture of periods, peoples, and topics (both real and imaginary), this was the kind of curriculum that many progressive educators, as well as the 1909 AHA Committee of Eight report, criticized. Two years after the 1909 AHA report was issued, the 1911 DPS annual report still declared authoritatively that the curriculum included ancient and world history in order to "fill the pupils' minds with stimulating ideas."[96]

Despite this rather conservative approach to the curriculum content in the DPS, its educators took a more progressive approach to classroom teaching as they searched for more child-centered and active ways to teach children.[97] The DPS annual reports from the early twentieth century recommended kindergarteners visit a firehouse and first graders dramatize Columbus's landing in the Americas.[98] They recommended teachers use the project approach (that Kilpatrick would later popularize). For example, the goal of a unit on coffee was to teach children about "distant lands and races," production, transportation, and consumption.[99] One DPS annual report advised teachers to select narrow topics for study that would allow them to integrate, rather than isolate, the important facts of an event so that children could understand the event in a broader context.[100]

Home geography, the study of the local environment through exploration and observation, which had developed in the latter part of the nineteenth century, was often taught in the early twentieth century.[101] Much of home geography featured the study of topics thought relevant to children's lives. This content became the basis of the topics-based approach to elementary social studies that developed later. TC Professor, Richard E. Dodge, was an advocate of home geography. His popular geography textbooks established his reputation as one of the most highly regarded leaders in the geography instruction of the early twentieth century.[102] Home geography, which featured in all his elementary textbooks for the lower elementary grades, focused on social topics (e.g., the home, the neighborhood, streets and roads, local government, and transportation) and physical topics (e.g., rivers, soils, and the atmosphere). Dodge used the concept of family to explain complicated topics. For example, he compared government to the family:

> The work of the house is divided among the members of the family just as the work of caring for the city is divided among a number of men, each having a special task. Thus a home is a little government, the simplest kind of government there is, and one that every child knows in his everyday life.[103]

While some proponents of home geography approved the use of social topics, they were less supportive of the near to far approach (e.g., home, school, community, state, and so forth).[104] According to Keith Barton, Dodge (and his co-author, Clara Kirchway) opposed this approach because they claimed it prevented students from studying distant yet relevant places (such as the origins of the products they used and consumed).[105] Yet Charles McMurry, the Herbartian scholar who wrote textbooks for many subjects, maintained that beginning with the child's interests and moving outward, the approach the 1895 NEA Committee of Fifteen report had endorsed, made the best pedagogical sense.[106]

There was no movement in the early twentieth century to discard the separate subjects of history and geography (including home geography) in the DPS, but the new concept of "social study" began to be used. In remarkably prescient language, the 1905 DPS annual report used the term "social study" to refer to lessons on the grocery, shoemaking, carpentry, and blacksmithing (similar to the home geography topics). For the third grade, the DPS curriculum described units on agriculture, animal husbandry, and sugar production as "studies in industrial life."[107] Moreover, the expanding communities approach was evident in the DPS geography curriculum that stated, "The general trend of the course is from the home outward....This is followed by a study of their home, city, county, state and nation."[108] Thus, long before the expanding communities approach became the centerpiece of the social studies curriculum, some DPS leaders recommended it as appropriate and logical for young children.

Of course, local protests, similar to the national protests, were raised against changes in content and pedagogy in the DPS. Some DPS educators worried that the pendulum would swing too far. The fear was that the facts-based curriculum, which had been criticized for its overemphasis on memorization, was now endangered. The 1912–13 DPS annual report, which urged memorization of facts in geography instruction revisions, cautioned, "Pupils now receive much general information, but their knowledge of maps and of location is far from exact."[109] Others raised concerns as well. In 1906, Dodge expressed concern that in moving away from memorization of places "we have gone too far" with the result that pupils have not "gained enough knowledge of the locational geography of the United States to understand the news of the day."[110] The debate over the child-centered curriculum versus the content-centered curriculum in elementary history and geography education, in Michigan as elsewhere, continued. As progressive education theories began to influence classroom practice, both sides, at the national and local levels, still conducted the debate in an either/or context.

The Emergence of Social Studies

Although "social studies" has its roots in the first decade of the twentieth century, it first achieved widespread recognition as a separate area of study (at least in rhetoric) following the publication of a report by the 1913–16 Committee on the Social Studies, a subcommittee of the Commission on the Reorganization of Secondary Education (CRSE).[111] The NEA and the U.S. Bureau of Education had jointly appointed the CRSE to examine secondary education and to make recommendations for change. Some education historians say the CRSE's innovative, even radical, recommendations marked a critical turning point in the history of U.S. education.[112] Others argue that the recommendations of the Committee on the Social Studies did not differ significantly from earlier AHA recommendations.[113]

Perhaps the CRSE's most important contribution was its listing of the "Cardinal Principles of Secondary Education."[114] These principles became the foundation of secondary education in the years ahead, even though few of the principles were really academic. The seven principles were health, command of fundamental processes, worthy home membership, vocation, civic education, worthy use of leisure, and ethical character. The intent of the principles was not to divide the curriculum into subjects but rather to provide overarching principles to guide each subject. The focus of these general guidelines was less on the advancement of knowledge and more on social education, citizenship training, and social progress.[115]

The Committee on the Social Studies (hereafter the Committee), which was one of the CRSE's subject-specific subcommittees, issued three social studies reports focused on social education, citizenship training, and social progress.[116] Echoing the New Historians' ideas on history instruction (in fact, the New Historian, James Harvey Robinson, was a member of the Committee), the Committee recommended that history study with immediate relevance to children's lives replace "old history" study.[117] The Committee continued to call for history courses but favored history study that was a mixture of social science, civics, and contemporary affairs.

Although the Committee's main interest was secondary education, its report, *The Teaching of Community Civics*, briefly referenced elementary education.[118] The course syllabus in the report listed historical documents for study (e.g., the Declaration of Independence and the Constitution), but priority was given to the study of thrift, teamwork, property rights, and the work ethic, and to instruction in the social, aesthetic, and religious life of the community.[119] One course goal was "to help the child know his community, not merely a lot of facts about it, but the meaning of his community life, what it does for him, and how it does it...."[120] Arthur Dunn, who was a co-author of the course and who would become a prominent civics educator, explained, "Every community also needs citizens who possess a large measure of social initiative and the power of leadership."[121]

It was clear the main goal of the community civics course and of schooling was the socialization of six- to twelve-year olds. "The school should also lead [the child] to see how the grocer, the iceman, the policeman, the postman, and many others in the larger community outside of the home and the school enter into his life and contribute to his welfare and the welfare of others."[122] The course listed a number of topics: health, protection of life and property, recreation and education, civic beauty, wealth, communication, transportation, migration, charity, corrections (criminal punishment), and the conduct and financing of governmental and volunteer agencies. The course promoted the "project learning" approach to teaching these topics, using multidisciplinary viewpoints.[123]

There is no discussion in the community civics course about the study of history and geography or 'about any reflection such study might lead to. "Community Civics" was about daily life and getting along with others rather than the specific purposes of government or how the study of the past informs the present. The purpose of the course, which was heralded as "almost indispensable" to the "new type of history," was to help the child choose a vocation.[124] This was a utilitarian view of education not envisioned by the educators and historians who had written the earlier national committee reports.

As Julie Reuben has shown in her description of citizenship in the Progressive Era, embedding citizenship education in community civics was a radical change from the approach nineteenth-century educators took.[125] Formerly, it was thought students learned to be good citizens by studying political institutions and by practicing democratic skills. Now the study of "community civics" meant encouraging students to participate in the local community. Lessons were no longer for the study of democratic principles; lessons were to teach children the habits of proper social deportment.

Local school districts soon felt the influence of the CRSE's recommendations, at least in theory (change at the classroom level was much slower). Cremin called the work of the CRSE "a pedagogical revolution" and in general a victory for progressive educators.[126] The U. S. Bureau of Education distributed twenty-seven thousand copies of the Committee's 1916 social studies report to educators across the country. [127] According to Edgar Dawson, a founder and leader of the National Council for the Social Studies, by 1923 the Committee's recommendations, which were widely accepted in U.S. schools, exerted as much, if not more, influence on education as the earlier AHA reports.[128] Some scholars argue that history, of all the social science subjects, was most influenced.[129] While the 1916 report did not actually call for "social studies" to replace history, many educators claim that was its effect as well as its intent. In the 1920s, many school districts created social studies departments that would conjoin the separate disciplines.[130] However, at the secondary level, history and geography were still taught as separate courses. At the elementary level, teachers generally continued to teach individual lessons in history and geography.

Education for Citizenship

Following the release of these social studies reports by the CRSE's Committee on the Social Studies, only two years before the United States entered World War I, educators and policymakers increased their emphasis on the importance of teaching citizenship in schools. Like most other Americans, they were swept up by the forces of patriotism and militarism. The rallying cry was that schools should teach patriotism and civic responsibility to all children, not just immigrant children singled out for assimilation or "Americanization." However, this new conception of citizenship, often packaged like the community civics course described above, was quite different from Reuben's description of progressive educators' "apolitical definition of citizenship."[131] Previously, civics courses in national government, which were only for high school students, taught the principles of democratic government. Now the community civics courses, which were for elementary students, encouraged community action.

In the Chicago Public Schools, for example, there was considerable enthusiasm for the community civics courses.[132] One Chicago school principal declared that historically the teaching of citizenship was "unorganized, indefinite, and incidental," and it was time to energize the civics curriculum.[133] Other Chicago educators supported teaching civics, even at the lower grades. One educator explained that civics "is the foundation upon which our entire system of education rests."[134] In harmony with the progressive educators' everyday-life-experience agenda, using an approach like the expanding communities approach (although not naming it as such), this same educator stated the purpose of civics education:

> Practical civics must begin with the phases of life which touch the child intimately, and radiate into circles of interest, which grow wider and wider. It must begin by direct personal contact with the activities of his own community. First hand acquaintanceship with the work of the garbage collector, the street sweeper, the policeman and the postman, forms a foundation upon which may be built an intelligent study of government and politics.[135]

However, some educators around the time of World War I took a more conservative approach to such changes in the curriculum. They thought citizenship could be effectively taught in geography and history classes. While history had often had this responsibility, the claim was rather novel for geography. Geography, the claim went, was the discipline most concerned with the "welfare of the human race"[136] because it dealt with the natural world and explained the linkage of phenomena such as city sizes with locations, and natural environments with cultures.[137] For instance, some educators thought geography field trips, which showed children the physical and cultural characteristics of their surroundings, taught them patriotism and nationalism.[138] Geography, it was said, had the same civilizing effect as history education by giving students "an understanding of human instincts, feelings, emotions, needs, and ideals which inspire human activities."[139]

By the early 1920s, many educators at the local level had begun adapting their history and geography lessons to include instruction in civic responsibility and social skills. For example, a course in the history of Chicago had a section on the difficulties of municipal waste disposal.[140] Other teachers used the activities in children's daily lives as teaching topics. The third-grade curriculum in the Chicago Public Schools stated, "The studies should include those street activities which every child sees going on about him, and which are the elements of the commercial life in which we live, and they should culminate in a study of the local business district and its relation to his home."[141] Thus, education for citizenship meant learning about the neighborhood grocer, the skilled carpenter, the helpful hardware man, and so on. These were lessons about harmonious life in an interdependent community.[142]

The AHA also joined the nationwide discussion on the importance of teaching citizenship. In the years 1917 to 1919, in a joint effort with the NEA and the National Board for Historical Service (an organization for history scholars), the AHA organized the Committee on History and Education for Citizenship in the Schools.[143] This committee was commonly called the Schafer Committee, after its chair, Joseph Schafer, Superintendent of the Wisconsin State Historical Society. Owing largely to the dissension among its members, this committee ultimately failed to gain approval for its recommendations for elementary, middle, and high schools.

The Schafer Committee generally supported two ideas about elementary education: (1) children should learn that the social world was one of progressive development; and (2) children should learn the value of evidence. Accordingly, "History rather than other subjects in the curriculum could best develop these two ideas."[144] The Schafer Committee's initial recommendations differed significantly from those offered by the AHA Committee of Eight. For example, the Schafer Committee recommended that elementary school children study ancient mythology, stories of early man, pre-Greek history, Egypt, and Palestine; the study of U.S. history was not recommended until grade seven.[145] While noting that some educators wanted to include American Indian myths, the Schafer Committee did not agree. Their ethnocentric claim was that such myths did not present the universality of human experience in the way the Greek myths did.[146] The Schafer Committee also strongly opposed the near to far approach endorsed by the CRSE's Committee on the Social Studies. The Schafer Committee argued that instead of expanding children's minds by introducing them to the strange and the new, the approach limited children's mental development. The Schafer Committee declared, "In these years the imaginative activity of the child is predominant, and it would seem a great pity to warp the child's normal development through an impatient insistence on the learning of family, community, and civic duties...."[147]

In the spring of 1919, the Schafer Committee solicited feedback on its recommendations from teachers. Teachers seized the opportunity, mainly to offer criticism. Their remarks about elementary school studies fell into three categories. First, the curriculum focused too heavily on European stories and topics; second, below grade seven, the curriculum neglected American history and civics; and third, the curriculum made no adequate provision for a "definite scheme of social studies" in junior high school.[148] There were various other criticisms, such as the complaint that too much emphasis was placed on "chronological" history and not enough on the "psychological states of the development of the child."[149]

Although the teachers' negative responses may have surprised the Schafer Committee, its members quickly realized they faced demanding revision work. Almost in desperation, Chairman Schafer confided to a fellow committee member, "I have lost pretty much all confidence in my ability to forecast what is wanted or needed in common schools and am prepared to make a new venture based very largely upon what I now know to be the desires of a good many school men."[150] The Committee then published a revised curriculum, with new recommendations, in the June issue of the AHA journal, *The Historical Outlook*. While history study was still emphasized, U.S. history was now the primary focus. First graders studied "the making of a community" (which included study of American Indians and pioneers), and second graders studied "the making of the United States" (which included study of the country's founding). Third through sixth graders studied U.S. history chronologically.[151] In terms of content, these revised recommendations were actually quite similar to those from the Committee of Eight of 1909. However, rather than the biographical approach recommended by the Committee of Eight, the Schafer Committee proposed the use of "problems" (e.g., "the problem of getting across the Atlantic") as the best way to interest students in the study of history.[152]

The AHA never endorsed the Schafer Committee's recommendations. Thus, while the recommendations had little influence on local curricula, interesting implications may be drawn from the responses to them. First, the revisions to the initial recommendations were the result of teachers' overwhelming preference for national history over world history.[153] Second, the Schafer Committee's rejection of the near to far approach revealed there were historians who strongly opposed that approach. Third, comments showed there was a consensus among the members (most of whom were historians) that history was the central and unifying discipline of citizenship education.

The National Council for the Social Studies

In the 1920s, however, there was a turning point in the struggle between historians and social studies educators. By the end of the decade, historians recognized that history was losing its pre-eminent position in the elementary curriculum. History was becoming a single subject in a multidisciplinary field. The National Council for the Social Studies (NCSS) was an important force behind this change.

Social studies educators had founded the NCSS following the tradition of other academic organizations such as the National Council of Teachers of English (founded in 1911) and the National Council of Teachers of Mathematics (founded in 1920). Unlike those single discipline organizations, however, the NCSS was a multidisciplinary organization whose members included teachers of history, economics, civics (political science), geography, and sociology. According to the NCSS, social studies had two tasks: education in the disciplines and education in citizenship.[154]

The history of the NCSS begins in 1921 when Earle Rugg (a Chicago high school teacher and a TC graduate student) and four social science professors met to organize "the association and cooperation of teachers of the social studies (history, government, economics, sociology, etc.) and of school administrators, supervisors, teachers of education, and others interested in obtaining the maximum results in education for citizenship from social studies."[155] In 1922, their new organization, now called the National Council for the Social Studies, added geography to its list of disciplines. Besides promoting citizenship education, the NCSS addressed the content and purpose of social studies, teacher certification requirements, new courses in community civics and democracy, and communication between education professors and professors of the history and the social sciences.[156] Immediately the simmering controversy between the historians and the social scientists began to boil. Harold Rugg (Earle Rugg's brother and fellow NCSS founder) declared, "It is not certain that all have learned that the social studies constitute a group of subjects which must be viewed as a group and not as separate disciplines, wholly independent of each other."[157]

The mission of the NCSS was to illuminate issues and solve problems in social studies education. The NCSS leaders thought patriotism, democracy, and good citizenship were best taught in social studies lessons rather than in history or geography lessons. Originally, the focus of the NCSS was secondary education although, as more elementary teachers became members, it broadened its scope to K–12 education.[158] In addition to addressing teacher certification requirements and communication problems between the education professors and the professors of history, geography, and other social sciences, the NCSS founders wanted to resolve the content and purpose conflicts in social studies and to introduce interdisciplinary courses.[159] History, which had always held a dominant position among the social sciences, was a particularly challenging problem in the movement to collect these separate disciplines under one umbrella. As the NCSS membership broadened from mostly high school teachers to K–12 teachers, its multidisciplinary sweep gained in popularity (see Chapter 3). In these years, at the high school level, U.S. history, civics and government, and economics were still taught as separate subjects (as they are today). At the elementary level, however, in policy and sometimes in practice, social studies was becoming a separate subject.

The Growth of Social Studies at the Local Level, 1916 to 1926

As education theory and practice began to address the idea of social studies and its progressive pedagogy, what did local school administrations recommend and how did teachers respond? Next we examine method and content in the public schools in Grand Rapids and Detroit as social studies began to influence their curricula. A study of the local level curricula reveals the challenges administrators faced with the new pedagogical theories and approaches. Although these curricular documents present only administrative recommendations, not requirements, they do offer valuable insights into the rhetoric of the times. They may also give us an idea of what and how teachers taught.

With regard to administrative policy on history and geography instruction, the GRPS annual reports from the early twentieth century were rather vague as far as preferred pedagogy, but the DPS annual reports revealed strong support for progressive teaching methods. Yet contemporaneous GRPS school surveys and DPS teaching commentaries were critical of the (traditional) teaching methods in use. Practice had not yet caught up with policy. As Barton found in his analysis of early twentieth classroom instruction surveys, conducted by educational experts, recitation in these years was the main method of instruction.[160] This finding is confirmed by the pedagogy in the GRPS where history study in the upper elementary grades was of "the usual question and answer type. The task of the pupils was to memorize the facts and then to give them out in the recitation in answers to questions."[161] Editorializing, the anonymous author of this GRPS survey stated:

> This fact-learning and recitation method is coming to be looked upon as less effective for the serious purposes of teaching history than the experiential method of re-living the reconstructed life of the past through the imaginative experience of reading in which the treatment is full, concrete, vivid and interesting. At the present time there is too much fact-learning and not enough historical experience.[162]

The situation was not much better in geography. The same GRPS survey stated, "Very little evidence was observed of the use of the problem-method of teaching geography."[163] It appeared that the GRPS had not yet adopted the progressive pedagogical approaches of student-centered teaching, learning by doing, and relating school content to the world outside school. History and geography instruction were still taught using the traditional approaches that many experts now increasingly viewed as ineffective.

Was there a similar gap between policy and practice as far as the adoption of social studies as a single subject at the elementary level in the GRPS and the DPS? In the DPS, it appeared the intent was to close that gap. In 1921, the DPS founded the Department of Social Science as part of its effort to replace the subjects of history, geography, and civics with social studies, and to develop social studies as a relevant area of study that would contribute to students' civic development. The DPS annual reports confirm this shift in policy with their prescription of stories for the lower elementary grades in which children would learn moral lessons and "aesthetic taste and appreciation."[164] As a supplement to their history and geography study, children in the upper elementary grades studied "social and industrial studies and civics" in order to learn the importance of economics, geography, and civics in society. They also studied the home tasks of cooking, sewing, and laundering before they studied industry and businesses.[165] Nevertheless, it appears teachers in both the GRPS and the DPS taught history and geography as they always had. Leah Spencer, the DPS Assistant Director of Social Science Education and a former geography teacher, commented, "For the first few years, the change in name [to social science] brought about no appreciable change in the teaching of social science. Geography was still taught as geography and history as history."[166]

Two DPS curricular guides from 1917 reflect this ambivalence about which social science subjects and which history lessons to teach and how to teach them. The history guide (grades seven and eight) took the traditional view of history study. Students should learn discrete knowledge units such as important people and events in history. The geography guide (grades three through six) was more progressive in that it emphasized thinking skills, collaborative work, and problem solving. This guide stated, "Understanding should precede memorizing," and "Children instinctively delight in ferreting out causes and studying results."[167] The geography guide also recommended lessons that taught process skills (reading and drawing maps) and lessons that developed concept skills (visualizing the "mental picture" of a city or a land mass). Both the history and the geography guides reflect, at least in rhetoric, the progressive philosophy of education in which lessons were child-initiated and teaching was child-directed.

The DPS Department of Social Science combined the departments of nature study, geography, history, and civil government. The Department's main founder, Arthur Dondineau, thought students knew little about contemporary political, social, and economic issues. He doubted "many children ever read a newspaper in 1921."[168] He thought a new curriculum was needed, especially a curriculum in which the children of newly arrived immigrant families were "schooled in a very different type of social scheme."[169] Traditional history instruction, Dondineau wrote, "will never teach the pupil how to vote nor will it teach him his duty to vote the year of his twenty-first birthday."[170] Yet, even as he supported citizenship training, Dondineau did not abandon certain elements of traditional history instruction: for example, birthdays of presidents were still celebrated in his curriculum.

Dondineau's main contribution to the DPS elementary curriculum during these years was the *Course of Study in Social Science: Grades One to Six* that he co-authored with Leah Spencer. The course still included history and geography, but it integrated them with the social sciences.

The purpose of the social sciences was to teach children to "partici-pate in the various social activities and institutions of our republican government now and in the future."[171] In addition, the course charged history instruction with a new purpose: "A study of the past is of value in so far as it assists in anlyzing [sic] and understanding our present social organization, how it came to be, its main defects, and in determining the future course of events."[172] In short, history and geography lessons were allowed a place in the DPS curriculum so long as they taught good citizenship.

Dondineau and Spencer's *Course of Study in Social Science* was an important milestone for social studies education in the DPS. Whereas once history and geography were the central focus of elementary social studies education, they now were only two of the many social science subjects, which included civics, elementary sociology, and basic economics.[173] In theory, such subjects in the DPS were organized in a "continuous and organic" whole under the heading of "social science" that taught participatory democracy, economics, and the natural world.[174] In his 1925 evaluation of the course, Henry Harap, TC Professor of Education, praised its innovative and "unified" approach to social studies.[175]

After its birth in the early decades of the twentieth century, slow-ly, often hesitantly, social studies developed in some elementary schools as a single subject that reflected progressive educators' and historians' philosophies of education and education psychologists' research on learning. Nineteenth-century history and geography lessons, both in content and in method, steadily lost influence at the elementary level as many educators, who rebelled against the dreary memorization of facts and dates, were beginning to see some of their progressive ideas about teaching promoted in school rhetoric and even realized in school practice. Contemporary social, economic, and political issues were creeping into the curriculum, with education for citizenship (increasingly defined as good behavior in school and in the community) always at the center of such study.

Yet, at its birth, the purpose and content of social studies education were still being formulated and debated. What was clear, however, is that many educators thought social studies would make the elemen-tary school curriculum more relevant and would better prepare students for their role as citizens. These were high hopes and expectations for a field of study just born.

Chapter 3

"Neither Fish nor Fowl": Social Studies in the Interwar Years

IN THE 1920S, when both history and geography were still taught as separate disciplines, educators began developing and promoting ideas for social studies programs. By the early 1940s, social studies was firmly established in the elementary curriculum in a form known as the fusion approach. In this approach, instead of studying the disciplines separately, children studied real world topics drawn from the social science disciplines. In both lower and upper elementary social studies, the primary goal was to prepare children to be good community citizens.

Many scholars argue that the success of social studies education is attributable to the efforts of the social studies advocates. Other scholars argue that this transformative pedagogical change was largely a response to the devastating economic crises and destabilizing political events of the interwar years.[1] Still other scholars question whether there really was a change in public education in these years of the magnitude that the social studies advocates claimed.[2] Yet, considering the nearly nationwide adoption of social studies as a separate subject in elementary classrooms, it was evident that elementary education had changed. The economic environment of the interwar years favored such change as educators began to reassess not only what schooling could do but also what schooling should do. For example, in 1933, the historian, W. G. Kimmel, explained, "Enormous pressure is being brought to bear at the moment for increased courses particularly in economic and social aspects growing out of the depression."[3] Perhaps because of this pressure, elementary social studies began to focus on social and economic topics such as employment, salaries, rent, taxes, and budgets, and the difference between necessities and luxuries.[4] The reasoning was that children should learn the principles of economics they would need to know as adults.

The political environment of the interwar years also favored change in schooling. Apprehensive about the rise of totalitarian governments in Europe, Americans renewed their sense of nationalism and their commitment to democratic principles. Many social studies educators, caught up in the same spirit, began promoting a new social studies curriculum that emphasized civic responsibility and national loyalty.

This chapter examines how social studies replaced the separate disciplines in elementary schools and why training in good citizenship supplanted instruction in disciplinary content. Teachers embraced the idea that teaching democratic principles and social skills was a better use of class time than teaching historic dates and events and abstract geography concepts like distance and scale. The newly developed social studies programs had this responsibility. The chapter also explains how and why, in the interwar years, the times were ripe for such change.

The Early Years of the National Council
for the Social Studies

The National Council for the Social Studies (NCSS), introduced in Chapter 2, was founded in 1921 as a subcommittee of the National Education Association (NEA). The NCSS was the most influential group of national educators to promote this new subject. However, initially the NCSS had little influence on education. It was a far less prestigious organization than the American Historical Association (AHA), the American Economic Association, and the American Sociological Association. Unlike members in these organizations, the NCSS members were mostly K–12 teachers, and many were women; few members were college or university professors. Moreover, the NCSS did not have a journal. Its members had free subscriptions to the AHA journal, *The Historical Outlook*, but with no editorial or operational responsibilities, they lacked a platform for spreading their ideas.[5] Despite this lack of prestige, combined with financial problems and poor organization, the NCSS grew rapidly in the 1920s, possibly because it appealed to K–12 teachers from the many social science disciplines. By 1923, teachers from every state and Canada were NCSS members.[6] By 1928, the NCSS had 1,600 members.[7]

However, there was a problem with the "more the merrier" membership drive by the NCSS: how to reconcile the members' varied opinions and other loyalties. Many NCSS members were also AHA and NEA members. In a recent historical analysis, Murry Nelson, who was an active member of the NCSS, reflected that, in part, the NCSS's "directionless" reputation was the result of its early alliance with the AHA and the NEA. Thus, the NCSS, with its diverse membership, was "neither fish nor fowl."[8] On the one hand, this all-inclusive identity attracted a large and supportive membership of educators and academics. On the other hand, and more problematically, the NCSS's vaguely conceived mission and broadly stated goals poorly defined the organization and its ideas.

The close linkage between the NCSS and the AHA meant that for many years the two organizations held joint annual meetings and AHA members took leadership roles in the NCSS. However, it was an uneasy alliance. Earle Rugg complained resentfully that the AHA stalwarts "froze us out."[9] In 1935, Edgar B. Wesley, NCSS President, reflected on the relationship between the NCSS and AHA: "For years following the organization of the [NCSS] in 1921, it met at the back door of the American Historical Association and was regarded and treated as a poor relative...the typical historian was indifferent, condescending, or scornful of the Council." Wesley acknowledged that there were some historians who were sympathetic toward and "tolerant" of the NCSS. One such historian was the history professor, August C. Krey, who attended the sessions devoted to teaching. However, Wesley observed that few other AHA members supported the NCSS.[10]

In turn, AHA leaders were skeptical, even fearful, of the growing influence of the social studies movement that the NCSS advocated. In 1923, Edward Cheyney, AHA President, warned against social studies reorganization in the secondary schools. He wrote that history as a subject had suffered an "indefinite and unsatisfactory outcome; and uncertainty has been heightened by the emphasis placed on the other social studies by the NEA's report of 1916, and by the vigorous efforts made by the advocates of those studies to substitute them for history in school curricula."[11] As Hazel Hertzberg concluded in her history of social studies, a major problem for the NCSS was always its relationship with the academic professionals whom it marginalized even as it courted them.[12]

One reason that AHA members took leadership roles in the NCSS was to maintain their influence over history education in the schools.[13] Edgar Dawson wrote that the AHA historians feared history would be replaced by a "patchwork collection of unrelated and unsystematic material."[14] By the late 1920s, the historians' fears seemed justified. Social studies education was becoming established in public schools throughout the country. In the same year the NCSS offered several programs at the annual NEA conference, which was held in July so that more members, especially teachers, could attend.[15]

Despite their struggle over the future of history and social studies education, the NCSS and the AHA maintained their edgy relationship into the 1930s. In their last joint project—the American Historical Association Commission on the Social Studies (hereafter the Commission), whose "lavishly funded" work spanned 1929 to 1934—the AHA and the NCSS put aside their differences, at least ostensibly, in an attempt to define agreed-upon goals and structures for history and social studies education.[16] With the publication of its sixteen volumes, the Commission made a significant contribution to the advancement of social studies education. However, its final volume led to a controversy, described in the next section, which overshadowed all its other work.[17]

The American Historical Association
Commission on the Social Studies

The work of the Commission has more relevance for secondary education than for elementary education. However, an analysis of the Commission's work offers insight into the thinking of its members (and indirectly of their contemporaries) on the history versus social studies debate. Moreover, in several volumes the authors addressed elementary social studies education.

Scholars disagree about the Commission's conclusions on the history versus social studies debate.[18] However, Herbert Kliebard's explanation is well-reasoned. According to Kliebard, the conclusions were "an implicit compromise" between social studies and history, in which social studies won in name and history won in content.[19] A statement by Charles Beard, the author of the first volume, *A Charter for the Social Sciences*, supports this claim. Beard argued for "a skillfully wrought mosaic rather than subliminal coalescence in which the separate disciplines would disappear and completely lose their identity as law, politics, economics, geography, and history."[20] Moreover, the sixteenth and last volume, *Conclusions and Recommendations of the Commission*, by the Commission and August C. Krey, published in 1934, took an even stronger position in favor of separating the disciplines. The Commission and Krey declared, "The Commission repudiates the notion that any general or comprehensive social science has been created which transcends the disciplines themselves."[21] However, as this section shows, the nature of the history versus social studies debate was different in elementary education than in secondary education.

Given the strong representation of AHA members on the Commission, it is not surprising the Commission prioritized history among the social science disciplines. Beard wrote about the disciplines: "crowning them all is history."[22] However, the Commission favored the New Historians' conception of history study (see Chapter 2). This meant instruction in societal problems and democratic principles. History, according to Beard, was the "cement" that bound the other disciplines into a "workable unity," despite their "stubborn and irreducible elements."[23] This was history study that social studies educators could support.

The Commission members had different opinions about the pedagogy used in elementary social studies. Beard, for example, was skeptical of the near to far approach (the basis of the expanding communities approach) because he thought "the immediate may prove to be most complex, the remote most simple."[24] On the other hand, the Commission and Krey endorsed the approach:

[The child] progresses from the near to the remote in time and space, and from elementary sensory response to the most abstract forms of thought; he moves out from the family into the neighborhood, the commonwealth, the nation, and the world, and from the present to the most distant reaches of the past and the future.[25]

Belying its title, the *Conclusions and Recommendations of the Commission* made no explicit curricular recommendations. Years later, the historian and AHA President, Arthur Link, referred to the volume's "nonrecommendations."[26] In his history of social studies, David Jenness argues that the task of writing specific social studies curriculum was left to teachers and subject specialists. Both groups lacked the necessary authority and broad vision to put the Commission's ideas into practice. The result in schools was a kind of "curriculum 'chaos.'"[27]

Reviews of the Commission's work were generally favorable. Beard's "positively exciting" volume was praised for its "fundamental, authoritative material."[28] However, it was charged that the last volume promoted dangerous ideas, "collectivism" in particular. The volume stated, "Cumulative evidence supports the conclusion that in the United States as in other countries, the age of individualism and *laissez-faire* in economy and government is closing and that a new age of collectivism is emerging."[29] By "collectivism," the Commission meant cooperation and interdependence among citizens, not state ownership of production and property. The intention was that teachers would prepare students to work for the common good rather than to pursue only individual self-interest.[30]

However, many educators, administrators, and especially politicians interpreted "collectivism" as "democratic socialism" if not "communism." In a letter to Krey, Beardsley Ruml, Dean of the Division of Social Sciences at the University of Chicago, wrote, "We do not believe that the social sciences on any level should be used consciously for purposes of indoctrination or for the inculcation of standards, values, attitudes, no matter how generally accepted or apparently desirable."[31] Some Commission members agreed. Ernest Horn refused to endorse the final volume for a number of reasons, including his objection to its "pervasive influence of economic collectivism...."[32] In a letter to Krey, Bessie L. Pierce complained of the volume's "propagandist character": "I fear very much that should this report with its avowed sponsorship of inculcation of collectivism in the schools be published that it would destroy much of the validity of the other work of the Commission."[33] Pierce was right. As Kliebard and Novick have noted, the political controversy caused by the Commission's sixteenth volume far overshadowed the positive commentary on the other fifteen volumes.[34]

Despite the complaints and the controversy, the Commission's work helped confirm the place of social studies in the curriculum. As the years passed, however, social studies advocates introduced new elementary school curricula that had little resemblance to the programs many Commission members had envisioned.

The AHA Commission's Influence on Social Studies

Initially, the Commission's work inspired several new social studies programs, including Krey's 1938 social studies program for rural schools. His program, which centered on the child's expanding surroundings and personal experiences, was the study of "food, clothing, and shelter, transportation and distribution, family, church, school, communication, health, and recreation."[35] Fay Rogers, an elementary school teacher, revised Krey's ideas in her 1938 social studies program based on a geographic, social, and cultural survey of urban Minneapolis. The Commission's work was an inspiration for Paul Hanna's *Building America* magazine (see Chapter 4). Many well-known writers, including social studies educators, contributed articles to the magazine that dealt with utilitarian topics such as food, machines, transportation, health, communication, power, recreation, and housing. These topics were thought useful for preparing children for their roles as consumers and voting citizens.[36]

For example, Paul T. Rankin, Supervising Director of Instruction in the Detroit Public Schools, described how mock elections in schools taught students about local and national elections.[37] Paul Hanna described how a school in White Mill, Virginia, tried to improve living conditions in the community by teaching students the democratic process and civic engagement.[38] Such classroom instruction in civic participation and responsibility reflected Beard's idea that the "environment can be changed within limits by individual and social action."[39]

Because the Commission made no specific recommendations for social studies programs, its pedagogical influence on social studies was largely theoretical and, at times, even antithetical to its intentions. The social studies educators, Howard Wilson and Edgar Wesley, complained that the Commission's "nonrecommendations" were "designed to promote and perpetuate the chaos and confusion in the social studies rather than synthesize the scattered and diverse trends."[40] Lacking direction from the Commission, other organizations could, and did, write social studies programs that abandoned the Commission's support for the disciplines. However, one of the Commission's "nonrecommendations" was influential even if it was altered in its implementation. Elementary schools enthusiastically embraced the expanding communities approach that Krey had in essence endorsed (however, without the disciplinary backbone Krey supported).

The AHA continued its involvement in secondary history and social studies education through the 1940s.[41] However, its influence had begun to wane. After the publication of the Commission's sixteen volumes, the AHA gave up its leadership role in the NCSS and ended its work with elementary social studies. The NCSS demonstrated its independence from the AHA in 1935 when it held its first annual meeting and in 1936 when it published the first issue of its own journal, *Social Education*.[42] As Dawson stated, in the 1930s the NCSS assumed "full responsibility for leadership in a united attack on the problems in its field."[43] From now on, social studies educators would control the future of elementary social studies education.

The NCSS and Elementary Social Studies

The NCSS gained its independence when the AHA began its retreat from K–12 social studies education in the late 1930s. At that time, the NCSS still lacked a clear vision for elementary social studies. Challenged by the complexity of organizing the social studies curriculum, NCSS members in the interwar years struggled to find an agreed-upon message.

The NCSS publications (bulletins, curriculum series, and yearbooks) are among our best sources for leading educators' ideas about social studies education in these years. *The Future of the Social Studies*, edited by James A. Michener (the Pulitzer Prize novelist), published in 1939, is particularly noteworthy.[44] The NCSS Committee on Curriculum wrote this book in response to the request to make recommendations for "attacking the problem of the social-studies curriculum."[45] The book's contributors were among the most well-known social studies educators of the time: R.O. Hughes, Mary Kelty, I. James Quillen, Earle Rugg, Harold Rugg, and Howard Wilson. Michener wrote an introductory chapter for the book titled "The Problem of the Social Studies."

While reflecting agreement on some issues (e.g., endorsement of the expanding communities approach), the book also revealed the contributors' varied opinions on other issues. There were many disagreements about the curriculum content, including the choice of topics (also known as scope) taught in the expanding communities approach. For example, should "home life" be the study of residential construction, family economy, or of household cleanliness and safety? Looking at this grab bag of proposed social studies topics, Michener concluded, "for the questions of *what to teach* and *when to teach it* there are no clear answers."[46]

Despite its internal dissension, the NCSS was clearly the leading social studies organization in the 1930s, a position it still holds today. When the NCSS assumed the editorship of the AHA's journal, *The Historical Outlook*, now renamed *Social Education*, NCSS members at last had their own journal. *Social Education* was addressed to the "practical needs of teachers and to the realities of classroom" and dealt with the disciplines of history, geography, government, economics, sociology, and social psychology.[47] The journal's focus was social studies curricula, teaching methods, textbooks, and student evaluations. However, as the "voice" of the NCSS, the journal had, and has, many problems, some of which may stem from the breadth of its mission. According to Louis Vanaria, the journal "may be striving for an impossible objective when it attempts to cover all grade levels from kindergarten through college in dealing with social science content, methodology, curriculum organization, and significant contemporary problems."[48] In accommodating so many areas of social studies education, the NCSS tried to please everyone but seemed to please few.

The NCSS and the Fusion Curriculum for Social Studies

As described above, NCSS members disagreed on how to teach social studies as well as on social studies content. In her review of the social studies debates conducted in the NCSS yearbooks, Dorothy McClure Fraser identified three curricula in social studies education in these years: (1) the "separate-subject curriculum" (often referred to as the "correlation" curriculum) in which history and the social sciences (geography and civics) were taught as separate subjects; (2) the "fusion of the social-studies subjects curriculum" in which lessons were structured around topics, issues, geographic areas, or time periods (e.g., the fusion of science and health in social studies); and (3) the "integrative curriculum" in which subject content was organized into "blocks of work" that blurred the lines between subjects.[49]

As Fraser noted, there was considerable overlap among the three curricula, particularly the fusion curriculum and the integrative curriculum.[50] The principal difference between these two curricula was that the integrative curriculum ignored disciplinary boundaries. However, in practice, educators referred to the two curricula interchangeably, perhaps because both sharply contrasted with the separate-subject curricula. Because most social studies educators in the interwar years referred to the fusion curriculum, that is the term used in this chapter.

In the early 1930s, the NCSS tried to persuade its members and other educators to support the fusion curriculum. One strong supporter was Howard Wilson. In the first NCSS yearbook, *Some Aspects of the Social Sciences in Schools*, published in 1931, Wilson addressed the advantages and disadvantages of the fusion approach.[51] He concluded, "Fusion has rendered real service to the social studies by its insistent and often dramatic demands that the curriculum must be made as nearly functional and as nearly learnable as possible."[52] A true fusion approach, Wilson argued, began by breaking down subject divisions. Thereafter, the curriculum should include only content with a "direct, functional value in training pupils for the socio-civic activities of current living," organized into "natural units of learning."[53] His prescription was for the junior high level, but it was also relevant at the elementary level where the fusion curriculum was steadily gaining support.[54]

Many teachers in the 1930s used the fusion curriculum in their classrooms. Fraser cited data from city school systems and from teacher questionnaires showing that, beginning in the 1930s, the fusion curriculum dominated in the lower elementary grades. However, Fraser found that teachers in the upper elementary grades generally taught history and geography separately, although they used "some degree of fusion" as well.[55]

Since neither the integrative curriculum nor the fusion curriculum followed the traditional disciplinary organization (of the separate-subject curriculum), NCSS educators also developed "scope and sequence" methods to track social studies lessons from grade to grade. "Scope" (generally, the content or topics of studies) has been interpreted variously. For example, Paul Hanna, a strong advocate of the integrative curriculum, conceived of scope in the expanding communities approach as the "basic human activities" (e.g., recreation, transportation, and communication). Other NCSS educators conceptualized scope as life competencies such as critical thinking and social participation.

The NCSS favored the expanding communities approach for the "sequence" (the curriculum progression in and between grades). This was the sequence some AHA Commission members had endorsed. For example, Edgar Wesley charged that the main competitor to sequence, which he identified as the chronological curriculum design, was "probably a mistake" for young children because of their limited experiences and immature understanding of time and chronology. He approved the "near-remote" and "unquestionably sound" principle by which children moved "from the experienced to the unexperienced." Wesley warned, however, that the application of this principle in schools was difficult since the media had already exposed children to foreign lands.[56] More than he probably could have imagined, this difficulty only increased with time as the number and variety of media outlets grew and as children acquired greater access to these outlets.

By the 1940s, the fusion curriculum in social studies had largely displaced the separate-subject curriculum of history and geography in the lower elementary grades. Yet some aspects of the separate-subject curriculum remained, particularly its emphasis on holidays and special days, the study of the flag, and stories of American heroes. The NEA's 1936 yearbook, which was devoted to social studies, noted that American heroes and holidays were taught in kindergarten through third grade.[57] In some form, U.S. history, particularly in its citizenship focus, still had a place in elementary education. However, few NCSS members challenged the fusion curriculum.

The Fusion Curriculum and the
Expanding Communities Approach

When schools across the country adopted the fusion curriculum in social studies at the lower elementary level, supporters claimed it aligned with the whole child pedagogy that views the curriculum holistically rather than piecemeal. Other education theorists applied Gestalt psychology (a psychological theory that views the learner as a whole person, emphasizing affective growth, and challenges behaviorism) to curriculum theory.[58] These theorists thought the curriculum should reflect life as it is, irrespective of its defining and limiting boundaries. As life is not structured into discrete disciplinary categories, but is rather organized by issues, institutions, and events, (e.g., production of goods, warfare, education, and racial unrest), its study properly crosses disciplines. Similarly, they argued, education cannot be tidily bundled as units of information. Therefore, according to some child psychologists, the fusion curriculum was best suited to teach children in a way that corresponded to their life experiences.

In addition, the fusion curriculum requires that elementary school teachers have only a general knowledge of history and geography. Thus, at the NCSS annual meetings in the interwar years there were special sections for elementary school teachers that included "hands-on demonstrations" and visits to model classrooms in the host cities.[59] The NCSS also formed education committees that developed magazines and newspapers for social studies classes and other materials for economics lessons at the elementary and secondary levels.[60]

What, then, was a specific unit of study (the scope) in the lower elementary fusion curriculum that used the expanding communities approach? The question is as valid today as it was in the interwar years. A good example is transportation, which was a favorite topic of community study. In fact, an NCSS transportation unit on aviation was the subject of an entire chapter in the 1941 NCSS yearbook.[61] This unit described sample activities the teacher might use: field trips, model airplane construction with blocks, aviation stories, and pilot-passenger role play. The unit's goals were to familiarize children with social situations and to explain the community's concern with safety. Educators believed that the study of aviation would also teach responsible civic participation, cooperation, and respect for authority — in short, what it took to be a good citizen.[62] As conceived of in this unit, the good citizen was no longer defined simply in terms of patriotism, nationalism, and the American Creed.

This revised definition led to objections to the fusion curriculum and the expanding communities approach in social studies, particularly by those who wanted to preserve the separate identities of history, geography, and civics in the classroom. They argued, for instance, that the curriculum and the approach were illogical and untested by research.[63] In general, however, the resistance was rather weak, and recommended alternatives did not differ significantly. It seemed the social studies curriculum, at least at the lower elementary level, was too popular to permit any serious challenges even if its implementation was not always smooth.

The most contentious area was the fourth- and fifth-grade curricula. While there was a general agreement that social studies in the lower elementary grades should focus on the home, school, and community, some educators were reluctant to adopt the fusion curriculum, using the expanding communities approach, at the upper elementary grades. One Wisconsin educator and a NCSS yearbook contributor, Mary Kelty, described the fourth-grade curriculum as a state of "chaos."[64] The chaos was explained by the fact that many states required history and geography instruction in the fourth and fifth grades. In those states, it was nearly impossible to adopt the fusion (or an integrative) curriculum using topics and problems, especially given the large class sizes.

The Social Studies Curriculum at the Local Level

At the local level some educators tried to impose order on what many felt was the chaotic situation of social studies at the national level. Some local educators had specific proposals about which, how, and when social studies lessons should be taught. For example, the City and Country School in New York City and the Lincoln School at

Columbia University created innovative social studies programs for young children (see Chapter 2). In addition, public schools across the country had begun to develop and teach social studies programs. Among these schools were the Detroit Public Schools, the Grand Rapids Public Schools, the Cleveland Public Schools, the University of Chicago Laboratory Schools, and the San Antonio Public Schools.

As leaders and active members in the NCSS, educators in the Detroit Public Schools (DPS) took a prominent role in social studies reform in the interwar years. For example, in 1936, the City of Detroit hosted the annual NCSS meeting where the DPS Department of Social Science leaders promoted their courses as models for the NCSS social studies agenda. These innovative courses, which the DPS had developed in the 1920s and 1930s, reflected a significant change from how social studies was taught in the early twentieth century, both in rhetoric and in practice.

In part, this change in social studies education was a response to national recommendations since the DPS administrators agreed with the NCSS on the broad principles of social studies education. However, the DPS took a more prescriptive and unified approach to social studies at the elementary level than the NCSS had envisioned in its recommendations. Yet adoption of social studies reforms in the DPS, as with most school reform efforts, was an evolutionary process. The DPS began social studies reform in the 1920s, but it was not until the mid-1930s that the fusion curriculum model that integrated history with the other social sciences was completed. This model is still used in elementary schools in the DPS and elsewhere.

According to accounts by Leah Spencer, the DPS Assistant Director of Social Science Education, throughout the 1920s most instruction in the DPS was fairly traditional in content and in method. Teachers were reluctant to adopt the newfangled methods, and parents thought children should be taught "the basics." Even in classes inspired by progressive education theory, such as manual training, teachers often simply lectured from a textbook since it was impractical to use active learning projects in classes with sometimes as many as fifty or sixty students. William Reese's description of education in the 1930s aptly describes DPS education in the 1920s: "Most classrooms nevertheless remained teacher dominated, textbook driven, and subject-matter based."[65]

Before the 1930s, because of tradition and parent-teacher resistance, civics, history, and geography were taught as separate
disciplines in the DPS. Gradually, however, social studies, which
included economics, political science, and sociology, in addition to
geography, history, and civics, was introduced at the secondary level.
The DPS leaders wrote curriculum guides and developed schoolwide
activities for these new social studies classes. The DPS educators, at all
school levels, explained that instruction in the social studies was more
"informal," a description that meant there were more opportunities
for children to work independently with maps, globes, reference
books, and pictures.[66]

More changes in the DPS social studies curriculum occurred in the
mid-1930s. One change—perhaps minor but revealing—was the
change in terminology: from "social science" to "social studies." For
years, C. C. Barnes, the Department Head (and a NCSS leader), had
resisted the national trend to rename social science as social studies.[67]
As a history of the DPS explains, "[Barnes] felt that 'science' had a
broader meaning than 'studies' and that, in Detroit, social science was
more than just a collection of related subject fields. Social science was
defined as the science of human relations."[68] Despite Barnes's resistance, by the mid-1930s the DPS Department of Social Science
became the Department of Social Studies.[69]

A more significant change in the DPS was its complete revision of
its social studies curriculum. In 1936, the DPS appointed a committee
to survey social studies teachers for suggested revisions, to examine
curricula in other states, to study national social trends related to
social studies, and to write a new curriculum. In 1937, the DPS
introduced a pilot program for the new curriculum in a few elementary schools. By 1940, all schools in the DPS had adopted the new
program.[70] This curriculum followed the sequence of the expanding
communities approach and used topics for its scope.

The new DPS social studies curriculum was much more child-
centered. Two examples are illustrative. In 1937, Stanley Dimond
(who had replaced Barnes as the Head of the DPS Department of
Social Studies) recommended a child-centered economics unit in
which children were asked questions such as "What things do you
need and want in life?" "What equipment did nature give you to get

these things?" and "Why can't you have all the things you want?"[71] This was an economics unit prompted by the grim realities of the Great Depression. The DPS educators aimed to teach children the value of thrift and saving. The DPS also introduced the child-centered focus of "Living Together" that was explained as follows: "The study of where and how the peoples of the world live, by what laws and governments they regulate their social relations, and especially the workings of American democracy, constitutes a large part of the day-by-day education of the children of the people."[72] The goal was that children in social studies lessons would learn to "work and play happily together."[73]

In conjunction with the movement toward more child-centered learning, the DPS social studies curriculum changed its emphasis on disciplinary content to the "whole child." Community life and citizenship were added to the curriculum. For example, "Home Economics," an experimental unit, had these four topics: "self-realization, human relationships, economic efficiency and civic responsibility."[74] Moreover, the DPS educators stressed "individual differences and the necessity of meeting the needs and interests of various groups of children. Only as the whole child is given all-around experience can we hope to build the richer and finer personalities that we all wish."[75]

Given these changes, there was less and less time in the school day for traditional history and geography study. And, in fact, when the DPS began encouraging students to be charity volunteers (e.g., for the polio fund drive and Christmas seals sales) and participants in "get out the vote" campaigns, there was still less time for such traditional lessons. Increasingly, the DPS educators thought they had both the obligation and the qualifications to make the curriculum relevant to children's lives outside school. This meant many new classroom projects and more extra-curricular activities. Compared to textbook learning, this was a new way of learning with an emphasis on the so-called seven attitudes and habits children develop from collaborative projects: tolerance, cooperation, obedience, industry, initiative, adjustment, and self-control.[76]

The changes in the social studies curriculum in the Grand Rapid Public Schools (GRPS) were similar to those in the DPS.[77] In the early 1930s, when the GRPS revised its curriculum, the "major accomplishment" was the integration of geography, history, civics, and practical arts into a single course (i.e., social studies) that "consider[ed] social problems in their entirety."[78] In the following years, social studies, as in the DPS, edged closer to citizenship education. A GRPS superintendent report stated, "The slogan of our social studies curricula might well be preparation for citizenship through participation in a cooperative fashion in worthwhile activities."[79] Like the DPS, the GRPS took a pedagogical approach that featured the "whole child." The report claimed:

> Education today means the adjustment of the individual to a changed and rapidly changing world. It is therefore recommended that provision be made for a continuing revision of the courses of study, keeping in mind that a curriculum is the total experience of the child as an individual and as a member of a group.[80]

The Cleveland Public Schools District was another urban school district that adopted a social studies curriculum similar to the DPS and the GRPS social studies curricula. In its social studies curriculum, which was described as "living together," the Cleveland Public Schools focused on group and community relations and the local environment. Teachers used the near to far approach to teach these topics. The 1936 Cleveland Public Schools superintendent's report stated:

> This understanding of the many services rendered in the community and the growing interdependence of people with the accompanying need for cooperation, and an appreciation of the things he [the child] meets in his everyday experiences are developed through the social studies program in the primary grades. The degree to which these understandings and appreciations function with the child will be evident in his conduct toward other people, in the classroom, on the playground, at home, and in the community.[81]

The 1939–40 Cleveland Public Schools superintendent's report explained that children's "egocentric" nature made the study of the larger community necessary. The report stated, "Before he enters school, the child is the center about which his small world revolves. He tends to be selfish and unaware of the larger social group of which he must become a part."[82] Much like the values the DPS children learned in the "getting along" curriculum, children in the Cleveland Public Schools learned that "wars settle nothing" and that "people may find other and better ways of settling their quarrels."[83] Children in the Cleveland Public Schools had history lessons only in the upper elementary grades. In these lessons, as in all social studies lessons, the goal was to cultivate children's habits and attitudes of industry, promptness, courage, unselfishness, and tolerance.[84]

In some schools and school districts, the focus on citizenship skills was less overt but still present. The University of Chicago Laboratory Schools charged elementary social studies with the responsibility of developing in students the "desirable social understandings, attitudes, and behavior."[85] Kindergartners and first graders studied topics such as the family, the neighborhood, farm life, transportation, and communication. Second and third graders studied the environment, American Indians, Vikings, and the history of Chicago. Fourth graders began the study of history and geography study with lessons in how societies had evolved from prehistoric times to the American Colonial period. At all levels, the purpose of social studies was to introduce students to social problems and issues in a world that was constantly changing. Teachers used a number of different, child-centered strategies and activities in social studies (e.g., story writing, dramatization, drawing and modeling buildings, and excursions).

The objectives for elementary social studies in the public schools in San Antonio, Texas, were derived from six of the seven Cardinal Principles of Secondary Education (see Chapter 2) that the NEA committee had proposed in 1918: ethical character, good citizenship, vocational efficiency, health, home membership, and use of leisure time.[86] Elementary social studies in San Antonio was the study of history, geography, health, character education, and citizenship. First graders studied children's games, toys, and pets as well as family life in the city and on the farm. Second graders learned about life and occupations in their own communities and in countries around the world. Third graders studied "primitive life" (such as the lives of American Indians and tree dwellers) and their city, past and present. Fourth and fifth graders studied their state and country. In all grades, teachers used learning activities influenced by progressive pedagogy (e.g., building a wagon, playing store, going on field trips, and forming a Junior Conservation Society). A San Antonio public school administrator summarized the goals of the social studies lessons for the child: the "value of social studies lies not so much in what he learns as how he reacts, how he learns to think, and how his attitudes and ideals are affected."[87]

At the local level, it seemed that teaching disciplinary content was secondary to engaging children in lively, participatory activities. Content-dominated history and geography lessons had been transformed to child-centered lessons on social harmony and good citizenship. And the student, not the teacher, was now the pedagogical focus. Rote learning and textbook drill decreased as innovative teaching methods, which engaged and stimulated learners, increased. Critics still charged, however, that disciplinary content learning suffered as a result.

Looking to the Future of Social Studies

Social studies gained a powerful foothold in U.S. education in the years between the two World Wars. However, even in the elementary schools, history was sometimes still taught as a separate course. According to Novick, social studies never completely displaced history in the school curriculum (especially at the secondary level).[88] He argues that a main reason social studies advocates never produced a coherent program of study, despite its near absorption of history, was their recognition that many school board members suspected social studies had a radical agenda. In addition, inertia, always an impediment to educational reform, often slowed acceptance of social studies reforms. Yet, during the interwar years, to the regret of many historians, U.S. schools in general marginalized history study in the classroom. In fact, in many schools, the social studies curriculum simply swallowed history. In 1935, the historian, Carlton J. H. Hayes, bluntly declared, "It is now *de rigueur* to regard history not merely as a step-sister of the social sciences but as an ugly and fallen sister, one whose very name should be avoided in polite circles and when referred to at all should be mentioned apologetically and with blushes."[89]

The diminished place of history in the social studies curriculum was especially evident at the lower elementary level. Topics that had little basis in any discipline (i.e., "living together," and "getting along") pushed history (as well as geography and civics) aside. Decades later, Diane Ravitch dismissed such lower elementary social studies as "tot sociology."[90] When history was taught, it was a simplified form of "new history" (see Chapter 2) that claimed history should be relevant to, and reflective of, contemporary life. If the discipline of history was the ugly stepsister of the social studies disciplines, then the new field of social studies was surely Cinderella.

Chapter 4

"Romance or Reality": Paul Robert Hanna and the Expanding Communities Approach

BY THE 1940s, social studies was taught in most elementary classrooms. However, social studies leaders and school administrators struggled to create a coherent social studies curriculum. They agreed that the primary goal of social studies was to teach citizenship skills but were uncertain how to go about it. Which lessons and which activities would help students achieve that goal? The many ideas that were proposed, particularly at the upper elementary level, only increased the confusion. Social studies needed a coherent scope and sequence that teachers could follow. It also needed a set of curricular materials (e.g., textbooks and teacher resources) that would present the scope and sequence.

Paul Robert Hanna responded to this call with his expanding communities approach for social studies. Hanna used the term expanding communities of men (later shortened to expanding communities), but others have used terms such as expanding environments and widening horizons for the same concept. Generally working independently from the National Council for the Social Studies (NCSS), Hanna, a professor of education for over thirty years, first at Teachers College, Columbia University (TC) and then at Stanford University, wrote highly coherent, logical, and systematic programs for social studies. In speeches, articles, letters, and especially textbooks, he promoted the expanding communities approach in elementary social studies, combining it with the topics-based content of the "basic human activities."[1] Hanna's textbooks were remarkably successful. In part, the success was owed to his publisher, Scott, Foresman and Company (hereafter Scott, Foresman), who attractively packaged his curriculum into accessible and manageable programs of study for teachers. Moreover, his books resulted in many imitations and helped secure Hanna's expanding communities approach as the dominant organizing framework for elementary social studies that is still in use today. Some scholars have labeled this framework the "de facto national [social studies] curriculum."[2] The approach appears today in state content standards, social studies textbooks, and social studies methods textbooks.[3]

When supporters and critics describe Hanna as the father of the expanding communities approach, they overlook some earlier developments. As previous chapters showed, in the nineteenth and early twentieth centuries, history instruction and especially geography instruction often used an approach similar to the expanding communities approach. In that instruction, children progressed from studies of the schoolyard to units about the community, the state, and beyond. These accounts were far from the well-developed materials created by Hanna. Nevertheless, there are hints of the approach in many earlier curricular guides and textbooks.[4] Even at the time of the Virginia Curriculum project, Hanna's first official foray into large-scale curricular design, some form of the expanding communities approach appeared in nearly half the school curriculum guides in the United States.[5]

Hanna was not the original creative force behind the expanding communities approach. However, he did turn the very loosely defined social studies curriculum that had developed in the 1920s into a well-organized program of study. Moreover, he applied a new content structure, or "scope," as he and his colleagues called it, to the expanding communities framework by adding distinct topics of study. The old expanding communities framework described the "sequence" of study (from the home, to the school, to the neighborhood, and beyond) mainly in geography lessons (and, in the twentieth century, in some social studies and civics lessons). Hanna's scope, in contrast, focused on a set of basic human activities; these activities, not the individual disciplines, were the main source of curricular content.

The social studies programs Hanna developed were innovative in many ways. To describe the ideas behind his highly ordered, logical framework that taught students about their world, he preferred the term "social education" to "social studies." He argued that "social studies" suggested memorization of names, places, and dates, whereas "social education" reflected the commitment to helping students live as citizens in a democratic society.[6] He thought that if school focused on the social institutions and relationships in their everyday lives, children could better deal with real-life problems, develop happier family relationships, help conserve the environment and natural resources, and achieve higher standards of living. For Hanna, instruction in the recitation of historical facts and the memorization of geographic place names did not further the goals of social reconstruction.

The sociopolitical context of the time greatly influenced the design of Hanna's programs. He developed his social studies programs during the cataclysmic years of the Great Depression and World War II when severe economic and social turmoil, threats posed by foreign dictatorships, and fears of domestic social and political unrest convinced him that citizens should be actively involved in the governance of their country. Hanna was also profoundly influenced by the social reconstructionists, such as George Counts and Harold Rugg, who were convinced that schools, with teachers as leaders, could prepare the way for substantial social and economic change.[7] Hanna thought education had the power to change society for the better.

However, Hanna's social studies programs, especially those at the lower elementary level, often did not fully reflect his ideas about education. The elementary social studies programs he created reflected little of this social reconstructionist spirit. Nor did they reflect the academic rigor that Hanna argued was essential in education. Some scholars such as Martin Gill have argued that Hanna's contributions were revolutionary: "It was a new notion that elementary children should and could study under as intellectual a rubric as was Hanna's design."[8] It is true that Hanna developed a very sophisticated system—in design—for elementary social studies. However, the topics of study in his programs generally lacked the academic rigor he claimed was necessary. This chapter describes this inconsistency between theory and practice in Hanna's work.

Despite this inconsistency, Hanna's social studies programs had a lasting influence in elementary schools at home and abroad. His role in elementary social studies education warrants a separate discussion from other national developments in social studies education because of his unique influence. By bringing purpose, coherence, clarity, and accessibility to elementary social studies education, Hanna shaped elementary social studies education in ways still observable today. This chapter draws upon Hanna's writings (his academic scholarship, curricular, materials, and personal correspondence) as well as studies on Hanna by Jared Stallones and Martin Gill.[9]

Hanna's Background and Early Influences

Hanna was born in 1902 in Sioux City, Iowa. His father, a Methodist minister, taught him compassion for people faced with "the ills of society," and his mother taught him the Deweyan belief in the power of learning acquired through firsthand experiences.[10] Hanna studied philosophy at Hamline University in St. Paul, Minnesota. He then earned a Master of Arts degree in school administration from TC in 1925, after which, at age twenty-six, he became Superintendent of Schools in West Winfield, New York. Although he tried to make curriculum changes, ultimately he felt discouraged in this position because of a "lack of match between the curriculum and what these children were interested in or what their lives were like."[11] He held this position for less than two years.

Encouraged by William Heard Kilpatrick, his mentor and a renowned child-centered progressive educator, Hanna returned to TC in 1927 to pursue a doctorate in education, with an emphasis in curriculum. While studying for his doctorate, he also taught in TC's laboratory school. From 1929 to 1935, he was a professor at TC where he studied and worked with a number of education giants including Kilpatrick, John Dewey, Harold Rugg, Jesse Newlon, and George Counts.[12] Although each of these men influenced Hanna to some degree, Counts and Kilpatrick were particularly important in shaping his ideas: Counts on the role of education and Kilpatrick on curriculum design.

Hanna attended the 1932 Progressive Education Association conference where Counts delivered perhaps the most famous speech ever presented at an American education conference: "Dare Progressive Education be Progressive?" In the speech, Counts challenged America's progressive educators to take the lead in radically changing society. Using such forcefully prescriptive words as "imposition" and "indoctrination," Counts bluntly asserted that teachers had a fundamental role in forming students' minds. Teachers, he declared, could never be neutral. Given the social problems associated with the collapse of the U.S. economy, Counts demanded that teachers take sides in the struggle to reshape and rebuild the country. Children, he said, had to "be lifted out of the present morass of moral indifference, be liberated from the senseless struggle for material success, and be challenged to high endeavor and achievement."[13] Influenced by Counts's ideas, Hanna called for social studies programs that would develop students' commitment to improving society. In comments that appeared in *The New York Times,* Hanna criticized schools for failing to address social problems. In addition, he blamed educators for their failure to teach topics that had relevance to children's lives outside school.[14]

Of Hanna's colleagues, Kilpatrick had perhaps the most influence on Hanna as far as education practices although he drew selectively on Kilpatrick's ideas. To a certain extent, Hanna supported the project method that Kilpatrick promoted, but he also worried that a curriculum based solely on activity learning diluted academic content.[15] Thus, Hanna never fully positioned himself in the child-centered wing of progressive education that Kilpatrick led.

Hanna's experience at the Lincoln School, the TC laboratory school founded in 1917 with the financial backing of John D. Rockefeller, was an important influence on his thinking about curriculum design. Hanna worked at the school under the guidance of its director Jesse Newlon, former Superintendent of the Denver Public Schools, who was known for his work in curriculum design. Newlon was particularly well-known for his innovative approach of including teachers in the curriculum design process, an idea Hanna later took in a curriculum project in Virginia.[16]

When Hanna joined the Lincoln School, he found its program of study inadequate. The inadequacy was not that the program lacked a curriculum. Indeed, the Lincoln School leaders claimed to be devoted to "curriculum making." They had even written a book outlining detailed plans for units of work that had been prompted by requests from visitors to the school. This book included units of study that had been developed over ten years: for example, studies of life on the farm for first grade, city life for second grade, China for third grade, food for fourth grade, water transportation for fifth grade, and time for sixth grade.[17] Each unit drew upon various disciplines; for example, the "Life on a Farm" unit taught concepts in writing, literature, science, numbers, geography and history, household arts, fine arts, industrial arts, music, physical education, and desirable habits of thinking and acting.[18] As such, this unit (as well as the others) integrated the disciplines and was guided by the general purpose of "help[ing] the child understand life about him" and making him become "more conscious of himself as a member of a social group...."[19] The Lincoln School staff reasoned that by third grade, children were interested in "the larger life of the world."[20]

Despite the Lincoln School's devotion to curricular design, evidenced by the considerable effort undoubtedly required to write the units, Hanna found the program of study disjointed and the units disconnected from year to year. For Hanna, this lack of an overall system seriously detracted from the quality of the education. More troubling, Hanna found this unstructured approach was actually a source of pride for teachers. One hears his dismay in a comment he later made on the teachers' point of view: "To acknowledge you had a design was to hang your head in shame."[21] While Hanna recognized that the Lincoln School's reputation rested on the work of some "magnificent" teachers, these "prima donnas," as he called them, clearly frustrated his attempts to impose any kind of structure on their free-flowing, imaginative activities.[22]

At the Lincoln School, Hanna helped reorganize the school administration, studied the curriculum, formed a parents' club, and wrote curriculum brochures. In this work, Hanna learned the importance of a highly structured curriculum that addressed children's interests and helped them connect school learning with life experience.[23] The social studies curriculum he developed at the Lincoln School was based on extensive surveys he made of children's interests (the teachers identified the interests).[24] Organized by grade level, the curriculum listed specific topics or units of work, such as airplanes and the zoo in kindergarten, and cities, colonial life, and pioneer life in fifth grade. In a state curriculum project a few years later, Hanna and others broadened this curriculum design to include general content areas such as transportation, production, and recreation.[25] This project is described after a summary of Hanna's ideas about education.

Hanna's Educational Philosophy

Hanna does not fit neatly into any category of education philosophy. He was an eclectic thinker who drew upon several progressive education philosophies in developing his own philosophy of education. During the early years of his curriculum work, he expressed a commitment to both subject matter content and children's interests. Admitting to an attraction to Kilpatrick's ideas, he drew upon aspects of the project method in his curricula. However, unlike Kilpatrick, Hanna did not believe students' interests should determine the academic content. Moreover, he questioned whether it was possible to identify children's interests. He once remarked that much of the learning educators that claimed evolved from children's interests was actually material the teachers were interested in.[26]

Thus, Hanna thought that neither approach (that is, the emphasis on the child to the exclusion of the curriculum, or vice versa) adequately prepared the young citizen for participation in a democratic community. In this respect, he was responding to the social meliorists' call for schools to remedy society's ills. Like Rugg, Hanna thought schools had the power and capacity to teach individuals to be responsible members of their communities. He agreed with Counts that schools had the social responsibility to teach the values and knowledge that students could use to reform society. This belief in the power of schools to change society for the better distinguished this wing of progressivism from that of the child-centered progressives who believed the purpose of education was to encourage children's creativity and freedom of expression. In contrast, Hanna, among others, including Rugg and Counts, thought education's primary purpose was to improve society.

Hanna used the terms "romantics" and "realists" to label and distinguish the advocates of the two opposing philosophies of education.[27] He acknowledged that the two groups had the same goals: to give each individual the opportunity to acquire values and pursue dreams that would give meaning to life and thereby to achieve "the good life." Yet he claimed the romantics and the realists used very different pedagogies.[28] Romantics sought to shelter children from life's harsh realities by taking them to the distant past where bold knights battled evil, where courageous seafarers explored uncharted waters, and where Greeks and Romans lived in the Golden Age of art and architecture. Such content, the romantics argued, allowed children to escape the sometimes-harsh reality of modern life and also nurtured their creativity and individuality. Realists, in contrast, sought to prepare children to face challenging socioeconomic conditions (e.g., unequal life opportunities) by teaching them about the scientific and technological advances that transform daily life.[29]

Although Hanna saw some value in the romantics' ideas, he was clearly one of the realists.[30] He disapproved of lessons that focused on ancient history and the romantic past because they could not give children the knowledge, the skills, or the will needed to change society. Even worse, this idyllic past, with its heroes and adventurers, was too remote from the lives of school children, many of whom lived in poor and very unromantic conditions. Hanna wrote, "It is not a matter of whether or not these children *should* have creative experiences; but it is a question whether or not they can have creative experiences living as they do in hunger, in depressing surroundings, below a subsistence income level."[31] According to Hanna, a "cultural reconstruction" in education was needed to confront the problems of economic inequality so that all Americans could pursue happiness.[32]

A constant in Hanna's education philosophy was the idea that social studies could teach students how people live, work, and govern in societies. As he stated in 1942, "We must develop geographical, historical, economic, and social understandings which show plainly the interdependence of all peoples, the basic human needs common to all, and the rights of all to share in the satisfaction of these needs." To achieve these goals at the elementary school level, children needed to appreciate the interdependence among families, schools, and neighborhoods. Hanna continued,

"Only by giving boys and girls actual experience in working together for a common cause can we expect them later to take a constructive part in building a world community."[33]

Like other educators in the 1930s, Hanna was strongly influenced by the sociopolitical context of the time, in particular by the Great Depression. Reflecting on this period, Hanna stated, "I kept thinking about the inadequate preparation that we American citizens had had. We didn't understand what was happening. We didn't know the causes and effects of our political, social economic system."[34] Because of this concern, Hanna created a curriculum that he thought was relevant to children's lives and that might prepare them for such social and economic upheaval.

In promoting his ideas, it is important to note that Hanna consistently claimed he wanted teachers to emphasize content from the social studies disciplines. Like Dewey, Hanna thought he could balance the child-centered approach with the content-centered approach. Late in his career, in 1954, he reflected:

> I cannot agree with those who say, "we teach children, but we do not teach subject matter." Children learn something and we are definitely concerned that this something be good subject-matter. I cannot agree with some who say that any content is of equal value with any other or that content generally must be subordinate to process. Both content and method—both the stuff of culture and the nature of childhood—are indispensable to a balanced curriculum.[35]

However, in his social studies textbooks, Hanna promoted an education goal that he thought was even more important than the goal of balancing the child and the curriculum. The purpose of education was to nurture in students the willingness and capacity to effect positive change in the world. Yet, as the next sections show, Hanna met various obstacles in writing a curriculum that would achieve this purpose.

The Virginia Curriculum Project:
The Seeds of the Expanding Communities Approach

In 1931, Hanna's TC classmate, Hollis L. Caswell, began work as a consultant on curriculum design for the State of Virginia. Caswell was a faculty member at George Peabody College in Nashville, Tennessee, and had previously been involved in curriculum design in several southern states.[36] Working with Caswell and others, Hanna, as a consultant for the social studies section, began developing the approach that would be his most well-known contribution to elementary social studies education. Despite his recollection that he was the leader of the social studies section, in reality Hanna was a member of a team of researchers on the Virginia Curriculum. The following discussion quotes from Hanna's article in *Progressive Education* about the Virginia Curriculum as well as from the report by the Virginia State Board of Education (*Tentative Course for Virginia Elementary Grades I–VII*). In his article, Hanna took considerable credit for the design of the social studies curriculum (and by extension, for the expanding communities approach). However, the report and the design were by no means solo efforts by Hanna.[37]

Dr. Sidney B. Hall, the newly appointed State Superintendent for Instruction in Virginia, initiated the project that had as its goal a comprehensive revision of the school curriculum in Virginia. As David Hicks and Stephanie van Hover recount, Hall considered this work "a magnificent adventure" because the revision replaced textbook memorization and lecture with active, student-centered instruction.[38] The project was indeed visionary in many ways, although like most educational innovations, it was sharply criticized.

Hanna and the research team began by studying the responses to questions about children's interests that Caswell's researchers posed to more than ten thousand Virginia teachers. The data gathering procedure was problematic because the researchers took an indirect approach to identifying children's interests (they asked the teachers, rather than the children, about these interests). The responses, Hanna wrote, surprised him because they showed children generally were interested in the same topics, year after year, rather than in different topics as they moved from grade to grade. Hanna said he could find "no rhyme or reason" for the sameness of their interests. He said he felt "stumped" and "defeated" in his quest to write a curriculum that showed a logical progression of ideas and content and that was based on children's actual interests.[39]

Despite this initial disappointment, Hanna and the team continued their efforts to create a well-defined, unified structure for elementary social studies. They were inspired by the curricular content, or "scope," in President Herbert Hoover's commissioned report, *Recent Social Trends in the United States*.[40] In 1929, President Hoover invited a group of eminent scientists and social scientists to compile a national survey that would present "a central view of the American problem as revealed by social trends" and that would address the interrelationships of these seemingly disparate trends.[41] Published in 1934, the Hoover report contained twenty-nine chapters on social, political, economic, and business topics with titles that included "Utilization of Natural Wealth," "Crime and Punishment," "The Status of Racial and Ethnic Groups," "The Family and its Functions," "Recreation and Leisure Time Activities," and "Education." Although the report, with its grounding in the disciplines, influenced Hanna's organization of the social studies topics, he moved beyond that structure in name and in focus, both in the Virginia Curriculum and in his textbooks.

Hanna and the team wanted to make the social studies topics age-appropriate (i.e., accessible and relevant to their lives). Therefore, they selected eleven (later reduced to nine) major topics or functions of social life (the basic human activities) that were simplified versions of the Hoover report chapters. These activities were: "protection and conservation of life, property, and natural resources"; "production of goods and services and distribution of the returns of production"; "consumption of goods and services"; "communication and transportation of goods and people"; "recreation"; "expression of aesthetic impulses"; "expression of religious impulses"; "education"; "extension of freedom"; "integration of the individual"; and "exploration."[42]

The activities were defined as "those unitary life experiences that the specialists have broken up and classified into such subject-matter fields as history, geography, civics, economics, sociology, political science, esthetics, ethics, anthropology, individual and social psychology."[43] In teaching these activities, teachers could focus on the child's everyday world rather than on the remote and often theoretical world of disciplinary study. As Hanna explained, social studies in this form was not "a fusion of related elements from each field" but rather a "unified whole-problem approach of the child," organized by a series

of fundamental social issues.[44] The study of social studies, in other words, should take an integrated approach that dealt with situations children might encounter.

Whereas proponents of disciplinary learning had compartmentalized these activities as separate fields (e.g., history and geography), Hanna integrated certain aspects of them, much in the tradition of the integrative and fusion curricula (see Chapter 3). Although he thought the activities should be based in the disciplines, Hanna did not advocate separate study of the disciplines. He thought this approach was too boring and too removed from the contemporary world of children.[45] He wrote that he also objected to the traditional separation of the disciplines because the social sciences were not discrete units of study. Furthermore, he thought teachers were insufficiently educated in all the social sciences. He explained:

> I struggled for a long time to get some kind of structure that did not represent merely the traditional categories of economics, political science, sociology, anthropology, history and geography, *because these would scare most teachers not having had anything in these fields.* So I wanted some terms with which they were more familiar, like transporting, communicating, educating or recreating.[46]

Teachers, Hanna thought, were better prepared to present lessons on everyday activities. They lacked the in-depth knowledge of legends, myths, and historic events needed for content lessons.[47] The solution to this dilemma was to simplify the social studies curriculum of activities as a "scope" that most elementary school teachers were qualified to teach.[48] Yet, as Caswell noted later, teachers also struggled with this approach.[49]

In addition to designing the curriculum "scope," Hanna also designed a curriculum "sequence." The sequence, or the progression of children's learning as they advance in the grades, was to evolve as his expanding communities approach. Taking inspiration from several sources, he devised a logical and practical order for the approach: a circle of expanding domains called communities. One source was Charles McMurry's "cultural epochs" idea.[50] Another source was Harold Rugg's idea about how young children learn as exemplified by the following statement by Rugg (and his collaborator, Louise Krueger): "The content of the course in the initial years must be based largely upon [the child's] personal life and that of the environment immediately around him...the child in school, home, the neighborhood and the local community."[51] Within the communities, Hanna created "centers of interest" for each grade. At the elementary level, these interests were "home and school life" (grade one); "community life" (grade two); "adaptation of life to environmental forces of nature" (grade three); "adaptation of life to advancing physical frontiers" (grade four); "effects of inventions and discoveries upon our living" (grade five); and "effects of machine production upon our living" (grade six). Hanna would later rename the "centers of interest" the "expanding communities of men."[52]

After his work on the Virginia Curriculum, Hanna continued to focus on the concept of the community. He wrote numerous journal articles and encyclopedia entries on the community and its relevance for education. For Hanna, a "community" was a group of people who inhabited a defined geographical space, who shared common values, traditions, and commitments, and who developed ways of communicating.[53] Hanna explained that individuals inhabit multiple, "interdependent" communities (e.g., family, school, neighborhood, and city or town) simultaneously.[54] He wrote, "This is the way a child's communities grow, and this same outward thrust from the home and family to larger arenas and larger numbers of people is paralleled in the history of the growth of mankind's communities."[55] According to Hanna, the curriculum should be rooted in children's everyday, community experiences: "After the child bursts the bounds of the block or the township, his world begins to expand rapidly as he comes into contact with more people living in larger and larger arenas."[56] He explained that children do not leave one community as they enter the next; instead, the child's world continually expands.

After developing the expanding communities approach (the sequence), Hanna interwove it with the human activities (the scope). He created a grid with the twenty-six topics on one axis, labeling them the "major functions of social life" (also identified as the basic human activities). On the other axis, he plotted the "centers of interest." Thus, when the functions were linked with the centers of interest, children learned new material in each grade. Hanna thought this design was far preferable to a design in which, for example, children read about the same topics year after year and studied discipline-based subjects.[57]

The Virginia Curriculum, with its "scope and sequence" grid, was published as a course of study in 1934.[58] The questions (one question per grid square) generally reflected a topics-centered focus. The intent was that each topic question would help children understand the complexities of their world.[59] For example, in grade one, under the activity of "providing recreation," the question was "How can we have an enjoyable time at home and school?" In grade four, under the activity of "consumption of goods and services," the question was "How does frontier living modify and how has it been modified by the production and distribution of goods and services?"[60] Although this question was historical, it did not contradict Hanna's view of the role of history in social studies education since he thought some historical knowledge of social institutions and issues was necessary in order to understand contemporary life. As Hanna explained, "The major emphasis, it seems to me, must be on analysis of life today and the designing of a new social order which guarantees the basic structure in which the good life will be possible for all."[61]

The Virginia Curriculum introduced a new teaching structure for social studies by combining the sequence of the expanding communities approach and the scope of the basic human activities in a highly ordered program of study. In recognition of the idea that social studies includes "those fields of human experience that deal with man to man relationships considered in the subjects of history, geography, economics, civic, sociology, and psychology," Caswell and Hanna organized the social studies curriculum around "concepts and materials [that] are drawn from these fields and integrated by the learner around large centers of human interest." They stated, "This course of study accepts this unitary view as contrasted with that of history, civics, geography, etc. pursued as separate fields of subject matter."[62]

Caswell and Hanna thought this new curriculum would simplify teaching social studies since teachers would require less academic preparation. In practice, however, the curriculum was not easier for the Virginia teachers. Caswell concluded teachers were unprepared to teach it.[63] As he explained, "Many teachers, as now trained, do not have adequate background in the content subjects to deal with many aspects of centers of interest...."[64] Even with the replacement of the social science disciplines with topics, the Virginia teachers had to know quite a lot about subject matter content as well as how to teach it. Caswell and Hanna observed that even with additional education in the disciplines, there was no guarantee that the teachers could teach the new curriculum.

There was another problem with the Virginia Curriculum that critics have pointed to. Hanna was deeply committed to social equality and democratic principles. He even believed this new curriculum, with its contemporary content, would help promote "cultural reconstruction," the notion that everyone could "attain the good life."[65] Yet the Virginia Curriculum did not directly reference such issues despite Hanna's commitment to social reconstructionism. One might argue that no curriculum at the time dealt with the complex social issues of poverty, racism, and privilege. However, some of Hanna's contemporaries, particularly educators who promoted intercultural education (see Chapter 5), addressed social issues in the curriculum recommendations they presented in the early 1940s.[66] One possible explanation for the omission of social issues in the Virginia Curriculum is that Hanna and his colleagues thought these issues were too complex, emotionally and cognitively, for young children. Another explanation may be that Virginia educators, politicians, and the general public may have thought certain social issues were just too controversial for school curricula.[67]

Despite these criticisms, as well as the implementation difficulties, the Virginia Curriculum was successful in many ways. Hicks and van Hover conclude, "The Virginia Program came to represent a model for statewide curriculum revision that was influenced by the leading educational ideologies of the period, dependent upon the participation of teachers, and responsive to the context of the time."[68] In the years ahead, Hanna's new curriculum would achieve remarkable success on a national, even worldwide, scale.

Hanna and Scott, Foresman and Company: Textbook Publications

After the publication of the Virginia Curriculum, Hanna's reputation in curriculum study and design was assured. He joined the Society for

Curriculum Study and was elected its president in both 1934 and 1935. In 1934, he gave six speeches on curriculum planning to state and regional groups.[69] Most importantly, in the early 1930s, various textbook publishers, including Macmillan, Houghton Mifflin, and Scott, Foresman, offered him textbook contracts. He accepted the Scott, Foresman contract because this publisher allowed him to work alone instead of in partnership with his TC colleagues.[70] Hanna's decision to work alone was timely and fortuitous. In 1935, he took a position as Associate Professor of Education at Stanford University's School of Education. It was an environment that allowed him to escape the shadow of the TC giants and to establish his own identity as a scholar.[71] The single-author contract with Scott, Foresman provided the impetus and the means for Hanna to begin a new phase in his career.[72]

However, as Gill claims, venturing into textbook publishing was "not necessarily the next logical step for Hanna."[73] Then, as now, the academic community valued research-based scholarship more highly than textbook publication. However, according to Gill, Hanna had a vision that was more compelling than peer recognition (or even the obvious financial rewards of textbook publishing). With textbooks, Hanna saw the opportunity to create a "totally integrated and coordinated elementary social studies textbook series that dealt with both the child's interest and the child's role as an apprentice participant in the social activities of man."[74]

Under contract with Scott, Foresman, Hanna began writing a series of textbooks that would quickly fill a market niche in elementary social studies education.[75] His contract was to write a social studies series for grades one to three as part of the Scott, Foresman Curriculum Foundations Series. This series would be part of a carefully constructed twelve-year social studies program that Hanna would lead.[76] Hanna's efficient and logical approach to organizing the curriculum impressed the Scott, Foresman staff and management, including upper-level executives.[77]

Although Hanna, as the lead author, had the main responsibility for the social science ideas in the textbooks, two co-authors assisted him: Genevieve Anderson, an elementary principal in New Orleans, who had written mathematics textbooks, and William Gray, a reading specialist at Scott, Foresman who, with Harry Johnston, Scott, Foresman's lead editor for its reading series, had developed curriculum materials based on reading textbooks.[78] Hanna had successful and long-lasting work relationships with both Anderson and Gray.

Scott, Foresman, the leading publisher of reading textbooks in the country, used these textbooks as models for its other textbooks (e.g., social studies, health and personal development, science, and numbers). Therefore, Hanna had to harmonize the style and language of his social studies textbooks with the language and style of the publisher's other textbooks. This meant Hanna had to use certain vocabulary words and a prescribed number of new vocabulary words in each of his books. For example, 249 "carry-over words" (words readers could recognize by sight) and 25 "new words" (e.g., words based in social studies such as "community") were required in his second grade book.[79] Hanna almost always agreed to these language demands although it seems he found them somewhat limiting. He stated he believed more in "content count" than "vocabulary count."[80]

Hanna's elementary school textbooks were *Peter's Family, David's Friends at School,* and *Susan's Neighbors,* all of which focused on family and school life.[81] These books clearly reflect the spirit of the multidisciplinary approach that Harold Rugg had used in his social studies textbooks.[82] Rugg, Hanna said, had certainly "influenced my curriculum thinking because I could see that the separate subjects—history and geography—were inadequate for living in a modern society in which knowledge of economics, political science, sociology, etc. were just as important as history and geography."[83]

However, Harry Johnston at Scott, Foresman discouraged the Rugg influence. He disliked the elementary social studies textbooks by Rugg (and his co-author Louise Krueger) because he found them too theoretical and too impractical.[84] After Hanna signed the Scott, Foresman contract, Johnston warned Hanna about the Rugg influence:

> The Rugg books are a perfect example of what happens without the critical ability and constructive help of a well qualified author who every day is battling instructional problems in an average public school system. The books have scholarship and a great deal of downright cleverness and ingenuity. They lack, however, evidence of realistic contact with the ordinary average school....[85]

In general, the topics in Rugg's textbooks were rather intellectually sophisticated. The books dealt with historical and social science
concepts (e.g., exploration, the growth of cities, the history of architecture, the history of telling time) and described people and places far
removed from the child's immediate world. For example, *Communities
of Men* featured chapters on villages in Africa, Asia, Germany, and
England.[86] Yet the books also had a certain charm. One book invited
its readers on a fantasy voyage of discovery: "The *First Book of the
Earth* will take us on many adventures. We shall whiz through space
on a magic cloud and see our sun and our moon among the millions
of stars of the heavens."[87] The *Rugg Social Science Series* was adven-
turesome as well as cognitively demanding for students and pedagogically challenging for teachers.[88] Possibly as a result of Johnston's
warning, Hanna's textbooks, by contrast, were noted for their simple
descriptions of traditional families engaged in everyday activities.

Hanna claimed that, in general, Scott, Foresman gave him considerable authorial freedom: "I have had from the beginning at top
management level complete understanding and support." Continuing, he stated that he wanted the relationship with the publisher to be
"a marriage for life."[89] In some ways, Hanna's education philosophy
was similar to that of his publisher. For example, and quite importantly, his expanding communities approach was consistent with the
publisher's approach to learning. In fact, the Scott, Foresman reading
series, the Elson-Gray Reading Program (which was in the Curriculum Foundation Series), also used the expanding communities
approach as an organizing structure.[90]

Gill's interview with Hanna and the 1935 and 1936 Hanna-Scott,
Foresman letter exchanges, however, suggest that this author-
publisher marriage was sometimes a troubled one. For example, Scott,
Foresman forced Hanna into a number of one-sided compromises.[91]
One important compromise concerned the substantive content Hanna
wanted and the lively, accessible content Scott, Foresman wanted. For
example, letters between the Scott, Foresman editors and Hanna
reveal the publisher's worry that "didactic material" might dominate
the text. The editors preferred a strong emphasis on sparkling stories
that captured children's interests.[92] However, despite their differences, Hanna was appreciative of the contribution by one editor,

Zerna Sharp, because, he admitted, she added "snap and sparkle which is so important in children's work."[93]

Nevertheless, Hanna maintained that the "snap and sparkle" touches should not be added at the expense of social studies content. He wrote his editors that he was worried the extensive attention devoted to a discussion of Christmas in *Peter's Family* seemed to "throw the emphasis off social studies materials."[94] When the editors replaced one factual vignette he felt was particularly important with a story about a rabbit eating forbidden grass and another story about a kitten riding a pony, Hanna wrote to Sharp:

> I am convinced in my experience that children want more factual materials about human relations and the objects and institutions about them and relatively less of the lighter animal-story materials. After all these pupils reading this book supposedly are interested in getting more information on how a school is run, not in reading more stories, to a great extent, irrelevant, on rabbits, horses, kittens, etc.[95]

Ultimately, Sharp reinstated Hanna's original vignette, but the tension between Hanna and the editors over content versus "snap and sparkle" was clear. On another occasion, Hanna bypassed his editors and complained directly to Willis Scott (President of Scott, Foresman) about the subtitle of the Curriculum Foundation Series. Hanna disliked the subtitle, *Everyday-Life Stories*, and wanted to use the subtitle, *Social Studies Texts*, instead. He thought the first subtitle was vague and asked if it could be changed.[96] However, early editions were subtitled *Everyday-Life Stories* although revised editions in the 1940s were subtitled *The Basic Social Studies Programs*.

Despite his wish to have more social studies content in his textbooks, ultimately Hanna agreed, if reluctantly, to Scott, Foresman's demands. In a letter to Johnston, Hanna worried, "My only feeling of inadequacy lies in the fact that there is too much story and not enough of the social studies concept." He continued, "I am sure you are correct, however, in saying that for these youngsters we need the spark and snap...."[97] Taking Hanna at his word, it appears he recognized that Scott, Foresman knew which social studies content would sell.

Why did Hanna so often agree to his publisher's demands since their effect was to diminish the content of his curriculum? A probable explanation is that the Scott, Foresman partnership resulted in both financial and professional rewards for Hanna. The success of his textbooks made him an influential figure in education circles. With an established reputation as a leading American educator, he became one of Stanford University's most famous professors. Furthermore, he likely understood that a mutually satisfactory relationship with Scott, Foresman could lead to the widespread dissemination of his social studies programs. He may have rationalized that compromising some of his commitment to social studies content meant more school sales and thus more acceptance of his programs.

Hanna's Textbooks: Content and Approach

All Hanna's textbooks followed the same pattern. Each book in the Everyday-Life Stories used the near to far trajectory for a particular social unit. From one grade level to the next, the books dealt with progressively larger social units: from the family to the school to the neighborhood. Local neighborhoods then formed the cities and counties that became regional communities, then national communities, and finally a world community. As Hanna developed his ideas in the 1940s and 1950s, he famously depicted the multiple communities in the concentric circles graphic that became known as the "expanding communities of men" or the abbreviated "expanding communities."

The primary focus in the Everyday-Life Stories was the family in its various communities, with particular emphasis on children. The stories described the family's work and activities (e.g., the father's salesman job and the mother's household tasks), vacations, holiday celebrations (e.g., Christmas), encounters with civic institutions, and experiences with the production and consumption of goods. All the stories depicted the family in the context of basic human activities. The rather minimal disciplinary content is geographic (e.g., community landmarks), economic (e.g., consumption and work), and civic (e.g., social harmony). However, this content was not deeply based in the disciplines. Moreover, history, which Hanna later explained was of no use in helping students understand contemporary issues, had no place in the stories.[98]

There is no indication in the editions of the Everyday-Life Stories from the 1930s that the parents in the family were affected by, or even aware of, the economic turmoil of the Great Depression, the possibility of world war, or society's racial divisions. The family's biggest dilemma was whether to move to an apartment in the city or to a house in the suburbs.[99] These stories, which reflected the racial and economic status quo in the United States, failed to even hint at the existence of such social problems. Although many controversial social themes, if not dealt with in sensitive, age-appropriate ways, are unsuitable in the lower elementary classroom, Hanna's depiction of American life as happy, simple, and conflict-free seems curiously optimistic, especially given his contention that children should know about the social realities of their times.

Hanna names the family in the series, without any suggestion of irony, the "White Family." There are no racial or ethnic minorities in his textbooks from the 1930s (this was fairly typical of textbooks of these years; Hanna's later textbooks featured some African Americans). The assumption seems to be that young readers' lives are very like Peter White's life. For example, one activity in the Teacher's Notes for *Peter's Family* suggests, "Each child may tell of the rooms in his own home."[100]

Because of this narrow view of the American family, Hanna's social studies textbooks have been criticized for their stereotypical characters, their sunny view of family life, and their assumption that Peter's family structure is the norm. However, Hanna's Caucasian, middle-class, Christian, and patriarchal family, which was presented as an ordinary American family, was consistent with the image presented in many other textbooks of the period. Another explanation for Hanna's traditional approach to family life was that social studies textbooks had to appeal to teachers, and most teachers resisted teaching children social reformist ideas (preferring to protect young children from society's ills).[101] Yet it is undeniable that this portrayal of family life was, as critics have charged, inconsistent with Hanna's often-voiced objection to the inequalities among groups of people and with his support for Counts's social reconstructionism.

Perhaps the most intriguing of all Hanna's books in the series is *Centerville*, for third graders, which described the town of Centerville: its businesses, roads and highway, farms, and school.[102] The book emphasized the interdependence of the producer and consumer, cooperative planning, the interrelationship of urban and rural activities, the use of applied science, the need for change in community customs and values, and the importance of civic-mindedness.[103] In its aggressive marketing campaign for the book, Scott, Foresman distributed marketing materials to reviewers that claimed *Centerville* was the first book to simplify complicated social concepts on a scale appropriate for the average eight-year-old.[104] For example, the promotional literature declared that *Centerville* showed how taxes pay for community goods and services, how life differs among communities, and how groups make decisions. According to Scott, Foresman, the book displayed "democracy at work" in a community when change creates problems requiring responsible solutions.[105]

One story in *Centerville* in particular illustrated how Hanna used the themes of community interdependence and civic responsibility to present his vision of the role of government. There was perhaps a dash of social reconstructionism in this vision. The narrative conflict concerns the poor condition of Centerville's main road that limits the mobility of the library on wheels, delays mail and newspaper delivery, and creates difficulties for farmers bringing products to market. The townspeople want to build a road through a farm owned by crotchety, old Farmer Banks (his name is a none-too-subtle reference to the failed financial institutions of the Great Depression). Eventually, they persuade Farmer Banks to permit the construction of a new road through his farm. In a triumph of community spirit over private property rights, Farmer Banks even donates land for a municipal swimming pool.[106]

Unless the teacher called attention to the social betterment message of *Centerville*, the average eight-year-old probably missed it and only enjoyed the happy ending. The message was not lost on adult readers, however. A 1938 review in *Time* magazine wrote of the book: "Aim of Centerville's subtle propaganda: to wean the younger generation from rugged individualism to cooperation."[107] Although the review was generally favorable, the magazine reviewer suggested Hanna's textbooks tended toward a "collectivist" bent, echoing the kind of criticism directed at the American Historical Association Commission on the Social Studies.[108]

To supplement these various reviews, the Scott, Foresman editors sought responses from the series' intended audience: schoolchildren.

Students were generally positive about *Centerville*. They appreciated the "realness" of the stories, thought the language was easy, and liked that there weren't tests every three pages (as in some other books). However, some students claimed they disliked Hanna's new, simpler direction for social studies and asked for more rigorous, sophisticated content. Other students were disappointed that there was not more of the imaginary, the distant past, and the unusual in the books. In his written replies to students and teachers, Hanna expressed his genuine interest in their comments, particularly the negative criticism, and sometimes even asked for further explanation.[109]

In fact, Hanna was eager to make his textbooks accessible to both students and teachers. He toured the country, visiting schools to promote his textbooks. These visits were inspired by his conviction that teachers needed help if they were to understand and use the expanding communities approach.[110] He also met with central curriculum staff members at the state and district levels and gave talks at the national meetings of the American Association of Colleges for Teacher Education. At these meetings, he presented his multidisciplinary approach to social studies and the rationale behind its sequence of study. He credited his textbook success partially to these promotional efforts rather than solely to the textbooks and their teacher instruction guides.

For Hanna, however, textbooks were only guides (although necessary ones). Teachers should use textbooks to direct students into more exploration and further study. Therefore, he included maps, student work pages, and pictures in his books in the hope that teachers could use such supplements to associate social studies concepts with their students' communities. Years later, Hanna explained how a third-grade teacher in Palo Alto, California, might have used these community ideas:

> We can focus on the BART [Bay Area Rapid Transit] system; we can focus on pollution; or we can focus on crime; or we can focus on the problem of recreation and the coastside effort at conservation and how it is going to affect the possibilities of recreation along the coast of San Francisco.[111]

In part, Hanna encouraged teachers to focus on social studies concepts in units directed to their communities because of the inherent limitations of his textbooks, which he acknowledged. The books were generalized for the entire country, featured representative (although stereotypical) characters, and focused on realistic but nonetheless fictional issues. Hanna's textbooks are not factual accounts, with history lines, biographies, or dates. Nor are they specific as to time, place, or issue. For national distribution, his books had to have fictional settings and characters that transcended time, place, and issue. To overcome this generic feature of the books—its typical American family in its typical American setting—it was the job of the teachers to adapt the books to the lives of their students. Yet it may be noted, it is the fictional aspect of his textbooks that appealed to young children, despite the incompatibility of this aspect with Hanna's idea that learning should reflect real life.

Hanna revised his social studies textbooks in the following decades, often changing their titles. As Stallones states, by the late 1950s, the series, now called the Basic Social Studies Program, had evolved to reflect his expanding communities approach more explicitly. The books, which were more discipline-focused, were now called *At Home, At School, In the Neighborhood, In City, Town, and Country, In All Our States, In the Americas,* and *Beyond the Americas.*[112] As Gill concludes, "Hanna had realized that he lacked sufficient depth in all the various social sciences he wished to incorporate into his textbook series."[113] In the revised editions from the 1950s, experts in the disciplines (for example, Clyde Kohn, a geography professor) were added as co-authors, and expository text replaced the narrative approach.[114] Chapter 5 returns to this discussion of how Hanna's textbooks and his relationships with disciplinary experts evolved.

The Success of Hanna's Social Studies Textbooks

Hanna thought his textbooks helped transform elementary education from its boring, irrelevant focus on the memorization of dates and places to a dynamic, engaging, relevant field of study founded on the most important principles of democratic citizenship (i.e., free exchange of ideas, love of country, and fair play). He credited the books, as well as the publisher's hardworking sales teams, with giving him the chance to promote his ideas nationally.

From the 1930s to the 1950s, school districts nationwide purchased Hanna's social studies textbooks. By 1941, his books had sold over one million copies, and by 1973, total copies sold were over ten million.[115] Reflecting on the mark he had made on social studies education, Hanna said:

> I have achieved the purpose that I had in mind which was to have American youth saturated with some kind of a multi-dimensional, multi-discipline, problem-solving, inquiring-oriented and all the rest of the things that I could say, to replace the old expository encyclopedic history separate, geography separate, and that was the pattern up until that time.[116]

He added:

> Nationally we sold the idea that there should be a multi-disciplinary approach to the social studies...we sold nationally the idea that it had to have some kind of a sequential design. Eventually I came up with the expanding communities of men which is now almost universally used, not only in this country but in many nations of the world.[117]

Hanna's ideas reflected the progressive commitment to relevancy and utility in the curriculum by using lifelike (albeit fictional) stories of situations, experiences, and communities that were familiar to children, with a sprinkling of charming silliness (e.g., a rabbit goes to school). Some critics charged that Hanna's books were boring and insipid, especially compared to the exciting, dramatic tales from legends and myths, and to the stories of history's heroes. Yet Hanna's stories suited the educational mood of the times. Some critics, such as Diane Ravitch, charge that was exactly what was wrong with them.[118]

Following the success of the Everyday-Life Stories in the Curriculum Foundations Series, Scott, Foresman contracted with Hanna to write a set of social studies textbooks for the upper elementary grades. The first book in the series was *Without Machinery* for fourth graders.[119] This book focused on people who work with their hands and included units on peoples from the South Pacific, Lapland, the Congo, China, and the American Southwest (the Zuni Tribe). Hanna and his wife even visited the American Southwest to witness firsthand the life of the Zuni and to take photographs and motion pictures for the book's illustrator to look at.[120] The second book in the series, also for fourth graders, *Ten Communities*, compared geography, industry, culture, history, and daily activities in various American cities (e.g., Atlanta in Georgia, and Waterloo in Iowa). The book had three purposes: first, to broaden students' conception of "community"; second, to show how society has moved from a pioneering to a technological culture; and third, to provide a starting point for the study of the local community.[121] With their emphasis on economics, these textbooks for upper elementary grades had more disciplinary focus than those for the lower elementary grades. The reason may have been the concern expressed by Hanna and other progressive educators that the schools had not prepared citizens for the Great Depression and had failed to teach its causes adequately.[122]

Hanna's textbooks for the upper elementary grades were less successful than his textbooks for the lower elementary grades. According to Hanna, Scott, Foresman had two explanations for this lack of success. At the lower elementary level, there was synergy between the reading series and the social studies series: school districts were inclined to purchase the social studies series if they had previously purchased the reading series. Moreover, at the upper elementary level, school districts were disinclined to abandon the traditional instruction methods in geography and history for the new methods promoted in the new series.[123] While the topics approach was enormously successful at the lower elementary level, in large part because history and geography were not major content areas in the curriculum, history and geography were still separate disciplines at the upper elementary level.

Despite this difficulty in extending his expanding communities approach upward into the upper elementary grades, Hanna enjoyed some success by extending it outward into other countries. Hanna took his ideas abroad (e.g., to the Philippines), hoping the world's educators would adopt his elementary social studies approach. Indeed, as Stallones remarks, Hanna's expanding communities approach became a "fixture in dozens of foreign school systems."[124] The premise of the approach, that children needed to learn about their immediate environments and then move in ever-widening communities, translated easily to other countries since the approach was not grounded in any particular time or place. Hanna thought his approach could prepare children for effective group living in any society by helping them identify, study, and address community problems.[125] He was convinced education was the key to building stronger, more democratic societies in the world as well as in the United States.[126]

What accounts for the longevity of Hanna's expanding communities approach that his social studies textbooks promoted? There are several explanations. First, the times in which Hanna wrote his books are relevant. In the 1930s, educators were concerned about the role of schools in a world challenged by economic crisis and political instability. Americans, who worried about foreign totalitarian ideologies and domestic social turmoil, wanted their children to become adults who actively participated in a democratic society. Hanna thought his books promoted this goal because they showcased economic and civic responsibility in familiar and local settings. When his fictional protagonists engage in everyday, apolitical situations, such as the farm and the grocery, they exhibit the behavior traits (e.g., cooperation, compromise, and civic responsibility) of good citizenship. This is the message educators and the general public wanted schools to convey.

There is also a market explanation for the popularity of Hanna's textbooks. The Scott, Foresman editors played an important role in popularizing Hanna's textbooks in the education community. By agreeing to their promotion recommendations and swallowing his preference for more disciplinary material, Hanna replaced much of his curriculum content with the "snap and sparkle" that sold textbooks. As Stallones observes, there was often a narrow line between Hanna's identity as promoter and as scholar.[127]

A third explanation for the success of Hanna's textbooks relates to twentieth-century changes in U.S. public schools, especially in enrollment numbers. A large demographic change created a profound crisis in teacher education because of the unexpected demand for more teachers as student enrollment increased. In the 1949–50 school year, for example, there were 25,111,000 children in elementary and secondary schools in the United States; only ten years later, in the 1959–60 school year, there were 36,087,000—an increase of nearly 44 percent.[128] Teachers had to be educated, and quickly, to meet this increase in the student population. Hanna's textbooks allowed elementary teachers with little in-depth disciplinary education to teach the basic social studies concepts. The focus on the "American Experience" in his curriculum did not require teachers to have extensive knowledge of history, civics, or geography. Their knowledge of "everyday life" was adequate. For Hanna, the everyday life curriculum focused on familiar concepts such as transporting, communicating, and recreating rather than on the "traditional" disciplines of history and the social sciences.[129]

Hanna had reason to worry that teachers lacked disciplinary knowledge. In 1930, half the nation's elementary teachers had only two years of study beyond high school (and 25 percent of them had even less education). No state required elementary teachers to have a college degree.[130]

Finally, the success of Hanna's books is explained by the "hybrid" nature of schooling that Larry Cuban describes as the process of embedding pedagogically progressive ideas within an otherwise traditional, teacher-centered classroom. As Cuban argues in his history of American teachers, progressive pedagogy has had little influence in classrooms except for the modest success enjoyed at the elementary level. Teachers have constructed "patchwork compromises" that blend child-centered practices, such as allowing students to work cooperatively and varying class activities. However, teachers have used these practices in the traditional school classroom where they make all decisions and rely upon traditional instructional tools such as textbooks.[131]

Hanna's textbooks supported this hybrid approach. Although his textbooks were innovative in their packaging of the social studies curriculum as basic human activities, they were very traditional in their teacher-centricity. Moreover, the read-aloud format of his books (i.e., standardized chapter arrangement and sentence construction) was similar to the reading books already in use, particularly the Dick and Jane reading series that Scott, Foresman published.[132] Hanna's hybridism of innovative packaging combined with traditional pedagogy was very attractive to teachers and to school districts.

Criticism of Hanna's Expanding Communities
Approach and Textbooks

There were, and still are, many critics of Hanna's expanding communities approach. Today's critics even hold the approach culpable for the present troubled state of elementary social studies. The main thrust of this criticism is that social studies, as taught by the expanding communities approach, overemphasizes the child's interests and experiences.[133] Yet Hanna was convinced he had avoided the exclusive, child-centered focus proposed by some progressive educators such as Kilpatrick. Hanna thought learning had to engage children while still providing content knowledge. In his philosophy of education, learning should be freed from the content-oriented approach traditionally associated with history and geography instruction. At the same time, learning should avoid pandering to children's whims.[134] In thus trying to balance "the child and the curriculum," Hanna saw himself as a follower of his mentor, John Dewey.[135] Yet Hanna's textbooks, which generally favored the child over the curriculum, did not reflect the intentions of many progressive educators as well as his own intentions. This inability to strike a balance between child and curriculum ultimately proved elusive to Hanna, and, as critics charge, resulted in sweeping consequences for social studies education.

Despite the popularity, even into the twenty-first century, of the Hanna-inspired social studies curriculum, the criticism continues. Scholars charge the social studies programs, rooted in Hanna's ideas, lack sufficient disciplinary content and are boring and redundant.[136] Moreover, extending their disapproval to Hanna, critics often point to the gap between his trust in education as a democratizing force for change and his work that supports the status quo in society. It is the "lost in translation" phenomenon, when rhetoric meets reality as theoreticians translate ideas into practice, that critics find disturbing. The charge has validity: many of Hanna's textbooks do not reflect his social concerns or his conviction that learning should have a strong content focus.

Hanna repeatedly claimed in his essays and speeches that students should be taught disciplinary content. He thought such content was compatible with a child-centered approach. However, as Stallones and others have noted, critics have long argued that Hanna placed too much emphasis on the child and too little on content.[137] As early as 1946, for example, TC Professor Isaac Kandel rebuked Hanna for favoring children's interests over traditional subject-content learning.[138] It is fair to say, as Kandel and others have complained, that Hanna's stories, which focus on children's daily activities and relationships, do little to advance students' understandings of broader aspects of civics, economics, geography, or history.

There were also severe critics among Hanna's contemporaries. As Stallones observes, Hollis Caswell, Hanna's one-time collaborator in Virginia, claimed Hanna's designs focused too much on children's social development and too little on their individual and creative development. Richard Gross, a social studies educator and Hanna's Stanford University colleague, pointed to the lack of psychological research behind Hanna's approach: no psychological theories justified the logic of moving from the known to the unknown. Gross also contended that the approach underestimated children's understanding of environments other than their own. Because of technological advances in television, radio, and other media sources, Gross argued, children have considerable knowledge of other people, other communities, and other lands.[139] Even Malcolm Douglass, one of Hanna's doctoral advisees, faulted his advisor's approach for its lack of intellectual rigor.[140]

In addition, there is considerable criticism of Hanna's textbooks for their failure to reflect his often-expressed commitment to social and economic equality in American life. The expanding communities approach, as conceived of by Hanna, was seldom used to address such issues. With the exception of the private versus community property conflict in *Centerville*, Hanna's lower elementary level textbooks ignored societal problems. These were textbooks written for America's public school students, many of whom were children of immigrants or children of migrants from the American South, living through the Great Depression and World War II. It is hard to imagine that such children could identify closely with the White Family and its conventional, middle-class life.

In the years following the huge success of his textbooks, Hanna continued to trust in the power of schools to instill democratic attitudes and to promote democratic decision making—a conviction originating in the social reconstructionism he had embraced many years earlier. Besides the Everyday-Life Stories about happy, largely unreflective family life, Hanna wrote curricula that reflected his conviction that schools could effect constructive change. His *Building America* (1935–1948) periodical series for junior high school, with its focus on sociopolitical problems, was daring. However, there was also criticism of these monthly magazine publications, in particular from the California Society of the Sons of the American Revolution.[141] As they had with Rugg's books, critics attacked the *Building America* series for its alleged communist sympathies.[142]

The *Building America* series was very different from Hanna's lower elementary level textbooks for young children.[143] This series presented a different picture of American life, with its more realistic themes and subjects, than the life enjoyed by his Everyday-Life family. It is probable that textbooks and programs by Hanna's contemporaries influenced the new series. Other textbook authors at this time were beginning to focus on intercultural education and were introducing sociopolitical themes in their books for elementary school children. For example, in the 1940s, the American Association of School Administrators, the NCSS, the John Dewey Society, and various U.S. school systems recommended and/or adopted curricula that addressed issues of racial and religious diversity with a focus on challenging ideas and interpretations of events.[144] It seems unlikely that Hanna was unaware of these efforts to tackle controversial although realistic topics in the elementary social studies program. However, had Hanna proposed to include such topics in his Everyday-Life Stories, it is highly doubtful Scott, Foresman would have approved the proposal.

The Lasting Influence of Hanna's Expanding Communities Approach

Hanna wanted to create a progressive social studies curriculum that would inspire civic responsibility in children. After trial and error, he found a structure that he thought advanced the best ideas of progressive education: the expanding communities approach as the sequence with the basic human activities as the scope. There is no doubt that his approach has had a significant and lasting influence on elementary social studies education. For decades, elementary school textbooks and national and state standards have reflected the dominance of this approach.

Hanna did not feature the disciplines (at least by name) in his original scope and sequence. However, by the 1960s, Hanna had added the study of six disciplines (anthropology, economics, geography, history, political science, and sociology) to his original social studies curriculum. He referred to these disciplines as "sunbursts" that were used for "floodlighting" his scope and sequence.[145] He argued that these foundational disciplines of social studies should play a greater role in the social studies programs than they had in the past. Yet, even in his sunburst design, the disciplines seemed more inspiration for the scope than expansion of the scope. His lessons still featured the basic human activities and paid little attention to historical study. He continued to defend his long-held position: "But the child's external world consists not just of events of the past; it is not history alone. The real world exists in the present."[146] Moreover, Hanna argued that teachers should not teach the disciplines independently. In a multidisciplinary approach, no discipline should dominate.

If widespread textbook adoption in U.S. schools is the criterion for success in education innovation, Hanna's success is unquestioned. Leading elementary social studies methods textbooks have used and praised the expanding communities scope and sequence. As social studies educator John R. Lee wrote, "The chart leaves the teacher great freedom for specifying particular goals and for selecting content from any of the social sciences. When a program is based on this pattern, the problems of providing continuity of experience from year to year are reduced."[147] However, if the criterion for success in education innovation is the intellectual development of children, then understanding Hanna's contribution is more complicated. On the one hand, Hanna helped make social studies curriculum relevant to children's lives in ways history, geography, and civics lessons may not have. On the other hand, the Everyday-Life Stories diminished the disciplinary content of the social science subjects. Citizenship education, for example, became learning to get along with others. Bland stories about idealized family life taught children little about their country's history or its problems.

Although Hanna was not the originator of the expanding communities approach, he played a key role in developing it, providing a philosophical (although not empirical) rationale for it, and popularizing it in his textbooks. His basic human activities approach also became a permanent part of many elementary social studies programs. The next chapter, which focuses on years during and after World War II, describes the development of competing elementary social studies programs. The chapter also explains how social, political, and economic forces provided a context that was highly supportive of Hanna's social studies programs and helped secure their position as the de facto elementary social studies curriculum.

Chapter 5
"A Revolution Is Needed": Social Studies in the Hot and Cold War Eras

IN THE MID-TWENTIETH CENTURY, two shocking events in the United States had a powerful, nationwide effect on public education. After the Japanese attack on the U.S. naval base at Pearl Harbor in Hawaii on December 7, 1941, and after the Soviet Union's launch of the first artificial space satellite, Sputnik, on October 4, 1957, there were comprehensive re-examinations of U.S. education policies and practices. Both events shook Americans' confidence in their country's military strength and in their political governance, and, following the second event, in their country's scientific capability. Politicians, educators, and citizens sought explanations and remedies. A primary concern was the country's education system. Were students properly taught the difference between democratic governments and totalitarian regimes? Was a more academically rigorous education system, especially in science education, needed? If U.S. education required reform, how should it be reformed, and by whom?

The Civil Rights Movement of the 1960s and 1970s also challenged the structure (e.g., the segregated school districts) and curriculum (e.g., the Eurocentric perspective) in U.S. education. More and more questions were asked. For example, should the largely White Anglo-Saxon Protestant curriculum include other cultural perspectives, especially those of minorities? Were supplemental programs needed to close the perceived achievement disparity between Black and White students? Should education directly confront issues of race, social class, power, and privilege? A spirit of reform arose that spread to many areas of the curriculum as educators, policymakers, and citizens began to ask more of the education system.

Although World War II, the Soviet Union's space program, and the Civil Rights Movement influenced U.S. education in many ways, curiously social studies in elementary schools was less influenced than other elementary level subjects and far less than social studies in high schools. Alternative social studies curriculum approaches and programs for K–12 were proposed in these years, including, for example, intercultural education, the "new social studies," Man: A Course of Study, and ethnic studies. However, because teachers lacked training and because of political opposition, among other factors, most of these approaches and programs were often short-lived in the elementary schools that experimented with them. None toppled the topics-based expanding communities approach from its dominant position in elementary social studies.

Yet there were changes of another sort. Despite promising initiatives for change in education, the social studies share of the elementary school day decreased, and the social science disciplines were increasingly de-emphasized. With only minor modifications, the elementary social studies curriculum, developed in the 1930s and refined in the 1940s, based in progressive ideology, continued as before. In 1981, Irving Morrissett, the Executive Director of the Social Science Education Consortium, reflected, "The stability of the dominant curriculum pattern for half a century and the relatively small lasting effects of the new social studies may give an indication of the most likely future of the social studies for the next decade or two: more of the same."[1] Many critics are convinced that this prediction from more than thirty years ago has been fulfilled. This chapter explains why none of the proposed alternative programs disrupted this stability in elementary social studies.

Elementary Social Studies in the 1940s and 1950s

In these two decades, most teachers of elementary social studies used the expanding communities approach (with a topics focus in the lower elementary grades and history and geography in the upper elementary grades). For his 1946 methods book in social studies education, Edgar Wesley examined objectives, instructional methods, curriculum materials, and assessment procedures in social studies lessons in grades one through six. He found the most "frequent" social studies topics in the grades were the following:

Grade 1: Home, family, school, community
Grade 2: Community, food, clothing, Indian life
Grade 3: Shelter, food, clothing, Indian life
Grade 4: Geography, state, and local history
Grade 5: American history, industries, geography of the United States and North America
Grade 6: European backgrounds, geography of Europe, Asia, and Africa[2]

Although Wesley favored the expanding communities approach, he saw there was a problem with its use in the classroom. Owing to "picture shows," newspapers, and radio, children already knew about places and even events far from home.[3] The popular media had expanded their horizons. Adding television to the media mix, another social studies scholar, Dorothy McClure Fraser, commented ten years later on the same problem:

> Do children really move from home to school to community to state to nation to world in their experiences? Or do not most of them push out the frontiers of their experience irregularly, jumping via television, radio, and other experiences from home to foreign lands and back to distant parts of their own nation, perhaps before they ever go to school?[4]

Despite this concern, Wesley, Fraser, and others thought the study of the local community contributed to children's social development. Children learned basic economics from reading about the grocer's and the milkman's jobs and about other people from visiting neighbors.[5] Social studies units, Wesley claimed, should address "the needs, interests, capacities, and wishes of the students, together with an understanding of their community and an awareness of contemporary developments."[6]

In his elementary social studies methods textbook, social studies educator, Ralph Preston, approvingly described the near universality of the expanding communities approach in U.S. schools. Preston wrote that students' learning should be "centered in the here and now [where] their learning is well rooted to the extent that it is concrete."[7] He favored the fusion organization over the separate-subject organization because it dealt with familiar topics children encountered outside school. Furthermore, several research studies (most of which were random design experiments, one with over two thousand students) had argued that the fusion organization resulted in higher academic achievement and provoked greater student interest.[8] Preston recommended using the expanding communities approach to teach topical "units" in the areas of community (e.g., community history), social-processes (e.g., conservation, transportation, production, and invention—topics similar to Hanna's basic human activities), foreign cultures and geographic regions (e.g., a minority culture in the community; a stable, peaceful, democratic culture) and history (e.g., holidays, early explorers, the westward movement).[9] Preston's inclusion of minority culture is noteworthy.

The expanding communities approach clearly dominated in elementary social studies in local school districts in these years. In his 1939 article on the Detroit Public Schools plan for social studies, C. C. Barnes firmly supported the approach.[10] He wrote that the expanding communities was used in "each successive grade" in order to "present a wider, more complex phase of that concept than the one before."[11] Barnes urged moving away from the traditional study of history, geography, and civics "toward an ever increasing study of practical, present-day civic, social, and economic life."[12] At both national and local levels, in social studies lessons children learned about the social networks and institutions they met everyday. There is no evidence, however, on how "complex" these phases were.

Wartime Elementary Social Studies Programs

In the early 1940s, in the war with Japan, Germany, and Italy, Americans renewed their commitment to democratic values and principles. Although educators responded in different ways to this renewal of patriotism and national unity, one common response was to call for better citizenship education. The National Council for the Social Studies (NCSS) issued a series of annual resolutions and several citizenship education guides for social studies with particular emphasis on international relationships. Some educators developed intercultural education programs that challenged the traditional programs dominated by the White Anglo-Saxon Protestant culture. The Detroit Citizenship Education Study concluded that if children were eventually to assume adult responsibilities in a participatory democracy, they required instruction promoting emotional stability.[13]

Although these pedagogical reform efforts resulted in more changes in secondary social studies education than in elementary social studies education, there was nevertheless an indirect influence on elementary social studies. Collectively, these efforts increased support for the goals and the curricula of the expanding communities approach. Noble ideas about racial harmony, good international relationships, and democratic principles could be adapted to the lessons in elementary social studies on how to get along with others.

The NCSS Wartime Programs

During and after World War II, the NCSS promoted citizenship education with an emphasis on instruction in sociopolitical issues, international as well as national. For example, some NCSS resolutions from these years dealt with the founding and mission of the United Nations. In 1942, the NCSS Commission on Wartime Policy published a pamphlet, "The Social Studies Mobilize for Victory," that promoted civic education as the "core" of social studies. Specifically, the NCSS called for greater focus on the differences between democratic and dictatorial political systems and on the responsibilities and privileges of democratic citizenship.[14]

In its sweeping proposals for reforming citizenship education, the NCSS suggested new topics for social studies education. For example, the NCSS recommended the study of family and interpersonal relationships. When schools added these topics to the social studies curriculum, there was, of course, less time for instruction in disciplinary content and disciplinary skills. The 1945 NCSS Resolution, which recommended teaching critical thinking, the scientific method, and evaluation of sources, also recommended that educators (and parents) work with youth organizations, churches, and public agencies to promote the emotional welfare of students. In addition, the Resolution stated that the goals of civic education were to teach the principles of interdependence (among nations) and democracy and to encourage the development of a social conscience in young people.[15]

In 1944, the NCSS Advisory Commission on Postwar Policy (C. C. Barnes, Stanley Dimond, and Paul Hanna were members) issued its report, *The Social Studies Look Beyond the War*, which urged educating students in local, national, and international problems and in world peace efforts. The report described a postwar social studies curriculum that focused on the aftermath of war, the importance of international organization and cooperation, and the need to preserve democracy.[16] While the report mainly addressed secondary education, it supported the expanding communities approach in elementary education. According to the NCSS, the approach could be used to teach racial, religious, and ethnic harmony by encouraging students to "extend their acquaintance from home and neighborhood to larger communities, with growing understanding of the new groups and people encountered."[17] To achieve these goals, the NCSS recommended lessons on different cultures (e.g., celebrations of festivals and holidays), the scientific facts on the races, and intercultural relationships.[18] The NCSS educators, among others, were beginning to realize that the social studies curriculum was too narrow.

The Intercultural Education Movement

Sometimes referred to as intergroup education, the mission of intercultural education programs was to teach core democratic ideals such as racial equality, the common good, and tolerance for cultural differences.[19] The NCSS, the American Historical Association (AHA), and the National Association for the Advancement of Colored People published curricular guides and textbooks for these programs. By the late 1940s, many urban U.S. school systems had implemented some form of intercultural education, although, with a few exceptions, these programs did not address the controversial matters of race, social class, power, and privilege that the developers of intercultural education were concerned with. Instead, most programs focused on the contributions of diverse peoples and on values such as tolerance and appreciation of racial and cultural differences.[20]

To some extent, intercultural education was incompatible with the expanding communities approach because of its emphasis on the unfamiliar, such as other cultures and other races. The creators of intercultural education produced evidence that young children were ready to learn about the differences between themselves and other people. For example, a 1947 study by Philadelphia's Bureau for Intercultural Education showed that young children were aware of and often understood sophisticated concepts such as stereotypes, personal conflicts, values, and rejection.[21] In contrast, the expanding communities approach emphasized the familiar, such as the people, places, and events in children's local communities.

However, both the expanding communities approach and intercultural education had a stake in teaching children how to get along with others. In the former, the others were classmates and family members; in the latter, the others were the people who lived and worked together in racially mixed communities. Given this commonality, tenuous as it may have been, it was natural that intercultural education programs were placed in elementary social studies where children learned socialization skills. These skills were the bread and butter of the expanding communities approach.

In practice, intercultural education in elementary social studies education lost some of its original focus. In the lower elementary grades, pro-social behavior (e.g., taking turns and playing fair) was emphasized. In the upper elementary grades, the contributions of diverse peoples were emphasized.[22] However, as implemented in schools, intercultural education's commitment to teaching tolerance of racial and ethnic diversity and to discussing issues of power and privilege was rather weak.[23] As a result, in two important respects most intercultural education programs disappointed.[24] By avoiding complex issues of race, culture, power, and privilege, intercultural education programs rarely promoted racial and ethnic tolerance. Some scholars argue that intercultural education programs may have marginalized minorities even more.[25] Additionally, with its focus on harmonious living, especially at the elementary level, intercultural education programs diminished the disciplinary focus in social studies still further.

For various reasons intercultural education eventually lost popularity. However, the movement is important in the history of social studies education as the predecessor of multicultural education, a similar education reform aimed at broadening the social studies curriculum.[26] Multicultural education (discussed later in this chapter) still exists in elementary social studies education although it too struggles with its identity. Does it dare to teach structural issues of race, social class, power, and privilege, or is it content to celebrate holidays, foods, and clothing of diverse racial and ethnic groups? In any case, both education reforms seemed to lose power when implemented in practice.

The Detroit Citizenship Education Study

Perhaps the most important research project to examine social studies education in these years was the Detroit Citizenship Education Study (DCES), conducted from 1945 to 1950. With its $425,000 grant (equivalent in 2012 to about $4,000,000), at the time it was the best-funded study of citizenship education in U.S. history.[27] The goals of the study were to assess students' citizenship knowledge, to examine citizenship instruction in the Detroit Public Schools (DPS), and to propose ways to improve civic education in Detroit and in the country.[28] Before beginning the study, the DCES defined citizenship: "The relations of the individual to his government, and, in addition, his relation to other members and groups in a democratic society."[29] It was clear that social studies education in the DPS had shifted from teaching disciplinary content and disciplinary skills to nurturing human relationships.[30] Troubled by their suspicion that students had only learned rote phrases about democracy, the DCES researchers recommended a more practical approach to citizenship education. The philosophy behind the approach was that citizenship education should be relevant to students' lives and should focus on current events.

The DCES made several recommendations based on its research. First, students should learn democratic principles, not by studying political systems and history, but by participating in school activities (e.g., student government and school-sponsored community projects). Second, students should become more effective problem solvers by learning how to handle conflict.[31] Third, students should directly experience their local environments by taking field trips to museums, factories, and government facilities.[32] Each DCES recommendation seemed applicable to every area of elementary education. Yet, as if by default, it became the responsibility of social studies to implement the recommendations, regardless of the effect on other social studies content. In fact, according to the DCES, the idea that "academic subjects are the most important aspect of a school...is false."[33] Explicitly, the DCES personalized education in citizenship in the context of students' lives.

For the DCES, citizenship education involved "emotional adjustment," defined as the emotional and social well-being of children.[34] To that end, the DCES presented portraits of "good" and "poor" school-age citizens ("poor" was also equated with "disturbed"). For example, Mary, a "poor" citizen, disliked her classmates, did not enjoy school, and was badly behaved. John, a "good" citizen, was friendly, earned good grades, and respected authority.[35] Healthy emotional adjustment, the DCES argued, was the "missing ingredient" in "poor" citizens.

Underlying the NCSS wartime programs, the intercultural education programs, and the DCES recommendations, was the belief that students lacked a clear and inspirational understanding of the democratic principles that defined the country. Therefore, it was the goal of education, in particular social studies education, to teach students those principles and at the same time provide them with the social skills and the emotional stability required of citizens living in a democracy. The social and emotional adjustment of children, as the task of education, influenced the life-adjustment movement that was popular in U.S. public education in the 1940s and 1950s. Like many other education reforms, life-adjustment education mainly focused on secondary education. However, its premise that school should be based in everyday living and should teach harmonious social relationships reflected, and thus reinforced, current trends in elementary social studies education.

Social Studies as Skills for Living

High school enrollment in the United States declined significantly during World War II. Although teenage enlistment in the armed forces was one reason for this decline, another was that many high school students went to work in factories that manufactured war materials. In an effort to keep students in school, educators developed and promoted practical, life-adjustment training designed to prepare students for work and life responsibilities.[36] This effort was similar to the work of the social efficiency advocates of the Progressive Era. Ronald Evans uses the term "new social efficiency" to describe this approach to education in the postwar years.[37]

In the 1940s and the 1950s, elementary social studies lessons (particularly for the lower elementary grades) in most U.S. schools focused on skills for social living. As one educator explained, "Teachers should not think of social studies as a subject-matter field but rather as a broad *area of experience* which serves to help children relate skills, arts, social sciences, and physical and biological sciences into one unified learning experience which has meaning for them."[38] The NCSS discourse on social studies had also begun to focus on skills for living. For example, there were chapters in the 1953 NCSS yearbook titled "Skills Needed for Social Competence," "Participating in Group Undertakings," and "Evaluating Self and the Group to which the Individual Belongs."[39]

Students at the upper elementary level studied the U.S. states, the United Nations, and some world history and geography (evidenced by curriculum guides, for example, in Grand Rapids, Denver, and Philadelphia). However, in their social studies lessons, students at the lower elementary level generally studied everyday-life topics associated with skills for living (e.g., family, clothing, neighbors). An example is a third-grade clothing social studies unit from the Kansas City Public Schools. Despite minor attention to the economics concept of production, the focus of the unit was clothing care and personal appearance.[40]

The post–World War II baby boom led to an enormous increase in school enrollment. By the late 1940s and early 1950s, children flooded the schools. As David Angus and Jeffrey Mirel argue, at the high school level many educators assumed more students meant more low-ability students. Based on this assumption, educators revised school curricula to add less academically challenging classes.[41] A similar argument could be made about lessons at the elementary level.

This influx of students meant many more teachers were needed. One appeal of the expanding communities approach was that elementary teachers could teach social studies without extensive education or preparation. Social studies was life skills; presumably teachers were competent at these skills and could teach them. Moreover, it was far easier to teach life skills than to teach abstract concepts in history and the social sciences, especially since many teachers lacked the education to teach those concepts. Elementary teachers were expected to teach in all the core academic areas and even in non-academic areas, such as art and music. Moreover, they were responsible for the social, emotional, and physical development of children. The assumption was that elementary school teachers only needed to know a little about a great many things; they did not need college degrees in history or in any of the social sciences. In fact, in 1942, only 12 percent of elementary teachers had college degrees (compared to 57 percent of junior high school teachers and 85 percent of senior high school teachers).[42]

Not everyone thought that elementary teachers needed only minimal education in the disciplines. As early as the 1940s, some educators and scholars questioned the quality and extent of teacher education. Paul Hanna, in comparing the four years of study required for teachers compared to the seven years of study/training required for pediatricians, asked why less education for the care of the child's mind was needed than for the care of the child's body.[43] As explained in Chapter 4, Hanna admitted that the expanding communities approach simplified social studies teaching for elementary school teachers; however, he also recognized that elementary teachers who followed the approach still had difficulty teaching its concepts and skills.

This concern about teacher preparation and education continued into the 1950s. For example, Ralph Preston argued that the transient nature of the teaching profession contributed to teachers' apparent lack of interest in the suggestions from subject specialists.[44] He explained:

> A sizable portion of today's elementary-school teachers consist of young women who are comparatively new to the profession and who view teaching as a fleeting activity between college and marriage; and of older women who, with their children grown, have returned to teaching.... Because of the unstable membership in the profession of elementary-school teaching, proposals of subject specialists may receive scant attention.[45]

As social studies became life skills, typically taught at the elementary level by teachers not particularly well educated to take overall responsibility for the social, emotional, physical, as well as intellectual, development of young children, concern among educators, parents, and others grew. This concern in part accounted for the development of "the new social studies" movement with its commitment to increased academic rigor.

The New Social Studies

In 1949, Mortimer Smith's book, *And Madly Teach*, caused considerable uproar. Although Smith was a businessman, not an educator, his book resonated with critics of American education. His book was a stinging attack on John Dewey and progressive education. Smith charged that such education promoted the practical over the intellectual in schools.[46] Of the similar attacks that followed, the most well-known is Arthur Bestor's *Educational Wastelands*.[47] Bestor criticized many aspects of American education, in particular progressive education and, as he claimed, its role in the decline of liberal education.[48]

Much of the criticism in these books and in the newspaper and journal articles that followed was of social studies education. For example, Bestor, who considered instruction in the "inner structure and logic" of the individual disciplines (e.g., history, literature, and languages) the solution to the problems in American education, argued that traditional history lessons should replace social studies lessons.[49] Allan Nevins, history professor and vehement social studies critic, wrote, "The lower school should offer a thorough elementary course...divorced from social studies, cosmic history and like fetters."[50] Whatever the truth of these charges (and some charges, especially the criticism of John Dewey, were unwarranted), politicians, educators, academics, and others took notice. The consensus was that the public schools would have to demand more of students academically.

The Soviet Union's 1957 launch of the satellite, Sputnik, was another reason for the attack on progressive education in these years. Americans were shocked, and frightened, by the seeming superiority of the Soviet Union's space program and, by extension, its science education program. Soon thereafter, the U.S. Congress passed the National Defense Education Act of 1958 that allocated more than a billion dollars to public school science education. Educators, scholars, psychologists, and disciplinary experts across the country partnered in the effort to reform K–12 science education. This effort focused on inquiry and discovery-oriented learning. Although both learning approaches had long been used in progressive education, now the attention turned to the special knowledge and skills associated with each of the disciplines.[51]

A 1959 conference, sponsored by the National Academy of Sciences, known as the Woods Hole Conference for its location at Woods Hole, Cape Cod, Massachusetts, is often credited with launching the reform movement referred to as the new social studies.[52] Jerome Bruner, a Harvard University psychologist, was the chair of the Woods Hole Conference (hereafter the Conference). The thirty-five Conference members were scholars (in history, classics, mathematics, and psychology), scientists, cinematographers, and educators. The Conference's primary task was to explore how to improve K–12 science education, but the Conference members also discussed general education topics such as curricula, teaching, and learning.

Bruner's short, powerful book, *The Process of Education*, summarized the Conference members' work and their vision of learning that focused on the fundamental processes of the disciplines.[53] Writing on behalf of the Conference members, Bruner stated, "the curriculum of a subject should be determined by the most fundamental understanding that can be achieved of the underlying principles that give structure to that subject."[54] Continuing, Bruner categorically declared disciplinary experts should be involved in decisions about the what, when, and how of instruction. For example, Bruner thought instruction in Frederick Jackson Turner's frontier thesis "requires the help of the scholar who has a deep understanding of the American past."[55]

Bruner also addressed the cognitive capacities of children. He claimed that "any idea can be represented honestly and usefully in the thought forms of children of school age...these first representations can later be made more powerful and precise the more easily by virtue of this early learning."[56] This concept of learning contrasted with the learning philosophy of the expanding communities approach that maintained children learned best from exposure to the familiar. In practice, especially in Hanna's lower elementary social studies textbooks, the expanding communities approach rarely challenged students cognitively; familiar, everyday topics–simplified and practical–were its content.

Bruner's book, as well as others' writings and statements, inspired the reform movement known as the new social studies, which, like many education movements, encompassed a great many efforts (at least one hundred projects were associated with this new reform movement). However, there were two unifying goals in these efforts: to bring greater disciplinary focus to social studies and to strengthen its academic rigor.[57] As a result, the disciplinary experts rather than the educators, who were often brushed aside or even excluded, led the movement.[58] Both government and science foundations, including the National Academy of Sciences and the National Science Foundation (NSF), invested enormous amounts of time and resources in the effort to improve school curricula.[59]

Although there had been similar reform efforts in the late 1950s, the reform effort of the new social studies was more successful in gaining support, especially after 1962, when the NCSS advertised "Project Social Studies" in its journal, *Social Education*. This advertisement called for research projects, curriculum study centers, conferences, and seminars related to social studies, funded by the NSF, the Ford Foundation, and the Carnegie Foundation.[60] Two waves of research projects resulted: the first from 1962 to 1967 and the second from 1968 to 1972.[61] In 1965, in its report on the reform efforts supported by Project Social Studies, the NCSS used the term "the new social studies."[62]

The new social studies marked an important period in U.S. educational history. As Evans argues, the new social studies movement "reengaged many historians and social scientists in development work and dialogue on school curriculum and teaching strategies after years of neglect and disinterest."[63] Despite its label as the new social studies, the movement actually focused on the individual disciplines such as anthropology and history instead of the multidisciplinary field of social studies. The movement also emphasized innovative pedagogical methods of inquiry and discovery learning.

However, as is often the case with education reforms, there was more change in rhetoric and policy in the new social studies movement than in practice. Although some teachers reported success with its methods (e.g., inquiry, concepts, and simulations), the use of the new social studies curricular materials and practices was neither widespread nor lasting.[64] By the mid-1970s, interest in the new social studies had waned. Many social studies scholars were harshly critical of this reform that they charged focused too narrowly on the separate disciplines and reflected too strongly the work and interests of professional historians and social scientists. Social studies scholars also claimed that the new social studies concentrated too heavily on education for citizenship and on students' interests and prior experiences.[65]

Another criticism was that the new social studies ignored the sociopolitical context of the Civil Rights Movement, the Women's Movement, and the opposition to the U.S. involvement in the Vietnam War. This lack of responsiveness to contemporary social and political movements, as well as implementation problems in the curricula, contributed to the early demise of the new social studies at the secondary level. In addition to inspiring "the newer social studies" at the elementary level (discussed later in this chapter), the new social studies movement resulted in several elementary level programs including the Anthropology Curriculum Study Project, the Developmental Economic Education Program, and Man: A Course of Study.[66] The last program is perhaps the most notable.

Man: A Course of Study (MACOS)

After the Woods Hole Conference, Jerome Bruner was appointed Director of the Educational Services's Elementary Social Studies Program that, among other things, created the imaginative and rigorous, although short-lived, program in the late 1960s and early 1970s called Man: A Course of Study (MACOS).[67] The history of MACOS reveals how politics and education may interact when controversial programs are proposed and taught.[68] However, MACOS is also of interest as an elementary social studies program that offered an alternative to Hanna's expanding communities approach. Peter Dow's account of the origin and failure of MACOS explains how public schools ultimately rejected this alternative program.[69]

MACOS was a social studies project that originated in a 1962 conference on social studies and the humanities at the Massachusetts Institute of Technology. Bruner was the MACOS project leader of a team of two anthropologists, a business professor, a psychologist, teachers, curriculum designers, twenty full-time researchers, and sixteen part-time specialists and consultants. Bruner supported a "less is more" approach known as "post-holing" in which students study a single culture over a period of time. The approach used artifacts, simulations, games, and case studies instead of traditional curricular materials such as textbooks. Using this post-holing approach, Bruner and his team developed units on salmon, baboons, herring gulls, Bushman, and the Netsilik Eskimos that were content-rich and discipline-focused (in the disciplines of anthropology, sociology, geography, and economics, among others). In all the units, the MACOS pedagogy emphasized inquiry: students asked questions in order to reach conclusions.

In two respects, the MACOS approach was consistent with Hanna's expanding communities approach. Both approaches emphasized the importance of recognizing children's interests in the selection of topics for study. Both approaches featured the interrelationships that allow society to function. However, in general, Bruner's ideas were a significant departure from the Hanna-inspired elementary social studies programs. Bruner rejected the expanding communities approach because he thought the focus on the familiar, ironically, was too complex and too abstract. He argued, for example, that understanding the postman's job required "excursions into the meaning of power, how it is constituted, and how power and force differ."[70] Instead, he recommended topics that made comparisons: man and higher primates, modern man and prehistoric man, technological man and primitive man, and man and child. These were topics with a "sense of mystery" that Bruner thought appealed to children.[71] However, many progressive educators wanted to replace this romantic sense of mystery with everyday realism.

Elementary teachers required considerable training if they were to teach the MACOS curriculum. Anita Mischler, who was in charge of teacher education for MACOS, described her shock at finding "that [elementary school teachers] were at the bottom in terms of college ability...[elementary education] recruited the least able people who had the greatest interest in security and not taking risks, provided [them] with the poorest education...and put them into work situations that discouraged any change."[72] To meet this challenge of the underprepared teacher, the MACOS team worked closely with teachers on the research and development of the new curriculum. The team experimented with the curriculum, assessed its implementation, and revised it in a second teaching cycle.

At first MACOS enjoyed enormous success. In his documentary film on MACOS, Charles Laird estimates the program was used with some four hundred thousand students.[73] Teachers and students in urban and suburban schools gave the program "glowing reviews."[74] Educators in Atlanta, Georgia, claimed the program motivated Black students.[75] In a study of 20 national social studies programs, conducted in 270 California classrooms, MACOS was rated superior to all other programs. The American Educational Research Association and the American Educational Publishers Institute gave Bruner awards for MACOS's impressive efforts in linking theory and research to the development of educational materials.[76]

Despite its rigorous and creative curriculum, its strong support by teachers, its appeal to children, and reports of its positive effect on student learning, MACOS failed to achieve widespread adoption. Peter Dow attributes the failure of MACOS to a decline in federal funding, to implementation problems, and, most of all, to complaints by politically and socially conservative groups who objected to its focus on cultural relativism and evolution and to content they found controversial (e.g., the "sex life of Eskimos").[77] Another reason for the failure of MACOS was that Americans had become less fearful of the Soviet Union's space technology. With President John Kennedy's "We choose to go to the moon" speech in 1962, heralding the revitalization of the U.S. space program, Americans' self-confidence in their scientific superiority returned. As Dow explains, "Now that the immediate threat of Soviet space dominance had passed, the urgency to change the schools soon evaporated, and we returned to the historic patterns of local control."[78]

Although the influence of MACOS on elementary social studies education was short-lived, the program is of historic interest since its pedagogy was very different from the structure of traditional social studies programs. As mentioned, disciplinary experts rather than educators developed MACOS. Moreover, MACOS curriculum content, which focused on the unfamiliar rather than the familiar, required that teachers have disciplinary knowledge and advanced instructional skills. Finally, although many thought MACOS was innovative, rigorous, and engaging, it could not withstand the challenge from politically motivated opponents. The expanding communities approach, in its blandness, generated no such opposition.

Other Efforts by Disciplinary Scholars in Elementary Social Studies Education

In another way, MACOS was an anomaly. Although the MACOS disciplinary scholars resisted partnering with educators in the design process, some social studies reformers tried to strengthen the partnership in other respects. The reformers' idea was that such a partnership, with a more rigorous academic focus, could teach students more competitive economic skills. An obstacle to such collaboration, however, was the reformers' suspicion that this was not a partnership of equals. The disciplinary scholars seemed to have more power. A report from the mid-1960s confirmed this suspicion. In the report, a historian wrote regretfully, "For too long historical scholars have been content to scorn the 'educationists'" alleged indifference to intellectual values, while educators have reacted with understandable resentment and defensiveness to the occasional and often poorly informed efforts of historians to speak to school problems."[79] Ultimately, this collaboration was not particularly productive since the disciplinary scholars had little lasting influence on elementary social studies.

In 1963, six social science professors founded the Social Science Education Consortium (SSEC). The SSEC's use of the term "social science education" instead of "social studies" suggests the professors' commitment to the individual disciplines traditionally included in social studies education. In 1966, the SSEC published *Concepts and Structure in the New Social Science Curricula*.[80] This publication, with its chapters on history, geography, anthropology, and political science, was intended to initiate an exchange of ideas about the place and structure of the social sciences in education.

Lawrence Senesh, a professor of economic education who wrote one SSEC chapter, thought even young children could understand complex ideas from economics, political science, sociology, anthropology, and geography if these ideas were presented in ways that related to their lives. Based on this conviction, Senesh developed a social science curriculum for grades one to six titled *Our Working World*.[81] The textbooks for this curriculum, like other elementary social studies textbooks, focused on families, neighborhoods, and communities. In fact, at one point Senesh expressed interest in collaborating with Hanna on his elementary social studies texts. Hanna, although impressed with Senesh's strong background in economics, already had a textbook consultant who was an economist.[82]

However, the level of learning sophistication in Senesh's topics and questions was higher than in comparable textbooks. For example, Senesh's textbooks dealt with taxes, budgets, specialization of labor, unemployment, public services, environmentalism, and governmental structure, all within the framework of the expanding communities approach. Senesh's program was one of the most influential of such social studies programs.[83] However, his textbooks were never competitive with mainstream social studies textbooks and went out of print in the mid-1970s.[84]

Other disciplinary scholars tried to reform K–12 social studies education, although they were generally unsuccessful. For example, in 1966, a committee of the Organization of American Historians (OAH) declared the historians' efforts to improve K–12 history education a failure, especially compared to "the recent curricular revolution in the natural sciences and mathematics."[85] The committee proposed a School History Projects Board with members from the OAH, the AHA, and the NCSS. However, the Board was never formed.[86] In 1970, with support from the NSF, the American Political Science Association formed a Committee on Pre-Collegiate Education. The goal of this committee was to encourage political scientists and educators to work together to write civics instructional materials for grades K–12. Like Senesh's program, this elementary program was based in the child's everyday life. For example, the study of politics was explained as "grounded in children's natural political life within the contexts of families, school, and peer groups but clearly focused upon universal experiences and perennial problems in the political life of mankind."[87] This elementary program was not competitive with the expanding communities approach either.

These collaborative relationships between educators and disciplinary scholars were often uneasy. In an interview in which he reflected on his life's work, Paul Hanna said that the social science experts had rebuffed his efforts in the 1930s to include them in the curriculum design process. He said he felt the disciplinary scholars "ostracized" him because he was foremost an educator. He saw no change in the 1940s. However, reflecting on a committee meeting held in the 1950s with geography scholars, he noted a difference in the attitude of the disciplinary scholars. Previously, he had found that he could not interest the political scientists and economists in elementary social studies.[88] Reflecting on a committee meeting with geography scholars in the 1950s, he said the "atmosphere was a 180-degree turn from what it had been ten years before. My colleagues in geography were delighted to welcome us…. We in turn, as educationalists, recognized openly that they had the content of their discipline both in concepts and in methods of inquiry."[89]

This was not an isolated incident. Hanna also noted that in the 1950s his social science colleagues at Stanford University, who were respected members in their professional organizations, worked "constantly with us in education." He explained their motivation: "They know that if they want, at the graduate level, economists or political scientists, and so forth, who have really for twenty years been maturing, the thing to do is to work with us, the educationalists, here in the primary grades right through high school."[90] Although Hanna's working relationship with his social science colleagues gradually improved, the collaboration produced only minor substantive changes in his elementary social studies programs.

The NCSS and the New Social Studies

There were clearly challenges to the content and structure of social studies education in the post-Sputnik years. The greatest challenge came from the increased emphasis on the individual disciplines, including those that fell under the social studies umbrella. Not long after the Sputnik launch, the NCSS renewed its commitment to social studies reform by issuing new materials for the social studies curriculum. In 1958, the NCSS issued a draft report describing the "troubled" times of social studies in the 1950s and that called for a comprehensive appraisal of social studies instruction.[91] The report candidly described the problems in social studies education: the general confusion around the term "social studies," the controversy over the relationship of the disciplines to social studies, the lack of effective national recommendations, and the poor quality of local recommendations. Moreover, the report charged that too many interests groups (especially those outside the field), each with its own agenda, were meddling in social studies.[92]

In 1968, inspired by Bruner's ideas about the structure of the disciplines, the NCSS published *Structure in the Social Studies*, a compilation of mostly previously published articles by various social studies educators and scholars.[93] In one chapter, the historian, Charles Keller, roundly criticized current social studies education for its lack of disciplinary focus: "The present unhappy situation results from the fact that 'social studies' is not a subject...too many social studies teachers have emphasized the creation of good citizens rather than the content and discipline of their subjects."[94] However, other contributors were less severe in their assessment of the current state of social studies. The book's preface warned that the articles "do not present a consensus."[95] This was an understatement.

Hanna was one of several contributors who disagreed with Keller. In his chapter "Revising the Social Studies: What Is Needed?" Hanna answered the question. Unsurprisingly, he thought the expanding communities sequence in combination with the basic human activities scope was the solution.[96] He explained his position:

> Those who propose to start the separate courses in history, geography, sociology, anthropology, economics, and political science in the elementary grades seem to us to violate the psychological principal [sic] that experiences with wholistic plans and structures for the field should precede experiences with partial plans and structures of the components.[97]

Given the conflicting views of its contributors, the 1968 NCSS publication did little to clarify the structure of social studies that its title seemed to promise. The continuing incompatibility and dissension between national educators who promoted the disciplines and national educators who promoted social studies, particularly at the elementary level, was plainly evident.

The Newer Social Studies

In the late 1960s, enthusiasm for the new social studies, with its disciplinary focus, diminished as other demands were made on public education in the United States. The changing sociopolitical environment of the late 1960s helped prepare the way for "the newer social studies," a term coined by Ronald Evans for the social studies programs that addressed real world, contemporary, and often controversial issues (e.g., urbanization, environmentalism, racism, and women's rights).[98] On the one hand, some ideas in the newer social studies (e.g., issues-centered education, inquiry learning, concept development, and values and values clarification) were an extension of ideas in the new social studies. On the other hand, the newer social studies introduced some new reform ideas such as the open classroom/open education and ethnic studies/multicultural education. The NCSS was a leader in these reforms with its publication of curriculum guidelines.

The 1971 NCSS Curriculum Guidelines

Prompted, in part, by the generally held perception that social studies was a field in confusion, the NCSS appointed a task force in 1969 to write curriculum guidelines. The Social Studies Curriculum Guidelines (hereafter the Guidelines) were published in 1971.[99] The task force was forthright in its charge to social studies educators: "*The National Council urges the profession to come to grips more directly with the social problems at hand and the personal concerns troubling young people and adults in every corner of this land.*"[100] The Guidelines called for the "enhancement of human dignity through learning and commitment to rational processes as the principal means of attaining that end."[101] Among the "enduring or pervasive" issues that should be studied, the Guidelines identified "economic injustice, conflict, racism, social disorder, and environmental imbalance...."[102] The Guidelines also recommended innovative pedagogical approaches such as "mini-courses...specially planned days or weeks focused on social problems, alternative courses of study" (although these examples were for secondary education, the emphasis on innovative approaches was for all K–12 education).[103]

The Guidelines took an intermediary position between the new social studies and the newer social studies. They emphasized four "curricular components": two components reflected the new social studies components (knowledge and abilities); two components reflected the newer social studies components (values and social participation). However, none of the four components dominated the others. The Guidelines explained, "Each nourishes the other."[104] Indeed, the task force members even admitted they sought a middle path between the new social studies and the newer social studies. The task force chairman wrote the NCSS President:

> Obviously, there are quite divergent viewpoints held by Council members, all the way from those who see social studies as nothing more or less than "pure" social science, to those who argue that social studies in fact has a structure of its own. We intended the document to walk a path somewhere between the various extremes.[105]

Thus, the task force argued that the disciplines merited study, although perhaps not "in their pure form":

> Broadly based social issues do not respect the boundaries of the academic disciplines. The notion that the disciplines must always be studied in their pure form or that social studies content should be drawn only from the social sciences is insufficient for a curriculum intended to demonstrate the relationship between knowledge and rationally-based social participation.[106]

In making this compromise, the Guidelines attempted to preserve the best of the new social studies while still adding fresh, imaginative, even radical ideas. The intentions were admirable: social studies should educate children to be responsible, social citizens. Yet this middle ground approach only complicated the practical work of achieving these intentions. In addition, some urban school districts and states were not even aware of the Guidelines.[107]

However, the Guidelines had some influence on social studies education. For example, John R. Lee's popular social studies methods textbook, published in 1974, reflects the spirit of the Guidelines.[108] The book describes methods such as inquiry and problem solving, and encourages values and attitude instruction. According to Lee, "the basic justification for teaching social studies is the contribution it can make to an individual's potential for acting wisely in human affairs."[109] For Lee, wise actions were "actions based on knowledge and judged as humane."[110] A 1974 compilation of seminal articles on elementary social studies published between 1969 and 1973 also showed the influence of the Guidelines: many articles explored the social, cultural, and ethnic characteristics of students, and how schooling could better meet the needs of diverse groups of students.[111]

Other Approaches in the Newer Social Studies

The newer social studies included several new, innovative social studies teaching approaches. Some approaches may be described as fads since they were short-lived and had little lasting influence. However, other approaches have become fixtures in many elementary programs. An examination of several approaches, whether fads or not, is important for understanding what was (and is) possible in elementary social studies. Four approaches (issues, inquiry, the Taba "concepts" approach, and values), rooted in the new social studies, were refined in the 1970s. The fifth and sixth approaches (open classroom/open education and ethnic studies multicultural education) were products of the newer social studies.

Issues-Centered Education

Americans faced an increasing number of controversial issues in the turbulent years of the late 1960s and early 1970s. Anti-Vietnam War protests, racial unrest, President Lyndon Johnson's War on Poverty, and the environmental effects of pollution were some of the better-known issues on the list. Some educators concluded it was time for social studies educators to make these issues topics in the curriculum.[112] The solution was issues-centered (also known as problem-centered) education that had its roots in some of the new social studies programs. One of these was the Harvard Social Studies Project, led by Donald Oliver, James Shaver, and Fred Newmann, which used an issues-centered approach for the secondary level curriculum. In this approach, students studied the history of an issue (e.g., diplomacy, international law, and population control), evaluated the multiple (often conflicting) perspectives on the issue, and then made value-based decisions.[113]

As interest grew in addressing urgent social and political issues in school, educators developed the issues-centered approach in an effort to make social studies more relevant. According to Anna Ochoa and Gary A. Manson, leaders in issues-centered education, an issue warranted inclusion in the curriculum if it was enduring, pervasive, or threatening.[114] Once an issue was included in the curriculum, students would analyze it from a social action perspective. Not only would students learn about the issue, they would acquire practice in making decisions, communicating effectively, and working collaboratively.[115] At the elementary level, issues-centered education could be simpler and less controversial while still aimed at the same goals. As an example of an issue for elementary social studies, Ochoa and Manson used the problem of students running in the halls. Students could analyze the problem, evaluate it in terms of independence, order, and safety, and then suggest solutions.[116]

Inquiry Learning

Inquiry learning grew out of Jerome Bruner's discovery learning, a theory that dealt with skills and motivation. Bruner thought that "mastery of the fundamental ideas of a field" meant understanding its general principles and developing a discovery-oriented attitude. He described discovery learning as "the development of an attitude toward learning and inquiry, toward guessing and hunches, toward the possibility of solving problems on one's own."[117]

In the 1970s, as social studies educators refined inquiry learning, the approach turned into the investigation of a question (sometimes students suggested the questions). Students posed hypotheses, gathered and analyzed data, and then evaluated the hypotheses and drew conclusions. In inquiry learning, conclusions might take the form of a convergent model (with one "best" answer) or a divergent model (with multiple, plausible answers). A fundamental premise of inquiry learning, then, is that the process of knowledge discovery is more important than the knowledge discovered. The approach, which is compatible with many other curricular approaches, is consistent with the constructivist theory of learning that gained popularity in the late 1980s. Inquiry learning is still used in many elementary social studies programs.

The "Taba Approach"

Not all social studies educators agreed that knowledge acquisition was secondary to knowledge discovery. Hilda Taba, a student of John Dewey and a leader in intercultural education as well, was one of the most influential advocates of teaching conceptual knowledge.[118] Considered a "nationally recognized authority on curriculum development and design,"[119] Taba developed what became known as "the Taba approach," which consisted of teaching key concepts (e.g., culture), organizing ideas (e.g., the intergenerational nature of culture), and facts (e.g., bowing as a cultural greeting in many East Asian countries).[120] This approach required students to think inductively and, as in inquiry learning, to ask questions and make analyses.[121] Taba emphasized that to understand concepts, students needed practice differentiating between examples and non-examples by asking if an example fit the concept's definition. Taba thought social studies education should teach students to understand and use conceptual knowledge rather than simply to recall factual knowledge.

After Taba's death in 1967, her followers continued to promote her ideas in the Taba Social Studies Program, emphasizing deep learning of organizing ideas and conceptual knowledge, using the expanding communities approach. According to a survey of one hundred school districts in thirty-six states, Taba's Program, like Senesh's *Our Working World* and MACOS, was one of the most influential of the new social studies elementary level programs.[122] Some contemporary social studies methods textbooks, such Walter Parker's, still feature the strategies of concept formation and concept attainment.[123] Other methods textbooks emphasize the importance of grounding lessons and units in networks of connected knowledge and of using "big ideas" to structure learning.[124]

Values Education

Values education was an approach developed in the 1960s in several new social studies projects. Louis Raths, Merrill Harmin, and Sidney Simon were among its advocates. The Harvard Social Studies Project used elements of this approach.[125] Analysis, discussion, and resolution of issues naturally involve values. In taking a position on an issue, a student often has to make value-based statements and make value-based decisions. However, few educators who supported the approach favored values indoctrination. The premise of values education, and its associated values clarification, was that students should learn to form opinions and make choices after thoughtful consideration of the issues. The best way to teach values was to present students with real problems requiring decisions. The problems might be political, social, or personal. In values clarification, students would learn to identify the values and attitudes behind their decision-making processes.[126]

Open Classroom/Open Education

In his 1970 book, *Crisis in the Classroom*, Charles Silberman, the journalist and scholar, criticized U.S. education and recommended open classroom/open education as a remedy.[127] As described by Silberman, the open classroom/open education movement (sometimes identified as informal education) called for a radical restructuring of the education system. The movement drew inspiration from the informal education approaches used in British primary schools after World War II.[128] As adopted in the United States, numerous students from multiple grade levels were grouped in a large, open classroom (often interior classroom walls were removed) where several teachers introduced student-centered projects that the students completed at their own pace. The open classroom approach encouraged teachers to work on particular skill sets with small groups of students, regardless of their grade level. There were no whole-class lessons, standardized tests, or formal curricula in the open classroom.

The goals of open education were consistent with many goals of social studies education. For example, open education aimed to promote the social-emotional growth of students individually and to support positive intergroup relationships. These were long-held goals of elementary social studies. Moreover, student-centered strategies popular in open classrooms (e.g., dramatic play, discussion, research, and simulations) were tried-and-true social studies strategies.[129]

However, criticism of the open classroom/open education approach was immediate and harsh. It was claimed there was little discipline and less learning in the open classroom. Typically, the media delighted in the controversy.[130] The back-to-basics movement in education in the late 1970s was a direct response to the open classroom/open education movement.

Ethnic Studies and Multicultural Education

The most enduring curricular approaches from the newer social studies era were ethnic studies and multicultural education. The main catalyst for these approaches was the demand for equal access to quality education, a demand which originated in the Civil Rights Movement and which challenged the education system. In response to this challenge, universities created Ethnic Studies departments, racist textbooks were banned in schools, more minority scholarships were awarded, and perspectives on history and society beyond the Eurocentric perspective were recognized.

Social studies educators also felt the influence of this sociopolitical upheaval in the United States. They thought social studies education should better address the social, economic, and political problems of the late 1960s and early 1970s. Although some educators resisted any change, many others took up the cause, once again, to reform social studies—its mission and content. According to Evans, the NCSS, in its journal and conferences, began to regard the student as a social activist rather than as a social scientist.[131] Thus, two new social studies approaches appeared: ethnic studies and multicultural education.

There are similarities between the two approaches. Both ethnic studies and multicultural education are based in several disciplines taught in social studies: for example, the disciplines of history, political science, and sociology. In addition, both approaches feature the cultural contributions of minority groups and promote equality in its various forms for people of all races, ethnicities, and social classes. However, ethnic studies programs generally focus on single groups who are identified by their race or ethnicity whereas multicultural education programs focus on other identifying factors such as social class, gender, and disabilities.[132] The criticism is sometimes made that, in their implementation, many educators view ethnic studies and multicultural education as curricular add-ons rather than as reforms to social studies education. This perception seems to trivialize their place in the social studies curriculum. Moreover, there has been a sharp divide between theory and implementation with both approaches.

Following the lead of higher education, ethnic studies programs were introduced in K–12 education after passage of the 1965 Elementary and Secondary Act (ESEA). In the 1970s, the Ethnic Heritage Program at the ESEA-supported Center for Ethnic Studies wrote thirty-nine social studies units on history, geography, society, economy, literature, art, music, drama, language, and general culture.[133] One social studies unit taught kindergartners to respect human differences and diverse family backgrounds and to learn by sharing experiences.[134] Such units originated in the citizenship studies, the life-adjustment movement, and the intercultural education programs of earlier years.

The goals of the new ethnic studies programs were to celebrate human diversity and to condemn racism. In 1969, the NCSS recommended the following curriculum materials: "The Negro in American History," "The Role of Racial Minorities in the United States," and "Minorities and the Social Studies."[135] In the same year, the DPS published a bibliography of books for use in K–12 classrooms. These were books that would give students "greater knowledge and appreciation of Afro-American history and culture."[136] The DPS superintendent from 1966 to 1971, Normal Drachler, actively campaigned to remove racist textbooks from the DPS and encouraged publishers to provide more multicultural materials for social studies and history, especially Black history.[137]

One of the leading proponents of these changes was (and is) James A. Banks, often described as "the father of multicultural education." Since the late 1960s, Professor Banks has written extensively on multicultural education. In 1973, he edited the NCSS yearbook on teaching ethnic studies.[138] He also chaired the NCSS Task Force on Ethnic Studies Curriculum Guidelines, which, in partnership with the

NCSS Ethnic Heritage Advisory Council, issued revised curriculum guidelines in 1976. These guidelines were identified as the NCSS vision statement on multiethnic education.[139]

Although these guidelines prescribed no curricular content or instructional approaches, they proposed four broad, philosophical principles to inform ethnic pluralism: the respect for ethnic diversity; the recognition that ethnic diversity ensures societal cohesiveness and survival; equal opportunity for all ethnicities; and the right of individuals to identify their ethnicity.[140] This document is important in the history of multicultural education because it reflects the NCSS's commitment to educational practices that value the contributions of ethnic groups (ethnicity defined by racial, cultural/religious, or national origin) and because it addresses how society deals with ethnic pluralism, both positively and negatively.

Many scholars argue that the ethnic studies programs and the multicultural education programs have had a major role in the reform of social studies education. It is true that elementary social studies textbooks (and methods textbooks) include more cultural and ethnic contributions.[141] However, other scholars argue that such textbooks do not deal with the more complex and troubling structural issues of power, privilege, and racism. Another concern that scholars have raised is that these new programs have really only been add-ons to a field that is already too comprehensive and too unfocused.[142] For these scholars, the result is unfortunate because they think such programs can be integrated meaningfully into elementary social studies goals and content.

In conclusion, during and after World War II, there were many changes in U.S. education as various reforms were imagined, developed, and implemented. Movements in social studies arose that introduced more citizenship education, higher academic standards, and greater recognition of the country's cultural, ethnic, and racial diversity. According to John Jarolimek, "No single set of ideas has emerged to provide the same excitement and energy for the field as the 'new social studies' did in the 1960s."[143] A number of interesting alternatives to the topics-based expanding communities approach have emerged from this spirit of renewal and reform that is reflected in the new social studies and in the newer social studies. Perhaps the most powerful and lasting of these social studies reform alternatives were those that broadened the social studies curriculum to include minority cultures and races.

Yet, despite the enormous social and political changes in these years, elementary social studies changed very little. This is a remarkable outcome since the goals of social studies education were based on the very issues and concerns behind these changes. Class time for social studies did not increase, children still reported that social studies was their least favorite subject, and the expanding communities approach continued its dominance.[144] Renewal and reform in social studies education, such as they were, were more practical than philosophical. Social studies teachers had access to more technology (e.g., films, globes, and television) and more multicultural resources, but they mostly taught the same elementary social studies from years past. None of the alternative social studies approaches replaced the expanding communities approach. In 1961, Charles Keller had written, "a revolution is needed, and soon." His call was mostly unheeded.[145]

In fact, these competing alternative approaches, while often exciting and daring, only increased the confusion in social studies education.[146] As a 1989 bulletin on the history and future of social studies education stated, "To assert that social studies was in disarray in the early years of the 1970s would be a generous assessment of the situation."[147] This disarray has had lasting consequences for elementary social studies. In the Eras of Educational Excellence and Accountability that followed, fewer and fewer minutes in the school day were devoted to elementary social studies, whether taught by the expanding communities approach or by any other.

Chapter 6

Social Studies at Risk: The Eras of Educational Excellence and Accountability

A NEW EDUCATION REFORM MOVEMENT arose in the late twentieth century that aimed to raise academic standards and to hold teachers and schools more accountable for student performance. The catalyst for this movement was the worry that the United States was losing the technological and competitive edge that had long assured its economic prosperity and military superiority. A corollary worry was that education had failed the country.

One of the most important documents in U.S. education history, the 1983 report by the National Commission on Excellence in Education, *A Nation at Risk: The Imperative for Educational Reform,* described American students' academic underachievement. The response to the report was an immediate call for local, state, and federal education reforms. A flurry of mandates, recommendations, and curricular revisions resulted, including new standards and accompanying assessments. In part, the report inspired The No Child Left Behind Act of 2001 (NCLB), which is a reauthorization of the 1965 Elementary and Secondary Education Act.

Three decades after *A Nation at Risk,* its effect on U.S. education remains a contentious issue. Supporters say the report began a much-needed conversation on the alleged mediocrity of public school systems in the United States. Critics say the report produced reforms that are highly political and skewed toward particular interests. For example, many scholars claim the resulting reforms, particularly the revision of the history standards, have damaged public education.[1]

The effect of the curricular reforms on elementary social studies is also controversial. As a result of the call for greater disciplinary focus in the curriculum, national education organizations and nearly all states have written standards for social studies that specify what elementary school children should be expected to know and be able to do, as well as willing to do. These standards, which in many states are grounded in the disciplines and address participatory citizenship in addition to knowledge acquisition and skills development, are challenging for teachers and students alike. However, there is little evidence to show the effect of these standards. In general, the states do not assess social studies for students in kindergarten through fourth grade. The critics who claim that standards-setting in elementary social studies has failed also charge that the goals of elementary social studies still conflict, the lessons are still too easy, and the multidisciplinary and interdisciplinary approaches are still too confused. The minimal federal funding for social studies research and curriculum design and the reduced instruction time for social studies in the school day have only exacerbated the troubled situation.

This chapter describes the reform movement in the "Era of Excellence" (the 1980s and 1990s) and in the "Era of Accountability" (2001 to the present) as it relates to elementary social studies. The chapter describes social studies standards-setting by national organizations and states, successes and shortcomings in the research and development of social studies programs, and, paradoxically, in the eras of education reform and change, the continuity of content and approach in elementary social studies.

Social Studies Education: From the Outside

In the late 1970s, a loose coalition of educators, politicians, and other citizens became increasingly concerned about the U.S. education system. The consensus was that major education reforms were needed. This concern, much publicized in the media, led to the back-to-basics movement, a broad education reform that had as its goals a renewed emphasis on reading, writing, and mathematics in elementary school, the revival of didactic instructional methods, the elimination of social promotion, and the substitution of academic subjects for electives and "frills." In many ways, these goals were a reaction to the perception that the education trends of the late 1960s and 1970s had weakened the emphasis on learning and had failed to prepare students for college or the workforce.[2]

A Nation at Risk used provocative rhetoric intended to warn, if not frighten, the public.[3] This highly critical report concluded the United States was at risk because of "a rising tide of mediocrity that threatens our very future as a Nation and a people."[4] The report called for greater coherency in content, more disciplinary rigor, better teacher preparation, and strengthened high school graduation requirements. Although the report's focus was secondary education, it provoked a call for back-to-basics in all K–12 education. At the time of its publication, the main criticism of the report was, besides its misuse of data, its flawed thesis. The claim was that the report wrongly called for an exclusive focus in education on achievement and international competition.[5]

The report did not single out elementary social studies for censure. However, other critics did. These critics described elementary social studies as a neglected and confused area, and some back-to-basics advocates even called for its elimination.[6] Nearly every evaluation of elementary social studies, from a variety of organizations and individuals, described the subject as trite, redundant with what children already know, narrowly focused, and lacking in rigor.

Three years after *A Nation at Risk* was published, William J. Bennett, U.S. Secretary of Education, turned the spotlight on elementary education. In his 1986 report, Bennett wrote that elementary education, including social studies education, was in "pretty good shape." However, he also wrote, "major reform is needed" in elementary education.[7] In particular, social studies education was failing in its responsibility to teach citizenship content and skills. The report explained, "The present social studies curriculum is too full of ersatz social science and too concerned about 'social living.'"[8] Bennett also recommended that social studies be more strongly based in the disciplines: "I suggest that we teach the knowledge and skills needed for life in a democratic society through three interrelated disciplines, the three pillars upon which our elementary school social studies curricula should be based: history, geography, and civics."[9] The report also proposed that elementary social studies should focus on fact-based history rather than on the symbol-based commemoration typified, for example, by paper turkey projects in classrooms at Thanksgiving.[10] While educators took note of Bennett's criticism, the report itself did not seem to influence or change elementary social studies education.

While social studies supporters could dismiss such criticism by conservative politicians, it was harder to ignore similar criticism from education scholars. The education researcher, John Goodlad, was one of the most influential critics of schools and schooling in these years. His book, *A Place Called School,* is considered the authoritative description of U.S. schools in the 1980s. In the book, Goodlad declared that elementary social studies was "amorphous." He concluded, "There appears to be much less certainty on the part of the schools, particularly at the elementary level, about either the importance of the social studies subjects or what should be taught in them."[11] He also criticized social studies instruction, which was patterned after instruction in the language arts, because much of its classroom activity was "listening, reading textbooks, completing workbooks and worksheets, and taking quizzes—in contrast to a paucity of activities requiring problem solving, the achievement of group goals, students' planning and executing a project...."[12] Goodlad also claimed that elementary school teachers, who rarely assessed students' social studies learning, did not greatly value social studies education.

In a 1983 journal article, Kieran Egan, the education philosopher, harshly criticized social studies education. In the article, he blamed John Dewey for the progressive trends in social studies education.[13] His criticism consisted of three arguments: a) the premise of the expanding communities was psychologically flawed; b) the socialization aim of social studies eroded other educational aims; and c) social studies was highly confused. Therefore, Egan concluded, social studies should be allowed to "quietly die."[14] Echoing earlier twentieth-century scholars, he claimed children are more interested in people, events, and stories from the past than those from their everyday lives. A few years later, Diane Ravitch added to the criticism with her assertion that no research base exists for the expanding communities approach.[15] The culmination of this criticism is that Egan, Ravitch, and others have called for replacing the expanding communities approach with a history-oriented approach—a recommendation that social studies educators resist, often fiercely.[16]

Social Studies Education: From the Inside

Other individuals and organizations, usually those more directly involved in social studies education, were both more optimistic about its future and less pessimistic about its deficiencies. While they agreed there were serious problems in social studies (e.g., too little direction and too little instruction time), their goal was to reform social studies education but without making major changes. For instance, the National Council for the Social Studies (NCSS) responded to the criticism of social studies education with guidelines and vision statements. The vision statements were long on romance and short on reality: they reiterated the oft-stated noble goals for the field but offered little guidance on how to achieve them. It appears the NCSS recognized that local school districts make implementation decisions in education.

Project SPAN (Social Studies/Social Science Education: Priorities, Practices, and Needs) was an early response to the criticism of social studies education. In 1978, the National Science Foundation funded Project SPAN, which was conducted by the Social Science Education Consortium. The aim of Project SPAN was to produce a series of reports on the status and future of social studies education.[17] The Project SPAN reports, although forthright in stating the challenges elementary social studies faced, were optimistic about its future. Like the reports by critics outside social studies, the Project SPAN reports noted the overwhelming and intractable dominance of the topics-based expanding communities approach in which there was a sprinkling of heroes, holidays, American Indians, as well as special topics (e.g., ethnic heritage, women, and careers) that were mainly just add-ons.[18]

The Project SPAN report, *The Future of Social Studies: A Report and Summary of Project SPAN*, presented goals for the K–12 social studies curriculum (described as the "desired state for the curriculum"). To achieve this "desired state," the report recommended that social studies lessons teach citizenship using the rich content of history and the social sciences, and teach critical thinking skills using analysis of social issues. Furthermore, social studies education should recognize the needs and abilities of students and should adapt to each school's community resources.[19] These goals were laudable, sensible, and consistent with the NCSS's vision for social studies. However, the goals were too broad for use as a blueprint for change.

In 1985, the American Historical Association (AHA) and the NCSS, later joined by the Carnegie Foundation for the Advancement of Teaching and by the Organization of American Historians, established the National Commission on Social Studies in the Schools to make recommendations for improvements in the field. In 1989, the Curriculum Task Force, appointed by the Commission, published its three-part report, *Charting a Course: Social Studies for the 21st Century*.[20] Part I of the report recommended approaches for twenty-first-century social studies, Part II described the research base, and Part III presented the views of history and social science associations (e.g., the Joint Council on Economic Education, the AHA, and the American Sociological Association). Like earlier NCSS reports, *Charting a Course* set various lofty goals for social studies education. For example, referring to the elementary grades, the report stated:

> In these formative years it is imperative that the social studies curriculum avoid superficiality and be well defined and relevant to the needs and interests of young learners. Many social studies concepts are abstract; nevertheless even very young students can begin to grasp these concepts if they are presented in active and engaging ways appropriate to their interests and cognitive development.[21]

While generally supportive of the expanding communities approach, *Charting a Course* cautioned against its exclusive use and its primary focus on students' immediate environment. The report also modified the fundamental principle of the expanding communities approach. Instead of the ever-widening circle of environments that the expanding communities approach was based on, the report encouraged moving "back and forth from what is familiar to the new" so that students could compare their lives and surroundings with those of others.[22] In addition, the report claimed that rigorous and "dense" social studies education should recognize "that children should not be taught the obvious."[23] The report stated, "Today's children know there is a far larger and more various world than their own neighborhood and community."[24] However, the report's criticism of the expanding communities approach was quite mild; it called only for tweaking the approach.

In 1985, another NCSS task force, the Task Force on Early Childhood/Elementary School Studies, published its report on social studies education in the lower elementary grades. This report set goals for social studies education and described current practices and the latest research. The pre-service education section of the report listed examples of exciting, rigorous, and meaningful elementary social studies lessons. The report also addressed some persistent problems in social studies education: the limited classroom time for social studies, elementary school teachers' doubts about their preparedness for teaching social studies, the scarcity of empirical research on how to teach social studies, and students' general lack of interest in the subject.[25] The report also warned, "An effective social studies program cannot be just a haphazard collection of unrelated activities. It must be organized systematically around concepts from history and the social sciences."[26]

These two NCSS reports presented an institutional vision of the future of elementary social studies. They also reflected the increasingly popular trend of representing what students should be expected to know and be able to do, as well as willing to do, as they advance in school. This trend developed into the standards movement in education in which organizations and individuals in core academic (and many non-academic) areas have developed content standards (also referred to as content expectations) for grades K–12.

The Standards Movement and Elementary Social Studies

The standards movement in the late twentieth century was an important turning point in the history of U.S. education, but it was not the first time educators had tried to establish a set of expectations for school children. Ravitch's history of education standards-setting shows that such movements (e.g., textbook selection, high school graduation requirements, and curricular patterns) began in the nineteenth century.[27] However, the standards movement in the 1980s and 1990s was the most widespread and best coordinated of these movements.

At the national level, a number of events reflected the broad interest in the standards movement. President George H. W. Bush's America 2000 Excellence in Education Act: Proposed Legislation, although not enacted as law, called for the creation of "world-class standards" in five core subjects: English, mathematics, science, history, and geography. In 1991 and 1992, the U.S. Department of Education funded private sector efforts to write voluntary content standards in the arts, English, civics, foreign languages, geography, and history.[28] Thereafter, the National Council on Education Standards and Testing (NCEST), which Congress established in 1991, promoted the standards movement in its report, *Raising Standards for American Education.*[29] This report recommended national content standards for the subjects identified in the America 2000 proposed legislation as well as state assessments to assess both student performance and the effectiveness of teachers' instruction.[30] Despite the fact that the NCSS had lobbied Congress and the NCEST to add social studies as a separate subject, social studies was not included.[31] Educators, policy makers, and the public supported improving student performance through the creation of national standards.[32] However, there was widespread disagreement about the process: supporters of national standards faced considerable opposition from many factions.[33]

In 1994, President Bill Clinton signed Goals 2000: The Educate America Act of 1994. Like the earlier America 2000 proposed legislation, Goals 2000 emphasized national content standards. Goals 2000, which was the work of a bipartisan coalition of state governors, set eight national education goals. These were goals for, among other things, student readiness, achievement, and completion, teacher preparation, and parent involvement. However, like America 2000, Goals 2000 did not identify social studies as a separate area of study. Rather, it listed several social studies disciplines in which students should demonstrate competency:

> All students will leave grades 4, 8, and 12 having demonstrated competency over challenging subject matter including English, mathematics, science,

foreign languages, *civics and government, economics,* arts, *history,* and *geography,* and every school in America will ensure that all students learn to use their minds well, so they may be prepared for responsible citizenship, further learning, and productive employment in our Nation's modern economy.[34]

Unsurprisingly, Goals 2000 was controversial. Critics complained about the slippery slope toward national education standards. Some members of Congress, and others, repeatedly challenged the funding of Goals 2000.[35] However, efforts were underway to create voluntary national content standards. The National Center for History in the Schools, the Council for Economic Education, the National Geographic Society, and the Center for Civic Education wrote voluntary content standards for civics and government, economics, geography, and history, respectively.[36]

The Voluntary National Content Standards

The voluntary national content standards for civics and government, economics, geography, and history are similar in several ways. They emphasize the knowledge content and skills of their respective disciplines, organized by grade clusters rather than by individual grades. In addition, although none of these content standards endorses the expanding communities approach or requires its use, all seem compatible with the approach. For example, the civics and government standards draw an analogy between personal governance and public governance; the economics standards begin with the study of personal behavior and choice; the geography standards address the influence of location and culture on human life; and the history standards use "a modification of the 'expanding environments' approach to social studies."[37]

Five clusters of questions organize the civics and government standards by the grade spans of K-4, 5-8, and 9-12. These questions deal with the role of government, American democracy, the Constitution, international relationships, and citizenship. The standards state, "Understanding what government does may be initiated in early grades by having students look at the governance of the family and school as analogous to the governance of the larger community and the nation."[38]

The economics standards are organized according to principles of economics (e.g., scarcity, decision making, and trade), with standards listed for grades four, eight, and twelve. The fourth-grade benchmarks require students to demonstrate understanding of the principles of economics in relation to their own lives (e.g., "List examples of penalties or negative incentives that discourage inappropriate behavior at home").[39] A reasonable assumption is that the standards' authors thought students could best understand such principles in the context of home and family.

The geography standards are organized by geography skills (e.g., reading maps, making geographic representations, and using tools). The standards also include cultural geography (e.g., how place and experience influence human life). The standards, which are for grades four, eight, and twelve, do not reference particular places or communities.[40] More generally, they refer to historical phenomena (e.g., "Explain patterns of settlement at different periods").

The history standards are divided among U.S. history content standards (for grades 5-12), world history content standards (for grades 5–12), historical thinking standards (separate standards for grades K–4 and 5–12), and K–4 content standards. History study begins with the study of families and communities and then moves to the history of the state or region, to U.S. history, and to the history of world peoples and cultures.[41] In addition to such diversity in historical content, the standards also emphasize disciplinary skills. The historical thinking standards address the skills that historians use in their work: "Chronological Thinking, Historical Comprehension, Historical Analysis and Interpretation, Historical Research Capabilities, and Historical Issues-Analysis, and Decision-Making."[42] There are even history standards for kindergarteners who are expected to consider multiple perspectives, evaluate the consequences of decisions, and interpret data.[43]

With the exception of the history standards, there was little organized objection to the voluntary content standards. However, a great deal of controversy arose around the history standards. Even before their release, conservative politicians and radio talk show hosts attacked their alleged political correctness and neglect of traditional U.S. history. In the revisions that followed these attacks, the authors of the history standards removed certain classroom activities but retained the focus on thinking skills and historical understandings.[44]

The NCSS Standards, Vision, and Curriculum Materials

There were no social studies standards in Americas 2000 or Goals 2000, nor did the NCEST make any social studies standards recommendations. However, the NCSS has developed national curriculum standards for social studies. In the early 1990s, prompted in large part by reports of education failures and the enactment of Goals 2000, the NCSS began drafting content standards for student learning. In 1994, the NCSS published its Curriculum Standards for Social Studies, which it revised slightly in 2010.[45] The NCSS contends that these standards, which are not intended as stand-alone directives for curriculum design, can guide state content standards. The NCSS standards are noteworthy for their thematic rather than for their disciplinary structure. However, some themes reflect a specific disciplinary focus (e.g., civic ideals and practices; time, continuity, and change; production, distribution, and consumption). Other themes are multidisciplinary (e.g., science, technology, and society; and global connections). The standards are grouped by early grades, middle grades, and high school (similar to the grade cluster organization of the voluntary content standards). Although the standards do not recommend the expanding communities approach by name, the influence of the approach is evident.[46]

The NCSS standards reflect its well-defined vision for the role of social studies in education. In 1993, a NCSS Task Force issued a vision statement that described the "powerful teaching and learning in the social studies" that the nation's students require. According to this statement, which showed the influence of constructivism, social studies education should be meaningful, integrative, value-based, challenging, and active.[47] This vision statement also reflected the work of Fred Newmann and his University of Wisconsin colleagues who showed that problem-based lessons requiring inquiry and higher-order thinking skills benefit both low- and high-socioeconomic status students on standardized and authentic assessments.[48] In 2008, the NCSS revised this vision statement for social studies but made few substantive changes.[49]

The NCSS has also developed a series of teaching videos (for elementary, middle, and high schools) as part of its Powerful and Authentic Social Studies (PASS) professional development program.[50] In a standards-based environment, the PASS program provides teacher instruction that includes discussion of curriculum design and assessment. PASS also offers interactive workshops and seminars and provides sample curriculum units.

In sum, although neither the voluntary content standards nor the NCSS standards mandate curriculum and instruction compliance, in various ways they have influenced the states' content standards. Both sets of standards, even if indirectly, reinforce the influence of the expanding communities approach that organizes learning according to the near to far principle. Moreover, schools and teachers have used both the voluntary content standards and the NCSS standards to write curricula and assessments.

State Content Standards for Elementary Social Studies

In recent years, nearly all states have developed their own education content standards including social studies content standards. With some exceptions, the social studies standards are built around the expanding communities approach that still dominates in social studies education. For example, the 1996 Michigan Curriculum Framework and the updated 2007 Michigan Grade Level Content Expectations use the expanding communities approach (e.g., kindergarten: "Myself and Others;" first grade, "Families and Schools;" second grade, "The Local Community," and so on) as the sequence.[51]

However, many state content standards, including those in Michigan, depart from the scope and sequence of the traditional expanding communities approach in two important ways. First, many state content standards set expectations for students' knowledge of civics and government, economics, geography, and history, for their learning skills in public discourse and decision making, and for their citizenship participation. For example, the Michigan standards emphasize "disciplinary content and processes and skills…" and "represent the essential core content of a discipline—its key concepts and how they relate to each other."[52] Second, many state standards widen the circle of the expanding communities beyond the present and the familiar. The social studies lessons sometimes feature people, places, and events from the past and from far away. Many elementary social studies methods textbooks now recommend this enlargement of communities in the expanding communities approach.

Nevertheless, some state content standards for social studies reflect an even greater departure from the goals of the expanding communities approach. For example, in several states the standards are more history-oriented. In California, Vermont, and Virginia, content standards are labeled "history and social science" instead of "social studies."[53] The Virginia Department of Education states, "History should be the integrative core of the curriculum, in which both the humanities (such as art and literature) and the social sciences (political science, economics, and geography) come to life."[54] The *Massachusetts History and Social Science Framework* integrates the four disciplines of civics, economics, geography, and history in order to teach "a coherent historical narrative."[55] First graders in Massachusetts, for example, learn national and world folktales, legends, and stories.[56] In California, Massachusetts, New Hampshire, Vermont, and Virginia, while there are still indications of the expanding communities approach (families, schools, neighborhoods) in the lower elementary grades, the stronger emphasis on history content is clearly evident.

NCLB and Elementary Social Studies

The NCLB Act of 2001, which essentially replaced Goals 2000, is an outcomes-based education reform that mandates evaluation of student performance according to measurable results. The NCLB goals include improving student performance and increasing teacher and school accountability. Under NCLB, federal funding to schools is linked to the achievement of these goals. NCLB requires the states to develop student content and academic achievement standards in mathematics, reading/language arts, and science, and to administer assessments in these subjects beginning in the third grade. However, social studies is not named in NCLB. Nor, under the assessment provisions, is social studies tested.[57] Social studies has always had less instruction time in the elementary classroom than "the three Rs"; following NCLB, social studies' place in elementary education is squeezed even tighter.[58]

There is concern that student learning has suffered as social studies has increasingly been marginalized in the elementary classroom. In 2009, the NCSS published a separate position statement for elementary social studies that argued that the marginalization of social studies for young students may have negative, long-term effects.[59] As is often reported in the media, compared to their peers in many countries U.S. students generally underperform on national tests of civics and history. Moreover, research indicates that as social studies is marginalized, "opportunities to learn" decrease.[60] Such opportunities are defined by the number of minutes of social studies instruction in the school day rather than, for example, by the amount of time needed for transitions, behavior management, and so forth. In social studies classrooms, these opportunities arise in content-focused learning activities.[61] This situation is especially problematic for students from low-SES backgrounds who are less likely to meet expectations for performance in history and civics than other students.[62] For the reasons stated above, NCLB receives a significant share of the blame for social studies' steady de-emphasis in elementary schools.

However, some social studies educators claim one section of NCLB has had a positive, if limited, influence on social studies education. There are three goals in the NCLB section titled "Education for Democracy Act": to improve civics education, to improve economics education, and to develop students' civic competence. To advance these goals, NCLB has awarded grants to the Center for Civic Education. These grants fund the following teacher professional development programs: We the People: The Citizen and the Constitution, and Project Citizen.[63] Although these programs are highly praised, at present no research is available on their effectiveness.[64]

In addition, NCLB's Teaching American History (TAH) program has awarded grants to schools for improvement in American history instruction. Schools have received funding that has allowed their history teachers to attend summer institutes and seminars, to travel to historic sites, and to take technology courses. Between 2001 and 2010, under NCLB, over one thousand such grants of about $1 million each were awarded. (The U.S. Department of Education significantly reduced the TAH grants program in 2011, and the 2012

U.S. budget eliminated it entirely.) However, there is scant research on either the success or failure of these grants. Sam Wineburg claims, "We have no idea after spending millions on the TAH program what works."[65]

One worrisome result of the TAH grants is that they have increased the long-standing curriculum dissension between the supporters of history education and the supporters of social studies education. The goal of the TAH grants was "to promote the teaching of traditional American history in elementary schools and secondary schools as a separate academic subject (not as a component of social studies)...."[66] This is not subtle language.[67] It could not be clearer that NCLB not only separates history from social studies but also envisions history lessons that are far removed from the lessons early twentieth-century social studies advocates imagined.

Social Studies Assessment, Curriculum, and Instruction (SSACI)

As of 2012, there are no national social studies standards for content and instruction. The only approximations to national social studies standards are the voluntary national content standards for civics and government, economics, geography, and history, and the NCSS Curriculum Standards for Social Studies (none of which is as specific as most state standards).[68] Although many state social studies standards sometimes refer to the NCSS standards and to the voluntary standards, the states, in maintaining their independence from national organizations, continue to determine the content of their standardized tests and thus their curricula.

In 2009, the National Governors Association Center for Best Practices and the Council of Chief State School Officers developed Common Core State Standards that are intended to "provide appropriate benchmarks for all students, regardless of where they live."[69] Currently, forty-five states have adopted the Common Core State Standards for Mathematics and English Language Arts. However, there are no standards for science and social studies in the Common Core State Standards. Some social studies advocates worry that the states' budgetary problems and the lack of consensus about the goals of social studies education may lead to the replacement of social studies with the English Language Arts Common Core State Standards.[70]

A positive development for social studies education is the movement called the Social Studies Assessment, Curriculum, and Instruction Initiative (SSACI). The National Governors Association Center for Best Practices and the Council of Chief State School Officers support the SSACI, as they do the Common Core State Standards. However, the work of the SSACI is separate from the Common Core State Standards. The primary goals of the SSACI are to design national social studies standards, to identify instructional resources, and to create assessments. Susan Griffin, Executive Director of NCSS, and Kathy Swan, Advisor to the SSACI, co-chair the task force for the SSACI.[71] This task force, which advises the SSACI, consists of leaders from fifteen national professional organizations (including the NCSS), state-level social studies consultants, assessment experts, and administrative personnel from state departments of education in twenty-one states.[72] Twelve disciplinary experts in civics and government, economics, geography, and history are writing the standards.

The work of the SSACI is more comprehensive than that of the Common Core State Standards since the SSACI plans to prepare instructional resources and assessments in addition to standards. Its "bottom up" design process, undertaken by a voluntary coalition of states, also differs from the approach used with the Common Core State Standards.[73] In a 2012 presentation, Kathy Swan, with her co-authors and SSACI consultants, S.G. Grant and John Lee, described the many complex problems of their task. They identified the most difficult problem, unsurprisingly, as the tension between disciplinary integrity and interdisciplinarity.[74] However, the SSACI leaders are hopeful they can overcome, or at least work with, these complexities and bring greater coherence to social studies education.

The SSACI standards, called the College, Career, and Civic Life (C3): Framework for State Standards in Social Studies, are scheduled for release for public comment in late 2012. Because the standards, which are not expected to address specific content, are written for grade spans (e.g., K–2 and 3–5) rather than for the individual grades, it is doubtful they will be adopted like the Common Core State Standards have been. Swan describes the standards as follows: "The standards include descriptions of the structure and tools of the disciplines as well as the habits of mind common in the disciplines.

The standards also include an inquiry structure and tools that are common in social studies. The full document provides a framework for states to select academic content to feature in curriculum."[75] The SSACI standards are sufficiently flexible that the states may add, subtract, or otherwise modify them as needed. It is as yet unclear how directly the SSACI standards will affect social studies education. However, it is clear that the SSACI has succeeded in focusing much-needed attention on social studies at the national level.

Alternative Programs to the Expanding Communities Approach

Many social studies scholars as well as others are openly critical of the expanding communities approach. Although their specific reasons may differ, as noted throughout this book, critics generally agree that the expanding communities approach is boring, trite, and redundant. They also find fault with its assumption that children cannot understand complex social phenomena, either from their daily lives or from remote time periods and distant places.[76] For example, Kieran Egan describes the expanding communities approach as "provincial trivia" that suppresses, buries, or atrophies "children's vivid mental categories in local detail...."[77] According to Egan, young children understand and are greatly interested in stories from outside their expanding communities. More recently, in a scathing critique from the Fordham Foundation, Bruce Frazee and Samuel Ayers hold the expanding communities approach and the pedagogical theory of constructivism responsible for forcing history, civics, and geography from the elementary curriculum.[78] Even the NCSS, the longtime supporter of the expanding communities approach, has expressed its doubts. The 2009 NCSS position statement states:

> The "expanding horizons" curriculum model of self, family, community, state, and nation is insufficient for today's young learners. Elementary social studies should include civic engagement, as well as knowledge from the core content areas of civics, economics, geography, and history.[79]

However, despite its charge that the expanding communities approach is "insufficient," the NCSS has not yet proposed an alternative approach. Although other organizations and other scholars have proposed alternative social studies approaches, few schools have replaced their programs with these alternative approaches (although some schools have adopted them as complements to their programs). There has been no large-scale adoption of any of these alternative approaches.

The following section briefly describes some of these alternative approaches that have developed in the last thirty years: Cultural Universals, Storypath, Service-Learning, Core Knowledge, Mini-Society, and Social Justice Education. Except for Core Knowledge, these approaches can be taught using the expanding communities approach.

Cultural Universals

Janet Alleman and Jere Brophy, who have conducted extensive research on elementary social studies, developed curricular materials for an elementary social studies approach they call Cultural Universals. Their cultural universals are food, clothing, shelter, communication, transportation, family living, childhood, money, and government.[80] The goal of the approach is to increase children's knowledge of these cultural universals that are rather like Hanna's basic human activities. Although Alleman and Brophy do not promote the expanding communities approach, they have designed their approach to be compatible with it.

In their research on how K–3 children think about their social world, Brophy and Alleman discovered, among other things, that children display historic presentism when talking about the past and chauvinism when talking about other cultures. They also found that children have little understanding of how geography influences people's lives and opportunities.[81] Alleman and Brophy think the nine cultural universals of their approach are well-suited for instruction in narrative format since they are the "fundamentals of the human condition" that all children experience.[82] The pedagogical approach of cultural universals, which is strongly rooted in the academic disciplines, counteracts presentisim and chauvinism with its focus on the commonalities of peoples across time periods and cultures.

Storypath

Margit McGuire adapted Storyline, a program that was developed in the 1960s in Scotland, as a social studies teaching approach. The U.S.

version, called Storypath, "uses narrative and role-play to engage children cognitively, operatively and affectively as they create meaning from experiences."[83] In the Storypath approach, students read or listen to engaging stories that lead them to ask questions, conduct research, and answer questions about social science concepts. The contexts of the stories are real events or community/economic structures such as neighborhoods or local businesses. In "living the story," students take roles and confront realistic life problems. For example, in a unit on communities, students play the mayor, city council members, and planning commissioners. The aim of the approach is to involve students in problem-solving situations typical of everyday life. McGuire argues that Storypath can be used to transform social studies learning from a "bland" and redundant experience to an "adventure."[84]

Service-Learning

A common theme runs through all forms of the Service-Learning approach: learning is acquired by working with others rather than for others. The approach is distinguished from community service projects by its emphasis on substantive learning through experience and by the reflection that accompanies that experience. In contrast, community service projects are often stand-alone events that are not integrated with the social studies curriculum. However, Service-Learning approaches, as described by Marilynne Boyle-Baise, Rahima Wade, and the National Service-Learning Cooperative, set societal goals for education that are "capacity-driven, community-respectful, and civically-oriented."[85]

Boyle-Baise says she was inspired by Arthur Dunn, a prominent early twentieth-century civic educator, who advocated "living one's civics."[86] Wade's *Toward the Common Good Curriculum*, which reflects many ideas of the Service-Learning approach, emphasizes substantive study of themes in civics, economics, geography, and history (e.g., exploration, conflict, and human rights), and involves students in "Civic Action Projects" in the school or community.[87] In its publication, *Essential Elements of Service-Learning*, the National Service-Learning Cooperative explained that the Service-Learning approach should focus on authentic community issues or problems, and should involve students in interactions with community members.[88]

Core Knowledge

In his 1988 best seller, *Cultural Literacy,* E. D. Hirsch Jr. argued that children were poor readers because they lacked cultural literacy—that is, the background information necessary for understanding what they read. To remedy this alleged deficiency, Hirsch prepared a long list of cultural references (e.g., historic facts and literary allusions) "that every American should know" and that children should be taught.[89] Several years later, he developed this idea, which had attracted the attention of educators and the general public, into the Core Knowledge Series (*What Your Kindergartner Needs to Know, What Your First Grader Needs to Know,* and so forth) and the Core Knowledge Curriculum. Several public schools (including preschools) in the United States and abroad now follow this curriculum that takes a history-oriented approach.[90] Unlike the three alternative approaches described above, Hirsch's Core Knowledge Curriculum is incompatible with the expanding communities sequence because it focuses on the past—facts, times, and places unrelated to the immediate environment.

There has been both praise and criticism of the cultural literacy approach to learning. A recent three-year study of one thousand elementary students in twenty New York City schools found that students in the Core Knowledge Program outperformed their peers at comparison schools who received standard instruction in reading (the instructional approaches varied among the schools, but most were described as "balanced literacy" approaches).[91] However, others have criticized the cultural literacy approach for its canonical approach to knowledge and for its emphasis on Western culture.[92] Still other critics say the Core Knowledge Curriculum is too ambiguous, too superficial, and too impractical for implementation in schools.[93] Although Brophy and Alleman agree with Hirsch that citizens should share a common culture, they criticize his approach. They argue the approach overemphasizes history, dwells too much on arcane facts, and fragments knowledge.[94] In response to such criticism, Hirsch and his co-authors have twice revised the core body of knowledge in the cultural literacy texts and have included more non-Western content.[95] However, many educators still object to Hirsch's authoritative approach to deciding which knowledge to include.

Mini-Society

In the early 1980s, Marilyn Kourilsky, UCLA Professor of Education, developed an economics program called Mini-Society for grades 4–6. The program teaches entrepreneurship, economics, and government using an experiential approach. In Mini-Society, students participate in an extended simulation in which they create a nation, form a government, design money, establish election criteria, and organize businesses. They study the principles of economics such as scarcity, incentives, businesses, cost-benefit analysis, competition, opportunity cost, and price. Lessons in the program, which are each thirty-five to sixty minutes, are taught at least three times per week for a minimum of ten weeks. Mini-Society assumes students must experience economic situations naturally (as natural as the classroom setting permits) before they can understand them. For example, at the beginning of a sample project, the teacher creates a scarcity situation in which students see that demand exceeds supply. Following the simulations, students discuss the concepts of supply and demand. Kourilsky also developed KinderEconomy+, a similar program to Mini-Society, for grades K–2.[96]

In her empirical studies on the effectiveness of Mini-Society, Kourilsky learned that elementary students of varying abilities benefit (i.e., they increased their economics knowledge) and that the program leads to improvements in their mathematical reasoning. She also found linkages between the program and improvements in students' economic decision making and in their attitude toward school and learning.[97]

Social Justice Social Studies

Various educators have designed social studies programs that address issues of inequality, racism, privilege, and power. These programs may be loosely grouped as social justice social studies. The origin of social justice education is often attributed to Paulo Freire, a Brazilian educator and a founder of critical pedagogy. In his famous book, *Pedagogy of the Oppressed*, Freire argued that education should allow the "oppressed" to overcome their powerless state. He also argued against the "banking model" of education in which knowledge is poured into the individual; in his view, the individual should be a co-creator of knowledge.[98] Intercultural education, ethnic studies, and multicultural education, described in Chapter 5, have similarities to social justice education.

Among the many social justice approaches to social studies, two are described here. One approach appears in publications by Rethinking Schools, a nonprofit, independent organization, founded in 1986, dedicated to publishing social justice instruction materials. Rethinking Schools publishes textbooks, policy books, and a quarterly journal titled *Rethinking Schools*. These publications cover many subject areas and many education topics. There is a particularly strong focus on social studies education, especially history. The publications present history from the perspectives of people traditionally underrepresented in historical narratives (e.g., working people, women, people of color, and children). The principal goals of this social justice approach are to help students acquire sophisticated knowledge of historical events, people, and movements, cultivate the skills needed to critically analyze historical events and actions, and develop the will and means to act for social change.[99]

Rahima Wade created a social justice approach that includes a series of teaching strategies.[100] These field-tested strategies derive from her analysis of interviews she conducted with forty teachers who used the strategies. The three themes of Wade's social justice approach are individual respect and responsibility, commitment to service, and concern for humanity and the environment. Wade recommended modifications to the traditional curriculum in order to feature these themes (e.g., in a unit on exploration, a teacher explained power and oppression; and, in a lesson on supply and demand, another teacher explained child labor).[101]

There are also certain curricular add-on topics that are linked to the social justice approaches (e.g., multiculturalism, conflict resolution, environmental education, peace studies, and drug education). Without a defined place in the curriculum, and because they relate to fundamental social studies issues such as human rights, the common good, and human/environment interaction, these topics usually find a home in social studies classes.[102] Indeed, there are rich possibilities for teaching civics and government with a social justice orientation and for teaching geography with a focus on environmental conservation.

However, the successful integration of these topics into the social studies curriculum is difficult, certainly time-consuming, and often beyond the capabilities of elementary teachers whose other responsibilities and pressures increase, day by day.

In brief, there is no shortage of alternative approaches to the expanding communities approach. Sometimes they are additions to the regular curriculum, and sometimes they are partial replacements in the regular curriculum. However, all such approaches require teacher content knowledge, teacher preparation time, teacher training, and student assessments. Moreover, both for adoption and implementation, all require courage, imagination, and persistence by teachers and administrators. Today a few public schools (and some private schools) use these alternative approaches to elementary social studies education. Nevertheless, although challenged, the expanding communities approach still prevails in most schools.

Research in Elementary Social Studies

In the Eras of Excellence and Accountability in Education, a natural assumption is that researchers and educators will investigate and evaluate the results of the various curriculum approaches. However, in general, the research in social studies has focused more on children's cognitive skills.[103] For example, Keith Barton and Linda Levstik have studied how children (grades K–6) understand historical time. They found that because children in these grades can grasp historical chronology, educators should rethink the neglect of history instruction for children in kindergarten through third grade and should re-evaluate how historical chronology is taught in the upper elementary grades.[104] Bruce VanSledright has researched how fifth graders learn history through inquiry into primary source documents.[105] Alleman and Brophy's study of children's understanding of a range of social science topics led to the development of their cultural universals approach. Research of this nature, examining how children make sense of history and the social sciences, is relevant for curriculum design.[106] Additionally, this research has contributed to the development of improved resources for teaching social studies (particularly history).

Despite the value of this research, there is a gap in the research as far as the effectiveness of elementary social studies programs.[107] Some studies explore children's preconceptions about social studies topics and teachers' use of social studies programs. Other studies document the inattention to social studies in the elementary grades. However, there are no rigorous, experimental studies that evaluate which approaches lead to higher student academic achievement, higher levels of civic competency, or other desired outcomes. The explanation may be that there are no national achievement assessments in lower elementary social studies (prior to grade four) and no measures of civic efficacy for either lower or upper elementary social studies.[108] Even if social studies assessments were a priority, there are no benchmarks to evaluate social studies instruction.

For decades, this lack of systematic research in elementary social studies education has been a problem. In its 1988 position statement, the NCSS noted the scarcity of research in elementary social studies education and called for systematic inquiry into teaching methodologies (e.g., thematic versus chronological approaches to learning and children's capability for understanding complex social concepts).[109] However, more than twenty years later, there is still relatively little research on whether the instructional approaches advance student learning in social studies. National datasets such as the Early Childhood Longitudinal Study include very few variables on social studies teaching approaches. Moreover, these datasets do not include student achievement scores for social studies.[110] Large-scale, experimental designs are needed (e.g., using random assignments of instructional approaches and various socioeconomic settings with diverse student populations). Such studies require significant funding; historically, funding for social studies research has been meager. The limited classroom time set aside for social studies further exacerbates the problem of conducting in-depth research in social studies.

In conclusion, there have been significant and well-documented changes in K–12 education in the Eras of Excellence and Accountability in Education. Yet, in general, there have been few positive changes in practice in elementary social studies education. The positive changes, such as they are, appear in classrooms where teachers have the commitment, support, and time to introduce alternative approaches. Even the interesting adaptations to the expanding communities approach that some schools use have not rescued social studies education. For the most part, the expanding communities approach is unchallenged. Harsh critics of elementary social studies claim that the field has stagnated for eighty years. In 1981, John Jarolimek predicted the revival of social studies: "We may anticipate a renaissance of interest in using social studies as the integrating center of the school curriculum."[111] So far, social studies education has not confirmed his prediction.

Conclusion

Opportunities for Twenty-First-Century Elementary Social Studies

SOCIAL STUDIES HAS BEEN A SUBJECT AREA, in various forms, in elementary education for nearly a century. While the goals of social studies education have been formulated, examined, challenged, and reformulated many times, they have always had a common theme: broadly speaking, social studies should teach civic competency and social responsibility. In 1916, the National Education Association report, often credited with officially introducing social studies in U.S. schools, declared social studies should teach "an appreciation of the nature and laws of social life, a sense of the responsibility of the individual as a member of social groups, and the intelligence and the will to participate effectively in the promotion of the social well-being...and the cultivation of good citizenship."[1] More than half a century later, in 1971, the National Council for the Social Studies (NCSS) declared the goal of social studies education was the "enhancement of human dignity through learning and commitment to rational processes as the principal means of attaining that end."[2] In 1994, and again in 2010, the NCSS stated the goal of social studies was "the promotion of civic competence—the knowledge, intellectual processes, and democratic dispositions required of students to be active and engaged participants in public life."[3]

These are ambitious goals for one subject in the elementary curriculum, not least because in social studies lessons, in two or three hours a week, at best—and often in less time than that—children are expected to acquire the knowledge and skills, as well as the social and cultural values, necessary for participation in a democracy. For various reasons, according to many educators, politicians, and other critics, elementary social studies education has not achieved these goals. Because social studies goals are often vaguely formulated, it is difficult to measure their achievement. In any case, because of the goals' future-oriented perspective, their achievement is best measured only many years after children have left elementary school. Because educators have quarreled constantly (often unproductively) among themselves, there is little consensus on how social studies should achieve these goals. Because other educators and scholars (e.g., historians and geographers) withdrew from the field in the mid-twentieth century, many social studies educators and scholars have been unrestrained in de-emphasizing disciplinary knowledge. Because social studies has often dealt narrowly with social skills, substantive topics such as power, privilege, inequality, and race have been minimized. Finally, because the expanding communities approach centers around the here-and-now, social studies lessons often lack imagination and mystery. The reality of everyday life has essentially edged aside the romance of the past and far away.

The problems in elementary social studies education are particularly grave for students of low socioeconomic status (SES). They are far less likely than middle- and high-SES students to receive instruction in social studies in the lower elementary grades.[4] Low-SES students also score lower on national tests of history and civics.[5] Meira Levinson has called attention to this situation in her theory on the "civic empowerment gap"—the disparity that favors middle- and high-SES students in terms of instruction in civic knowledge content, skills, behaviors, and attitudes.[6]

For as long as social studies has been in the elementary curriculum, it has been the object of criticism. Social studies scholars and educators have described the field as "confused"[7] and "directionless."[8] Others have been even harsher. Arthur Bestor mocked social studies as "social stew."[9] Herbert Kliebard concludes that social studies is "a vapid and barren rendering of the American heritage that contains little or nothing of the intense drama, arresting political conflict, and serious social inquiry that social studies as a school subject should embody."[10] Moreover, a widely held opinion is that, in practice, social studies is unable to integrate the social science subjects in the way theorists have proposed. At the secondary level, this gap between social studies theory and practice has been well-researched, but there is little such in-depth research at the elementary level.

Twenty-first-century educators, teachers, politicians, and policy makers who believe social studies can fulfill its long-held goals have several opportunities open to them. These opportunities arise from our knowledge of the past: from what has and has not worked in elementary social studies programs. The six opportunities described next, while not an all-inconclusive list, if seized upon, may help reform and therefore preserve elementary social studies. Scholars such as Janet Alleman, Jere Brophy, and Stephen Thornton have offered sound and practical recommendations for teaching social studies.[11] The six opportunities presented here, although they build on some of their ideas, derive mainly from the historic perspective of this book.

The first opportunity: Agreeing upon and revising goals. Thornton argues that "aims talk matters," and multiple voices (e.g., teachers, disciplinary experts, and education scholars) are part of this talk.[12] As explained in several chapters, in part the conflicts about goals, scope, and sequence have slowed the development of elementary social studies and marginalized it in the classroom. For decades, as educators, politicians, the media, and the public have criticized social studies, its advocates have been forced into the mostly defensive position of deflecting these attacks. By taking an offensive approach— acknowledging the troubled history of the field and working toward its improvement—social studies education may be transformed. As the history of elementary social studies shows, this is complex and difficult work that requires a large commitment of resources, both human and financial. Such complexity and difficulty, however, should be seen as a positive challenge. The Social Studies Assessment, Curriculum, and Instruction Initiative described in Chapter 6 is an important attempt to meet this challenge.

The second opportunity: Conducting education research. As described in Chapter 6, many social studies researchers have studied children's cognitive skills. Their findings on how children learn have led to various adaptations in the curricular materials and programs used in social studies lessons. However, more research is needed that addresses the effectiveness of these materials and programs in terms of student achievement and motivation. When assessment measures in these areas are developed, researchers can conduct experimental design studies that evaluate the new curricular approaches. Social studies research lags behind the research in other subjects. In times when scientifically-based research influences policy and practice, elementary social studies would benefit greatly from more empirical research.

The third opportunity: Improving the collaboration among social studies educators and disciplinary experts. A pattern for effective collaboration is found in the early to mid-twentieth century when historians and social studies educators served jointly on curriculum design committees that had as their purpose the strengthening of disciplinary content and the modernizing of teaching methods. As explained in several chapters, at times these relationships were tense and unproductive; but occasionally, when personal and philosophic differences were set aside, good, collaborative work resulted. Social studies educators know how to make content accessible, engaging, and student-centered. Historians and social scientists know how to enrich the curriculum by grounding it in disciplinary knowledge. If the two groups can respect each other's expertise and can agree on the goals for elementary social studies, they have the potential to transform social studies education.

The fourth opportunity: Challenging the expanding communities approach. There are alternative organizing structures that teachers can use in place of the dominant expanding communities approach. It is logical and natural to introduce abstract social science concepts in the context of children's lives, as the expanding communities approach does. Yet such an approach can be limiting. When everyday topics are the scope, rich content is often diluted or simply disappears. Since both the history supporters and the social studies supporters challenge the expanding communities approach, there is an opportunity for the two groups to seek alternatives. Because of the approach's dominance in the social studies curriculum, challenges to it require teacher/administrator patience and courage as well as professional development and other support. As detailed in Chapter 6, efforts to adapt, even replace, the expanding communities approach have shown promise.

The fifth opportunity: Improving social studies textbook selection. Textbooks strongly influence curriculum and instruction since they are teachers' primary instructional sources in the classroom. When social studies textbooks are muddled, bland, and lacking in disciplinary rigor, the instruction is likely to be so as well.[13] The analysis in Chapter 4 of Hanna's enormously successful textbook series demonstrates that publishers' concerns about marketability often dilute the emphasis on content. However, some publishers are beginning to recognize and respond to changes in the textbook market. There are alternative social studies textbooks available. Chapter 6 identifies several of these textbooks that encourage students to look at the human condition from different perspectives and to engage more actively with disciplinary content. Additionally, trade books (e.g., historical fiction, biographies, and informational texts) are useful supplements to textbooks.

The sixth opportunity: Integrating the elementary social studies and the literacy curricula. There is a growing recognition in recent years of the importance of the content area of literacy (defined as the level of reading and writing necessary to read and comprehend appropriate texts in a subject area, such as social studies or science). The authors of the English Language Arts Common Core State Standards recognize the value of such integration: the complete name of the document is the *Common Core State Standards in English Language Arts & Literacy in History/Social Studies, Science, and Technical Subjects*.[14] Initial research in the integration of literacy and social studies has shown that project-based learning may raise student achievement in both areas.[15] Caution is advised, however.[16] If such integration is too rapid or too comprehensive, social studies content may be distorted or diluted.[17] Hanna's textbook experience, in which he sometimes sacrificed authorial principle to editorial pressure (recounted in Chapter 4), suggests the danger in aligning social studies textbooks with an existing reading program. Nevertheless, successful integration may lead to authentic learning in both subjects.[18]

Those who would reform and revitalize social studies have sometimes called for "a revival," "a renaissance," or "a revolution." These six opportunities, if pursued, have the potential to bring about such change that joins social studies content with child-centered learning. The history of elementary social studies shows that social studies education can accommodate both the romance of the past and the reality of the present.

Since the founding of the United States, leaders have viewed education as a fundamental pillar of a democratic society. Nothing suggests that in the twenty-first century schools will lose their responsibility for preparing students to become informed and thoughtful citizens. A safe assumption is that social studies at the elementary level will continue to have that responsibility. No other area of the elementary school curriculum is a likely candidate. Nor is the complexity of this responsibility likely to diminish in a world where countries and their citizens daily face extraordinarily challenging national and global problems, among them voluntary and involuntary immigration, political unrest, human rights abuse, and environmental damage. The continuing neglect of elementary social studies can have no positive results. The children of our country—our youngest citizens—deserve better.

Notes

Introduction. Challenges for Elementary Social Studies

1. Detroit Board of Education, *Detroit Educational Bulletin: Research Bulletin*, no. 2 (1920), 15.
2. *No Child Left Behind Act of 2001*, Public Law, 107–110, 107th Cong. (January 8, 2002).
3. Center on Education Policy, "Instructional Time in Elementary Schools: A Closer Look at Changes for Specific Subjects," Washington, DC: Center on Education Policy, 2008, http://www.cepdc.org/_data/n_0001/resources/live /InstructionalTimeFeb2008.pdf.
4. Jere Brophy and Janet Alleman, "Early Elementary Social Studies," in *Handbook of Research in Social Studies Education*, ed. Linda S. Levstik and Cynthia A. Tyson, 33–49 (New York: Routledge, 2008); Paul G. Fitchett and Tina L. Heafner, "A National Perspective on the Effects of High-Stakes Testing and Standardization on Elementary Social Studies Marginalization," *Theory and Research in Social Education* 38, no. 1 (2010): 114–30; Judith Pace, "The Complex and Unequal Impact of High Stakes Accountability on Untested Social Studies," *Theory and Research in Social Education* 39, no. 1 (2011): 32–60; Lisa Winstead, "The Impact of NCLB and Accountability on Social Studies: Teacher Experiences and Perceptions about Teaching Social Studies," *The Social Studies* 102 (2011): 221–27.
5. Bruce Frazee and Samuel Ayers, "Garbage In, Garbage Out: Expanding Environments, Constructivism, and Content Knowledge in Social Studies," in *Where Did Social Studies Go Wrong?* ed. James Leming, Lucien Ellington, and Kathleen Porter, 111–23 (Washington, DC: Thomas B. Fordham Foundation, 2003); Diane Ravitch, "Tot Sociology: Or What Happened to History in the Grade Schools," *The American Scholar* 56, no. 3 (1987): 343–54.
6. Yali Zhao and John D. Hoge, "What Elementary Students and Researchers Say about Social Studies," *The Social Studies* 96, no. 5 (2005): 216–21.
7. Jere Brophy and Janet Alleman, "A Reconceptualized Rationale for Elementary Social Studies," *Theory and Research in Social Education* 34, no. 4 (2006): 428–54.
8. E. D. Hirsch Jr., *Cultural Literacy: What Every American Needs to Know* (Boston: Houghton Mifflin, 1987); E. D. Hirsch Jr., *The Making of Americans: Democracy and Our Schools* (New Haven, CT: Yale University Press, 2009).
9. For example, see Wayne Au, *Rethinking Multicultural Education: Teaching for Racial and Cultural Justice* (Milwaukee, WI: Rethinking Schools, 2009); Bill Bige-

low, Linda Christensen, Stan Karp, Barbara Miner, and Bob Peterson, eds., *Rethinking Our Classrooms: Teaching for Equity and Social Justice* (Milwaukee, WI: Rethinking Schools, 1994); Bill Bigelow and Bob Peterson, *Rethinking Columbus: The Next 500 Years* (Milwaukee, WI: Rethinking Schools, 2003); Rahima C. Wade, *Social Studies for Social Justice: Teaching Strategies for the Elementary Classroom* (New York: Teachers College Press, 2007).

10. Keith C. Barton, "Home Geography and the Development of Elementary Social Education, 1890–1930," *Theory and Research in Social Education* 37 (2009): 484–514; Jere Brophy, "The De Facto National Curriculum in U.S. Elementary Social Studies: Critique of a Representative Example," *Journal of Curriculum Studies* 19, no. 5 (1987): 511–26; David T. Naylor and Richard A. Diem, *Elementary and Middle School Social Studies* (New York: Random House, 1987).

11. John Dewey, *The Child and the Curriculum* (Chicago: The University of Chicago Press, 1902).

12. Raymond H. Muessig, "An Analysis of Developments in Geographic Education," *Elementary School Journal* 87 (1987): 519–30; Stephen Thornton, "Legitimacy in the Social Studies Curriculum," in *Education Across a Century: The Centennial Volume*, ed. Lyn Corno, 185–204 (Chicago: National Society for the Study of Education, 2001); Stephen Thornton, *Teaching Social Studies That Matters* (New York: Teachers College Press, 2005).

13. O. L. Davis Jr., "Understanding the History of the Social Studies," in *Eightieth Yearbook of the National Society for the Study of Education: Part II. The Social Studies*, ed. H. D. Mehlinger and O. L. Davis Jr., 19–35 (Chicago: The University of Chicago Press. 1981), 20, 28, 35.

14. On the historiography of social studies, see Barton, "Home Geography"; Davis Jr., "Understanding the History of the Social Studies"; Hazel Whitman Hertzberg, *Social Studies Reform: 1880–1980* (Boulder, CO: Social Science Education Consortium, Inc., 1981); Michael Lybarger, "The Historiography of Social Studies: Retrospect, Circumspect, and Prospect," in *Handbook of Research on Social Studies Teaching and Learning*, ed. James P. Shaver, 3–15 (New York: Macmillan, 1991); Stephen J. Thornton, "Continuity and Change in Social Studies Education," in *Handbook of Research in Social Studies Education*, ed. Linda S. Levstik and Cynthia A. Tyson, 15–32 (New York, Routledge, 2008); Christine A. Woyshner, "Introduction: Histories of Social Studies Thought and Practice in Schools and Communities," *Theory and Research in Social Education* 37, no. 4 (2009): 426–31; Christine A. Woyshner, "Notes Toward a Historiography of the Social Studies: Recent Scholarship and Future Directions," in *Research Methods in Social Studies Education: Contemporary Issues and Perspectives*, ed. Keith C. Barton, 11–39 (Greenwich, CT: Information Age, 2006).

15. Woyshner, "Introduction: Histories of Social Studies Thought"; Woyshner, "Notes Toward a Historiography."

16. Ronald W. Evans, *The Hope for American School Reform: The Cold War Pursuit of Inquiry Learning in Social Studies* (New York: Palgrave Macmillan, 2010); Ronald W. Evans, *The Social Studies Wars: What Should We Teach the Children?*

(New York: Teachers College Press, 2004); Ronald W. Evans, *The Tragedy of American School Reform: How Curriculum Politics and Entrenched Dilemmas Have Diverted Us from Democracy* (New York: Palgrave Macmillan, 2011); Jared Stallones, *Paul Robert Hanna: A Life of Expanding Communities* (Stanford, CA: Hoover Institution Press, 2002).

17. Paul R. Hanna, "Romance or Reality: A Curriculum Problem," *Progressive Education* 12 (May 1935): 318–23.

Chapter 1. Before Social Studies: Nineteenth-Century History and Geography Education

1. Carl F. Kaestle, *Pillars of the Republic: Common Schools and American Society* (New York: Hill and Wang, 1983).

2. Kaestle, *Pillars of the Republic.*

3. Horace Mann, "Twelfth Annual Report," in *The Republic and the School: Horace Mann on the Education of Free Men*, ed. Lawrence Cremin, 79-112 (New York: Teachers College Press, 1957).

4. Kaestle, *Pillars of the Republic.*

5. William J. Reese, *America's Public Schools: From the Common School to "No Child Left Behind"* (Baltimore: The Johns Hopkins University Press, 2005), 12.

6. Reese, *America's Public Schools*, 29.

7. Kaestle, *Pillars of the Republic*, 124.

8. Kaestle, *Pillars of the Republic*, 100–103.

9. Gerald F. Moran and Maris A. Vinovskis, "Schools," in *A History of the Book in America, Volume 2: An Extensive Republic: Print, Culture, and Society in the New Nation, 1790–1840*, ed. Robert A. Gross and Mary Kelley, 286–303 (Chapel Hill, NC: The University of North Carolina Press, 2010).

10. Reese, *America's Public Schools*, 29.

11. Gerald F. Moran and Maris A. Vinovskis, "Schooling, Literacy, and Textbooks in the Early Republic" (paper presented at the Conference on Reading and Publishing, 1790–1840, American Antiquarian Society, Worcester, MA, January 1998), 19.

12. John Rury, *Education and Social Change: Themes in the History of American Schooling* (Mahwah, NJ: Lawrence Erlbaum Associates, 2002), 79.

13. David Angus, Jeffrey Mirel, and Maris Vinovskis, "Historical Development of Age-Stratification in Schooling," *Teachers College Record* 90, no. 2 (1988): 211–36.

14. Rury, *Education and Social Change*, 89.

15. Marie Kirchner Stone, *The Progressive Legacy: Chicago's Francis W. Parker School (1901–2001)* (New York: Peter Lang, 2001), 68–70.

16. See Arthur B. Moehlman, *Public Education in Detroit* (Bloomington, IL: Public School Publishing Company, 1925), 105; Samuel Chester Parker, *A Textbook in the History of Modern Elementary Education* (Boston: Ginn and Company, 1912), 273.

17. For an analysis of Froebel's influence on the kindergarten movement, see Kristen Dombkowski Nawrotzki, "The Anglo-American Kindergarten Movements

and Early Education in England and the USA, 1850–1965" (PhD diss., University of Michigan, 2005).

18. William Reese cited an 1882 report sponsored by the U.S. commissioner of education on "common school studies" by John M. Gregory. The report stated that the seven basic subjects were spelling, reading, writing, arithmetic, geography, English grammar, and occasionally United States history. See Reese, *America's Public Schools*, 109.

19. Lawrence C. Cremin, *American Education: The Metropolitan Experience, 1876–1980* (New York: Harper & Row, 1988); Rolla Tryon, *The Social Sciences as School Subjects* (New York: Charles Scribner's Sons, 1935). A 1920 review of textbooks claimed that no "satisfactory" history text existed until the publication in 1822 of C. A. Goodrich's *A History of the United States*. See Alfred Lawrence Hall-Quest, *The Textbook: How to Use and Judge It* (New York: The Macmillan Company, 1920), 36.

20. John T. McManis, "History of Geography as an Elementary School Study," *Educational Bi-Monthly* 5, no. 5 (June 1911): 434–46; Mindy Spearman, "Race in Elementary Geography Textbooks: Examples from South Carolina, 1890–1927," in *Histories of Social Studies and Race, 1890–2000*, ed. Christine Woyshner and Chara Haeussler Bohan, 115-34 (New York: Palgrave Macmillan, 2012).

21. McManis, "History of Geography as an Elementary School Study," 436. David Jenness makes a similar argument: "…perhaps because in the early 1800s in America there appeared to be less 'past' to understand, while space seemed vast and mysterious." See David Jenness, *Making Sense of Social Studies* (New York: Macmillan Publishing Company, 1990), 222.

22. Stephen E. Ambrose, *Undaunted Courage: Meriwether Lewis, Thomas Jefferson, and the Opening of the American West* (New York: Simon and Schuster, 1996).

23. Ambrose, *Undaunted Courage*, 437.

24. Jacob Willets, *An Easy Grammar of Geography: For the Use of Schools* (Poughkeepsie, NY: P. Potter, 1814).

25. Woodbridge wrote a number of textbooks. See William D. Walters, "William Channing Woodbridge: Geographer," *Journal of Social Studies Research* 16–17, no. 2 (1993): 42–49.

26. William C. Woodbridge, *A System of Universal Geography on the Principles of Comparison and Classification*, 7th ed. (Hartford, CT: Oliver D. Cooke, 1836), x.

27. This statement was by Arnold Henry Guyot, a Swiss-American follower of Pestalozzi. Quoted in Jenness, *Making Sense*, 222.

28. See Anne-Lise Halvorsen, "Back to the Future: The Expanding Communities Curriculum in Geography Education," *The Social Studies* 100, no. 3 (2009): 115–20.

29. Spearman, "Race in Elementary Geography Textbooks."

30. Dorothy Ross, *The Origins of American Social Science* (Cambridge, UK: Cambridge University Press, 1991), 26.

31. For an example text, see Peter Parley, *Universal History on the Basis of Geography* (London: William Tegg, 1867).

32. George H. Callcott, *History in the United States 1800–1860: Its Practice and Purpose* (Baltimore: The Johns Hopkins University Press, 1970), 58.

33. Callcott, *History in the United States*, 57–58; Natalie Zemon Davis and Ernest R. May, eds., *The McGuffey Readers: Selections from the 1879 Edition* (Boston: Bedford /St. Martin's, 1998); Reese, *America's Public Schools*, 30.

34. Henry H. Vail, *A History of the McGuffey Readers* (Cleveland, OH: The Burrows Brothers Co., 1911), 2, 16.

35. Callcott, *History in the United States*, 57. Callcott cited William H. McGuffey, *McGuffey's Newly Revised Third Reader* (Cincinnati, OH: W.B. Smith, 1848) and eleven other readers. Some readers devoted up to 60 percent of their text to history topics.

36. William J. Reese, *The Origins of the American High School* (New Haven, CT: Yale University Press, 1995), 117–18, 137–38, 150–51.

37. Ross, *The Origins of American Social Science*, 26.

38. Noah Webster, "On the Education of Youth in America," in *Essays on Education in the Early Republic*, ed. Frederick Rudolph (Cambridge, MA: Belknap Press of Harvard University Press, 1965), 65. Quoted in Joseph Moreau, *Schoolbook Nation* (Ann Arbor, MI: The University of Michigan Press, 2003), 31.

39. Noah Webster, *An American Selection of Lessons in Reading and Speaking*, 6th ed. (Newport, RI: Peter Edes, 1789).

40. Moreau, *Schoolbook Nation*, 30–31.

41. See Goodrich, *A History*.

42. Reese, *The Origins*, 118.

43. Herbert Kliebard, *The Struggle for the American Curriculum, 1893–1958*, 3rd ed. (New York: Routledge, 1995), 4. See also Paul T. Rankin, ed., *Improving Learning in the Detroit Public Schools* (Detroit: The Board of Education of the City of Detroit, 1969). In fact, contemporary reviewers also thought mid-nineteenth-century texts were too dry and too general.

44. Barbara Finkelstein, *Governing the Young: Teacher Behavior in Popular Primary Schools in Nineteenth Century United States* (New York: Falmer Press, 1989).

45. Esther R. Perry, "The Educational Value of Seat Work," *Educational Bi-Monthly* 9, no. 4 (April 1915): 294–308.

46. Elmer Pflieger, "Social Studies," in *Improving Learning in the Detroit Public Schools*, ed. Paul T. Rankin, 481–99 (Detroit: The Board of Education of the City of Detroit, 1969).

47. Charles W. French, "The Departmental System in the Elementary School," *Educational Bi-Monthly* 1, no. 3 (February 1907): 264–72.

48. Callcott, *History in the United States*, 64–65.

49. McManis also thought Parley's books were notable exceptions to the trend of dull textbooks. John T. McManis, "History in the Elementary Schools," *The Educational Bi-Monthly* 6, no. 4 (April 1912): 325–28.

50. Parley, *Universal History*, vi.

51. Parley, *Universal History*, 3.

52. Callcott, *History in the United States*, 66.

53. Quoted in McManis, "History in the Elementary Schools," 323.

54. Sherry Schwartz explains that, in general, there is a long history in elementary education of using the local and the immediate to teach children complex social

concepts. Many educators think the study of the self and the local community is better preparation for democratic citizenship than the study of foreign lands and the remote past. If children understand their place in the world, they can then understand the past. Sherry Schwartz, "Finding the Expanding Environments Curriculum in America's First Primary Schools," *The Social Studies* 93, no. 2 (March/April 2002): 57–61; Sherry Schwartz, "The Origins of History's Mission in American Schools: A Case Study of Hannah Adams," *Theory and Research in Social Education* 29, no. 2 (2001): 212–37.

55. Johann Friedrich Herbart, *Herbart's ABC of Sense-Perception, and Minor Pedagogical Works* (New York: D. Appleton and Company, 1896).

56. Edward Austin Sheldon introduced the object teaching method in the United States. See Chara Haeussler Bohan and James A. Chisholm Jr., "Mary Sheldon Barnes: An Educator's Life in Historical Context," *Social Studies Research and Practice* 6, no. 2 (2011): 85–94.

57. Charles A. McMurry's pedagogical texts include McMurry, *The Elements of General Method, Based on the Principles of Herbart* (New York: The Macmillan Company, 1903); McMurry, *Special Method for Literature and History in the Common Schools* (Bloomington, IL: Public-School Publishing Company, 1898); McMurry, *Special Method in Primary Reading and Oral Work with Stories* (New York: The Macmillan Company, 1903). McMurry's texts for students include McMurry, *McMurry's Pioneer Explorers on Land and Sea* (New York: The Macmillan Company, 1904); McMurry, *Pioneer History Stories of the Mississippi Valley* (Bloomington, IL: Public-School Publishing Company, 1895).

58. McMurry, *Special Method for Literature and History*.

59. McMurry described how words in stories could be used in the study of phonics and how story content taught children cultural traditions and other topics, such as animals and nature. See McMurry, *Special Method for Literature and History*, 7–27.

60. McMurry, *Special Method for Literature and History*.

61. Leo W. Leriche, "The Expanding Environments Sequence in Elementary Social Studies: The Origins," *Theory and Research in Social Education* 15, no. 3 (Summer 1987): 137–54.

62. McMurry, *The Elements of General Method*, 70.

63. Charles Eliot, *Educational Reform: Essays and Addresses* (New York: Century Co., 1898), 145.

64. On Hall, see Dorothy Ross, *G. Stanley Hall: The Psychologist as Prophet* (Chicago: The University of Chicago Press, 1972).

65. Kliebard, *The Struggle*, 23–24.

66. G. Stanley Hall, ed., *Methods of Teaching History* (Boston: Ginn, Heath & Co., 1883), xii.

67. See Thomas D. Fallace, *Dewey and the Dilemma of Race: An Intellectual History, 1895–1922* (New York: Teachers College Press, 2011), 20–21, 44–46, for a discussion of cultural epochs theory, in particular John Dewey's interpretation.

68. The five stages are: (1) the hunting and fishing stage; (2) the nomadic, grazing, or domestic animal stage; (3) the agricultural stage; (4) the domestic labor stage; and (5) the factory-system or national economy stage. Parker, *A Text-*

book, 422. See also Charles E. Strickland and Charles Burgess, "G. Stanley Hall: Prophet of Naturalism," in *Health, Growth, and Heredity: G. Stanley Hall on Natural Education,* ed. Charles E. Strickland and Charles Burgess, 1–26 (New York: Teachers College Press, 1965).

69. G. Stanley Hall, "The Ideal School as Based on Child Study," in Strickland and Burgess, *Health, Growth, and Heredity,* 114–36.

70. G. Stanley Hall, "Child-Study and its Relation to Education," in Strickland and Burgess, *Health, Growth, and Heredity,* 74–90.

71. Hall, "The Ideal School," 125.

72. Hall, "Child-Study."

73. United States Bureau of Education, *Report of the Commissioner of Education for the Year 1897–98* (Washington, DC: Government Printing Office, 1899), 1282–85.

74. G.E. Partridge, *Genetic Philosophy of Education: An Epitome of the Published Educational Writings of President G. Stanley Hall of Clark University* (New York: Sturgis and Walton, 1912), 99–100. Quoted in Diane Ravitch, *Left Back: A Century of Failed School Reforms* (New York: Simon and Schuster, 2000), 70.

75. Ravitch, *Left Back,* 71.

76. Scientists, university scholars, politicians, and reformers from charitable organizations founded the American Social Science Association in 1865. The purpose of this new association was to promote social reforms and to advance scientific inquiry. See Ross, *The Origins,* 63.

77. Arthur S. Link, "The American Historical Association, 1884–1984: Retrospect and Prospect," *The American Historical Review* 90, no. 1 (February 1985): 1–17.

78. J. Franklin Jameson, "The American Historical Association, 1884–1909," *The American Historical Review* 15, no. 1 (October 1909): 13.

79. Joseph Watras, "Historians and Social Studies Educators, 1893–1998," in *Social Education in the Twentieth Century,* ed. Joseph Watras, Margaret Smith Crocco, and Christine Woyshner, 192–209 (New York: Peter Lang, 2004).

80. Novick has examined Americans' understanding of trends in European thought. See Peter Novick, *That Noble Dream: The "Objectivity Question" and the American Historical Association* (Cambridge, UK: Cambridge University Press, 1998), 21–46.

81. David L. Angus and Jeffrey E. Mirel, *The Failed Promise of the American High School: 1890–1995* (New York: Teachers College Press, 1999); Chara Haeussler Bohan, "Early Vanguards of Progressive Education: The Committee of Ten, the Committee of Seven, and Social Education," *Journal of Curriculum and Supervision* 19, no. 1 (2003): 73–94; Kliebard, *The Struggle.*

82. For more on Charles Eliot's role in the Committee of Ten, see Arthur G. Powell, *The Uncertain Profession: Harvard and the Search for Educational Authority* (Cambridge, MA: Harvard University Press, 1980), 24–27.

83. National Education Association, *The Report of the Committee of Ten on Secondary School Studies* (New York: The American Book Company, 1894).

84. The other seven conferences were: Latin; Greek; English; Other Modern Languages; Mathematics; Physics, Astronomy, and Chemistry; and Natural History

(Biology, including Botany, Zoology, and Physiology). National Education Association, *The Report of the Committee of Ten.*

85.   Kliebard states that while the Committee's recommendations were clearly in the vein of "liberal education for all," their recommendations were a "moderate" departure from the traditional nineteenth-century curriculum. He points to the Committee's attempt to demonstrate the same level of interest in modern studies that they had in classical studies. See Kliebard, *The Struggle*, 14. On the Committee of Ten, also see Lybarger, "The Historiography of Social Studies"; David W. Saxe, *Social Studies in Schools: A History of the Early Years* (Albany, NY: State University of New York Press, 1991), 39–41; Michael Whelan, "Albert Bushnell Hart and the Origins of Social Studies Education," *Theory and Research in Social Education* 22, no. 4 (1994): 423–40.

86.   National Education Association, *The Report of the Committee of Ten*, 198.

87.   National Education Association, *The Report of the Committee of Ten*, 163.

88.   National Education Association, *The Report of the Committee of Ten*, 190.

89.   National Education Association, *The Report of the Committee of Ten*, 181.

90.   National Education Association, *The Report of the Committee of Ten*, 209.

91.   National Education Association, *The Report of the Committee of Ten*, 211, 215.

92.   National Education Association, *The Report of the Committee of Ten*, 222.

93.   National Education Association, *The Report of the Committee of Ten*, 211, 221. There was less agreement among members of the Geography Ten than among members of the History Ten. See Edwin J. Houston's letter in National Education Association, *The Report of the Committee of Ten*, 237–49. One of Houston's many complaints was that not enough attention was paid to physical geography in the elementary grades.

94.   Tryon, *The Social Sciences*, 13–14.

95.   National Education Association of the United States, *Correlation of Studies, Report of Sub-Committee of the Committee of Fifteen* (Bloomington, IL: Public-School Publishing Company, 1895), 28.

96.   National Education Association of the United States, *Correlation of Studies*, 31.

97.   National Education Association of the United States, *Correlation of Studies*, 53.

98.   National Education Association of the United States, *Correlation of Studies*, 33.

99.   The Committee of Seven, *The Study of History in Schools: Report to the American Historical Association by the Committee of Seven* (New York: Macmillan, 1899), v.

100.   The Committee of Seven, *The Study of History*, 446. See Chara Haeussler Bohan, *Go to the Sources: Lucy Maynard Salmon and the Teaching of History* (New York: Peter Lang, 2004).

101.   Jameson, "The American Historical Association."

102.   See Bohan, *Go to the Sources*, for an in-depth discussion of Salmon's life and her contributions to history education.

103.   The Committee of Seven, *The Study of History*, 511.

104.   Bohan, *Go to the Sources*, 63.

105.   The Committee of Seven, *The Study of History*, 513–15.

106.   The Committee of Seven, *The Study of History*, 511.

107. Salmon also addressed the correlation of history with other subjects. In an earlier report, she praised Germany's program, which resulted in a "compact articulated, organic system in striking contrast to our own." Salmon claimed that history's isolation in the school curriculum made it less meaningful for students. She argued that history should be taught in conjunction with geography and literature. See The Committee of Seven, *The Study of History*, 78.

108. The Committee of Seven, *The Study of History*, 516.

109. This report was not the only report to emphasize the study of other histories. A 1899 report by the New England History Teachers' Association recommended that, in addition to American history, children study Greek, Roman, and Norse myths and Hebrew, Greek, Roman, European, and English stories/biographies. See Parker, *A Textbook*, 413.

110. The Committee of Seven, *The Study of History*, 514.

111. Bohan, *Go to the Sources*, 75.

112. The Committee of Seven, *The Study of History*.

113. The Committee of Seven, *The Study of History*, 473.

114. The Committee of Seven, *The Study of History*, 473.

115. Woyshner, "Introduction: Histories of Social Studies Thought."

116. Detroit Board of Education, *Fifty-First Annual Report of the Board of Education of the City of Detroit* (Detroit: Detroit Board of Education, 1894), 185.

117. Detroit Board of Education, *Education in Detroit* (Detroit: Detroit Board of Education, 1916), 14.

118. Jeffrey Mirel, *The Rise and Fall of an Urban School System: Detroit, 1907-1981* (Ann Arbor, MI: The University of Michigan Press, 1993), 3.

119. W. L. Smith, *Historical Sketches of Education in Michigan* (Lansing, MI: W.S. George and Company, 1881), 37, 8. *Morse's Geography* was listed as the textbook used.

120. Detroit Board of Education, *Fifty-First Annual Report*; Detroit Board of Education, *Fifty-Second Annual Report of the Board of Education of the City of Detroit* (Detroit: Detroit Board of Education, 1895). The 1894 Report mentions stories from history, myths, and fables as material for use in oral language study.

121. Detroit Board of Education, *Fifty-Second Annual Report*, 39.

122. Detroit Board of Education, *Fifty-Second Annual Report*, 39.

123. Detroit Board of Education, *Fifty-Second Annual Report*, 36.

124. Detroit Board of Education, *Fifty-Second Annual Report*, 36.

125. Detroit Board of Education, *Fifty-First Annual Report*, 149; Detroit Board of Education, *Fifty-Second Annual Report*, 130.

126. Detroit Board of Education, *Fifty-Second Annual Report*, 37.

127. Students read these texts in their language lessons: Scribner's *Geographical Reader-Europe*, *Our World Reader*, and *No. 1-Europe*; Eggleston's *First Book in American History*; Hawthorne's *Tanglewood Tales for Boys and Girls*; and a biography of Nathaniel Hawthorne.

128. Detroit Board of Education, *Fifty-Second Annual Report*, 165-78.

129. The texts included readers on Africa, Australia, and Asia as well as Tompkin's *Life of Franklin*, Foster's *Life of Abraham Lincoln*, and Longfellow's *The Courtship of Miles Standish*.

130. Detroit Board of Education, *Fifty-First Annual Report*, 175.

131. The seventh-grade reading curriculum included Eggleston's *A History of the United States and its People*, Holmes's *Grandmother's Story of Bunker Hill and other Poems*, and Dickens's *A Christmas Carol*.

132. Students studied Barnes's *Brief History and Government Manual*. They also read Dole's *The American Citizen* and wrote essays on history and government.

133. Detroit Board of Education, *Fifty-Second Annual Report*, 38.

134. Frederick Wheeler, *Proceedings of the Board of Education 1899–1900* (Grand Rapids, MI: Grand Rapids Board of Education, 1900), 60.

135. Grand Rapids Board of Education, *Annual Report of the Board of Trustees for the School Year 1865–66* (Grand Rapids, MI: Grand Rapids Board of Education, 1866), 16.

136. Grand Rapids Board of Education, *Annual Report of the Board of Trustees for the School Year 1889–90* (Grand Rapids, MI: Grand Rapids Board of Education, 1890), 99.

137. See *Harper's School Geography* (New York: American Book Company, 1885). This oversized book featured a large amount of factual information such as geographic definitions, description of locations within and outside the United States, and colored maps (as well as relief maps). It also listed a series of recall questions after each section and included directions for making maps. The methods texts for teaching geography included Francis W. Parker, *How to Study Geography* (New York: D. Appleton and Company, 1894) and Charles Francis King, *Methods and Aids in Geography* (Boston: Lee and Shepard, 1889).

138. Although history was not listed as a formal course of study until eighth grade, the reference library at the Central Grammar School had a number of history textbooks on its shelves.

139. Grand Rapids Board of Education, *Annual Report of the Board of Trustees for the School Year 1884–85*, (Grand Rapids, MI: Grand Rapids Board of Education, 1885), 11.

140. Grand Rapids Board of Education, *Annual Report of the Board of Trustees for the School Year 1884–85*, 10.

141. Grand Rapids Board of Education, *Annual Report of the Board of Trustees for the School Year 1892–93* (Grand Rapids, MI: Grand Rapids Board of Education, 1893).

142. Chalmers quoted the educator, B. O. Flower. See Grand Rapids Board of Education, *Annual Report of the Board of Trustees for the School Year 1892–93*, 11.

143. Grand Rapids Board of Education, *Annual Report of the Board of Trustees for the School Year 1893–94* (Grand Rapids, MI: Grand Rapids Board of Education, 1894), 103–44.

144. Grand Rapids Board of Education, *Annual Report of the Board of Trustees for the School Year 1893–94*, 80–81.

145. Grand Rapids Board of Education, *Annual Report of the Board of Trustees for the School Year 1893–94*, 77.

Chapter 2. Social Studies Is Born:
The Early Twentieth Century

1.   More than thirteen million immigrants came to America between 1901 and 1913. Eugene E. Leach, "1900–1914," in *A Companion to Twentieth Century America*, ed. Stephen J. Whitfield, 3–18 (Malden, MA: Blackwell Publishing Company, 2004).

2.   Robert H. Wiebe, *The Search for Order: 1877–1920* (New York: Hill and Wang, 1967).

3.   Leach, "1900–1914," 5.

4.   David B. Tyack, *The One Best System: A History of American Urban Education* (Cambridge, MA: Harvard University Press, 1974), 133–34.

5.   See Ellen Condliffe Lagemann, *An Elusive Science: The Troubling History of Educational Research* (Chicago: The University of Chicago Press, 2000), 96; Edgar B. Wesley, *NEA: The First Hundred Years* (New York: Harper & Brothers Publishers, 1957).

6.   Wiebe, *The Search for Order*, 120.

7.   Wiebe, *The Search for Order*, 119.

8.   Thomas D. Snyder, ed., *120 Years of American Education: A Statistical Portrait* (Washington, DC: U.S. Department of Education, Office of Educational Research and Improvement, National Center for Education Statistics, 1993).

9.   Bureau of Statistics and Reference, Detroit Public Schools, *Growth of the Detroit Public Schools* (Detroit: Bureau of Statistics and Reference, Detroit Public Schools, 1923).

10. Tyack, *The One Best System*, 230.

11. Kevin Boyle, *Arc of Justice: A Saga of Race, Civil Rights, and Murder in the Jazz Age* (New York: Henry Holt and Company, 2004), 71.

12. Boyle, *Arc of Justice*, 106.

13. Jeffrey E. Mirel, *Patriotic Pluralism: Americanization Education and European Immigrants* (Cambridge, MA: Harvard University Press, 2010).

14. Lagemann, *An Elusive Science*, 58–59, 70.

15. Edward L. Thorndike and Arthur I. Gates, *Elementary Principles of Education* (New York: The Macmillan Company, 1929).

16. Thorndike and Gates, *Elementary Principles*, 178.

17. Charles H. Judd, *Psychology of High-School Subjects* (Boston: Ginn & Company, 1915), 441.

18. In many ways, Judd's ideas on disciplinary learning were prophetic of those of University of Chicago Professor of Science, Joseph J. Schwab. See Joseph J. Schwab, *Science, Curriculum, and Liberal Education: Selected Essays*, ed. Ian Westbury and Neil J. Wilkof (Chicago: The University of Chicago Press, 1978).

19. Judd, *Psychology of High-School Subjects*, 376.

20. Judd, *Psychology of High-School Subjects*, 388.

21. Judd, *Psychology of High-School Subjects*, 378.

22. Sam Wineburg, *Historical Thinking and Other Unnatural Acts* (Philadelphia: Temple University Press, 2001), 30.

23. Judd, *Psychology of High-School Subjects*, 381.

24. Charles H. Judd, "Needed Revisions in Social-Science Instruction," in National Council for the Social Studies, *The Social Studies Curriculum*, 9–21 (Philadelphia: McKinley Publishing Company, 1934).

25. Lawrence Cremin, *The Transformation of the School* (New York: Alfred A. Knopf, 1961); Jeffrey Mirel, "Old Educational Ideas, New American Schools: Progressivism and the Rhetoric of Educational Revolution," *Paedagogica Historica* 39, no. 4 (August 2003): 477–97. Also see Arthur Zilversmit, *Changing Schools: Progressive Education Theory and Practice, 1930–1960* (Chicago: The University of Chicago Press, 1993).

26. Kliebard, *The Struggle*.

27. Cremin, *American Education*, 229. See also Susan F. Semel, "Introduction," in *"Schools of Tomorrow," Schools of Today: What Happened to Progressive Education*, ed. Susan F. Semel and Alan R. Sadovnik, 1–20 (New York: Peter Lang, 1999).

28. Larry Cuban, *How Teachers Taught: Constancy and Change in American Classrooms, 1890 to 1990* (New York: Longman, 1984), 61.

29. Bruce Ryburn Payne, *Public Elementary School Curricula: A Comparative Study of Representative Cities of the United States, England, Germany and France* (New York: Silver Burdett, 1905).

30. Charles W. French, "The Departmental System in the Elementary School," *Educational Bi-Monthly* 1, no. 3 (February 1907): 266.

31. French, "The Departmental System." Another strategy, although not generally adopted, was for elementary schools to follow the high school "departmental system" in which teachers specialized in and taught only one subject area.

32. David Tyack and Larry Cuban, *Tinkering Toward Utopia: A Century of Public School Reform* (Cambridge, MA: Harvard University Press, 1995).

33. Tyack and Cuban, *Tinkering Toward Utopia*, 182.

34. David F. Labaree, "Progressivism, Schools and Schools of Education: An American Romance," *Paedagogica Historica* 4, nos. 1–2 (2005): 275–88.

35. Kliebard, *The Struggle*.

36. Evans, *The Social Studies Wars*.

37. See Novick, *That Noble Dream*, 89–108. In footnote 12 (p. 92), Novick differentiates between the New Historians and the Progressive Historians. These labels, which are sometimes used interchangeably, differ slightly. Novick explains that the New Historians were the historians who used new methodologies; the Progressive Historians were the historians who interpreted American history in new ways. In this book, I use New Historians because that is how Robinson identified himself and other historians at Columbia University.

38. Ernst A. Breisach, *American Progressive History: An Experiment in Modernization* (Chicago: The University of Chicago Press, 1993), 2.

39. Novick, *That Noble Dream*, 92.
40. James Harvey Robinson, *The New History* (New York: The Free Press, 1912). Some scholars at the time claimed Robinson's theories were only revisions of Frederick Jackson Turner's frontier study ideas. Therefore, there was nothing "new" in them. See Clarence Alvord, "Review of The New History," *The Nation* 94 (1912): 457.
41. On the "New Historians," see Novick, *That Noble Dream*; Hertzberg, *Social Studies Reform*.
42. Robinson, *The New History*, 24.
43. Novick, *That Noble Dream*, 89.
44. American Historical Association, *Annual Report of the American Historical Association*, 1900, 37–47.
45. William H. Mace, "The Value of Observation in History," *Educational Bi-Monthly* 3, no. 2 (December 1908): 124–27. Mace also wrote history methods textbooks and elementary textbooks. See, for example, William H. Mace, *Method in History, for Teachers and Students* (Boston: Ginn & Company, 1902; William H. Mace, *Stories of Great American Leaders* (Chicago: Rand McNally & Company, 1941).
46. Mace, "The Value of Observation," 126.
47. Novick, *That Noble Dream*, 86–100.
48. Semel, "Introduction," in Semel and Sadovnik, *"Schools of Tomorrow."*
49. Marie Kirchner Stone, "The Francis W. Parker School: Chicago's Progressive Education Legacy," in Semel and Sadovnik, *"Schools of Tomorrow,"* 23–66; Stone, *The Progressive Legacy.*
50. Dewey described the relationship between democracy and education in his famous book, *Democracy and Education* (New York: The Free Press, 1916).
51. Stone, *The Progressive Legacy*, 27.
52. Stone, *The Progressive Legacy*, 24.
53. Jack K. Campbell, *Colonel Francis W. Parker: The Children's Crusader* (New York: Teachers College Press, 1967), 82.
54. Stone, "The Francis W. Parker School," 28–29; Stone, *The Progressive Legacy*, 64–72.
55. Dewey, *The Child and the Curriculum.*
56. John Dewey, *The School and Society* (Chicago: The University of Chicago Press, 1900), 150.
57. Dewey, *The School and Society.*
58. John A. Beineke, *And There Were Giants in the Land: The Life of William Heard Kilpatrick* (New York: Peter Lang, 1998). Some elementary schools used approaches such as the project method before Kilpatrick popularized it. See Ravitch, *Left Back*, 180.
59. William H. Kilpatrick, "The Project Method: The Use of the Purposeful Act in the Educative Process," *Teachers College Record* 19 (September 1918): 319–35.
60. William H. Kilpatrick, *Foundations of Method: Informal Talks on Teaching* (New York: Macmillan, 1925).

61. Hunter C. Goodrich and Ethel Black, "A Project in Civics," *Detroit Journal of Education* 1, no. 4 (June, 1921): 24–30; Ada E. Newman, "A History Project Worked Out in the North Woodward School," *Detroit Journal of Education* 1, no. 4 (June 1921): 47–49; E. D. Oglivie, "Report of a Project in Geography," *Detroit Journal of Education* 2, no. 2 (November 1921): 73–76.

62. Harold Rugg and Ann Shumaker, *The Child-Centered School: An Appraisal of the New Education* (Yonkers-on-Hudson, NY: World Book, 1928). See Chapter 8 for a discussion on the lack of curricular structure in progressive schools.

63. Rugg wrote a series of junior high school social science textbooks that were adopted across the country. The books were enormously successful until various business leaders accused him of promoting communism and of encouraging membership in communist youth organizations. See Ronald W. Evans, *This Happened in America: Harold Rugg and the Censure of Social Studies* (Charlotte, NC: Information Age Publishing, 2007).

64. Rugg and Shumaker, *The Child-Centered School*, 100–101. The authors describe how the study of boats draws on various subjects such as the industrial arts, history, geography, and the fine arts, among others.

65. James S. Tippett et al., *Curriculum Making in an Elementary School* (Boston: Ginn & Company, 1927), 31. Quoted in Rugg and Shumaker, *The Child-Centered School*, 104.

66. See Evans, *This Happened in America*, for a full discussion of Rugg's educational contributions.

67. Joyce Antler, *Lucy Sprague Mitchell: The Making of a Modern Woman* (New Haven, CT: Yale University Press, 1987), 250.

68. Lucy Sprague Mitchell, *Here and Now Story Book, Two- to Seven-Year Olds* (New York: E. P. Dutton & Company, 1921), 4.

69. Antler, *Lucy Sprague Mitchell*, 248.

70. Margaret Wise Brown, *Good Night, Moon* (New York: Harper, 1947).

71. Sherry L. Field, "Lucy Sprague Mitchell (1878–1967)," in *"Bending the Future to Their Will": Civic Women, Social Education, and Democracy*, ed. Margaret Crocco and O. L. Davis Jr., 125–47 (Lanham, MD: Rowman & Littlefield, 1999).

72. For example, see Lucy Sprague Mitchell, *Manhattan: Now and Long Ago* (New York: The Macmillan Company, 1934); Lucy Sprague Mitchell, *North America: The Land They Live in for the Children Who Live There* (New York: The Macmillan Company, 1931); Lucy Sprague Mitchell, *The People of the U.S.A.: Their Place in the School Curriculum* (New York: Service Center Committee, Progressive Education Association, 1942); Lucy Sprague Mitchell, *Young Geographers: How They Explore the World and How They Map the World* (New York: Basic Books, 1963).

73. Antler, *Lucy Sprague Mitchell*, 239; Susan F. Semel, "The City and Country School: A Progressive Paradigm," in Semel and Sadovnik, *"Schools of Tomorrow,"* 121–40.

74. Semel, "The City and Country School," 130.

75. Semel, "The City and Country School," 130.

76. American Historical Association, *The Study of History in the Elementary Schools: Report to the American Historical Association by the Committee of Eight* (New York: Charles Scribner's Sons, 1912). The Committee of Eight met from 1905 to 1909. Like the Committee of Seven, it began its work by seeking to learn more about the current conditions of history education in the schools. Members sent questionnaires to superintendents, and three committee members spent some months in England, France, and Germany observing elementary school teachers and schools. Also see Chara Haeussler Bohan, "Digging Trenches: Nationalism and the First National Report on the Elementary History Curriculum," *Theory and Research in Social Education* 33, no. 2 (2005): 266–91.

77. See the AHA Annual Reports from 1904–1906 and the Committee of Eight folder, box 260, the American Historical Association Records, 1884–1985, Library of Congress, Washington, DC (hereafter cited as AHA Records) for discussions relevant to the work of the Committee.

78. American Historical Association, *The Study of History*, v, ix.

79. American Historical Association, *The Study of History*, x.

80. The Report stated, "Our history teaching in the past has failed largely because it has not been picturesque; it has been an error to strive for a hurried survey of the whole field; we have repeated and enlarged the picture in successive years, but the charm of surprise and novelty has been lost and pupils have failed to appreciate the value of further elaboration when the initial interests has been forestalled." The Committee of Eight sought a remedy for this problem. American Historical Association, *The Study of History*, xiv.

81. American Historical Association, *The Study of History*, x.

82. Bohan, "Digging Trenches," 277, 287.

83. Bohan, "Digging Trenches," 277, 280.

84. Mirel, *Patriotic Pluralism*.

85. American Historical Association, *The Study of History*, 98.

86. American Historical Association, *The Study of History*, xii.

87. J. Montgomery Gambrill, "History in the Elementary Schools: Shall the Course of Study Recommended by the Committee of Eight Be Adopted in the Elementary Schools?" *The History Teacher's Magazine* 3 (February 1912): 30–32.

88. Armand J. Gerson, "The Social Studies in the Grades—1909–1929," *Historical Outlook* 20 (1929), 269.

89. Tryon, *The Social Sciences*, 28, 31, 27.

90. Bohan, "Digging Trenches."

91. Bohan, "Digging Trenches," 284.

92. Bohan, "Digging Trenches."

93. It is important to note that while we have these official school reports on recommended instruction, we have no information on the extent to which teachers followed them.

94. Detroit Board of Education, *Annual Report of the Superintendent 1904–1905* (Detroit: Detroit Board of Education, 1905), 142.

95. Grand Rapids Board of Education, *Annual Report of the Superintendent, 1901–1902* (Grand Rapids, MI: Grand Rapids Board of Education, 1902); Grand Rapids Board of Education, *Annual Report of the Superintendent, 1903–1904* (Grand Rapids, MI: Grand Rapids Board of Education, 1904).

96. Detroit Board of Education, *Annual Report of the Superintendent 1910–1911* (Detroit: Detroit Board of Education, 1911), 21.

97. Detroit Board of Education, *Annual Report of the Superintendent 1903–1904* (Detroit: Detroit Board of Education, 1904), 133–34.

98. Detroit Board of Education, *Annual Report of the Superintendent 1900–1901* (Detroit: Detroit Board of Education, 1901), 123–24.

99. Detroit Board of Education, *Annual Report of the Superintendent 1904–1905*, 71.

100. Detroit Board of Education, *Annual Report of the Superintendent 1903–1904*, 133.

101. Barton, "Home Geography."

102. For example, see Richard E. Dodge, *Dodge's Primary Geography* (New York: Rand McNally, 1910).

103. Dodge, *Dodge's Primary Geography*, 14.

104. Barton, "Home Geography," 499–500.

105. Richard E. Dodge and Clara B. Kirchway, *The Teaching of Geography in Elementary Schools* (New York: Rand McNally, 1913).

106. Charles A. McMurry, *Special Method in Geography from the Third through the Eighth Grade*, new ed. (New York: Macmillan, 1904), 5.

107. Detroit Board of Education, *Annual Report of the Superintendent 1904–1905*, 142.

108. Detroit Board of Education, *Annual Report of the Superintendent 1903–1904*, 134.

109. Detroit Board of Education, *Annual Report of the Superintendent 1912–1913* (Detroit: Detroit Board of Education, 1913), 76.

110. Richard E. Dodge, "The Political and Locational Factors in General Geography," *Educational Bi-Monthly*, 1 (December 1906): 139–41.

111. See Evans, *The Social Studies Wars*; C. Gregg Jorgensen, "Unraveling Conflicting Interpretations: A Reexamination of the 1916 Report on Social Studies (PhD diss., Utah State University, 2010); Saxe, *Social Studies in Schools*.

112. Angus and Mirel, *The Failed Promise*; Kliebard, *The Struggle*; Ravitch, *Left Back*.

113. Watras, "Historians and Social Studies Educators," 197.

114. National Education Association, *Cardinal Principles of Secondary Education: A Report of the Commission on the Reorganization of Secondary Education* (Washington, DC: U.S. Government Printing Office, 1918).

115. Saxe, *Social Studies in Schools*, 110.

116. Thomas Jesse Jones, *Social Studies in Secondary Schools: Preliminary Recommendations by the Committee of the National Education Association*, Bulletin No. 41 (Washington, DC: U.S. Government Printing Office, United States Bureau of Education, 1913); National Education Association, *The Teaching of Community Civics* (Washington, DC: United States Office of Education, 1915); United States Bureau of Education, *The Social Studies in Secondary Education* (Washington, DC: U.S. Government Printing Office, 1916).

117. United States Bureau of Education, *The Social Studies in Secondary Education.* See Watras, "Historians and Social Studies Educators."

118. Ravtich, *Left Back*, 127–29; Diane Ravitch, "A Brief History of Social Studies," in Leming, Ellington, and Porter, eds., *Where Did Social Studies Go Wrong?*, 1–5.

119. National Education Association, *The Teaching of Community Civics*. Also see Arthur Dunn, *Community Civics for City Schools* (Boston: D. C. Heath and Company, 1921).

120. National Education Association, *The Teaching of Community Civics.*

121. National Education Association, *The Teaching of Community Civics*, 9.

122. National Education Association, *The Teaching of Community Civics*, 189.

123. National Education Association, *The Teaching of Community Civics.*

124. National Education Association, *The Teaching of Community Civics*, 10.

125. Julie A. Reuben, "Beyond Politics: Community Civics and the Redefinition of Citizenship in the Progressive Era," *History of Education Quarterly* 37, no. 4 (1997): 399–420.

126. Lawrence Cremin, "The Revolution in American Secondary Education, 1893–1918," *Teachers College Record* (March 1955): 307. Also quoted in Ravitch, *Left Back*, 129.

127. Edgar Dawson, "Manuscript on the History of the National Council for the Social Studies," folder 27, box 2, series 1, National Council for the Social Studies Records, Dolph Briscoe Center for American History, University of Texas, Austin, TX (hereafter cited as NCSS Records).

128. Dawson, "Manuscript on the History of the National Council for the Social Studies," NCSS Records.

129. Angus and Mirel, *The Failed Promise*, 14–16; Ravitch, *Left Back*, 127.

130. For example, the Detroit Public Schools formed a Department of Social Science in 1921.

131. Reuben, "Beyond Politics," 400.

132. "Public School Civics," *Chicago Schools Journal* 2, no. 5 (January 1920): 6.

133. Peter B. Ritzma, "The Chicago Course of Study in Citizenship," *Chicago Schools Journal* 8, no. 1 (September 1925): 5.

134. E. Lori Brown, "Civic Foundations," *Chicago Schools Journal* 2, no. 5 (January 1920): 11–14.

135. Brown, "Civic Foundations," 11.

136. Fred K. Branom, "The Significance of Geography," *Chicago Schools Journal* 2, no. 7 (March 1920): 16.

137. Ida Giachini, "Project Lesson Outlines," *Chicago Schools Journal* 5, no. 3 (November 1922): 122–24.

138. Virginia C. Bell, "The Excursion as a Means of Improving Geography Teaching," *Chicago Schools Journal* 5, no. 7 (March 1923): 281–83.

139. Edward E. Hill, "Some Objectives in Teaching History," *Chicago Schools Journal* 4, no. 9 (May 1922): 328.

140. G. A. Heinrich, "Material for the Fifth Grade History Course," *Chicago Schools Journal* 7, no. 7 (March 1925): 14–25. The course description suggests it is a civil en-

gineering unit on how cities like Chicago dispose of waste rather than a historical analysis. Heinrich was a city engineer for Chicago as well as the father of a fifth grader. The principal of his daughter's school asked Heinrich to write the article.

141.　"Principles Underlying the Course of Study for the Kindergarten and Primary Grades," *Chicago Schools Journal* 4, no. 2 (October 1921): 52.

142.　"Principles Underlying the Course of Study."

143.　Saxe, *Social Studies in Schools*, 173–74.

144.　Daniel C. Knowlton, "Report of the Secretary and Papers Read at the Conference on the Report of the Committee on History and Education for Citizenship in the Schools," *The Historical Outlook* 11, no. 2 (February 1920): 73–76.

145.　"Preliminary Report of the Committee on History and Education for Citizenship in Schools," *The Historical Outlook* 10, no. 5 (May 1919): 273–98.

146.　See Jonathan Zimmerman, *Whose America? Culture Wars in the Public Schools* (Cambridge, MA: Harvard University Press, 2002), 23–24, for a discussion of how textbooks portrayed Native Americans.

147.　"Preliminary Report of the Committee on History and Education," 274.

148.　"A Report of Progress," folder Correspondence, 1919, box 768, AHA Records.

149.　Waldo Leland to Daniel C. Knowlton, 13 May 1919, folder Correspondence, 1919, box 767, AHA Records. Knowlton responded to Leland that he sympathized "the least" with this particular criticism because it was not "possible to harmonize a chronological treatment with a psychological approach." Daniel C. Knowlton to Waldo Leland, 14 May 1919, folder Correspondence, 1919, box 767, AHA Records.

150.　Joseph Schafer to Daniel C. Knowlton, 14 May 1919, folder Correspondence, 1919, box 767, AHA Records.

151.　"A Report of Progress. The Decisions Reached by the Committee on History and Education for Citizenship in the Schools, at its Recent Meeting in Washington," *The Historical Outlook* 10, no. 6 (June 1919): 349–51.

152.　Committee on History and Education for Citizenship in the Schools: Minutes of the Meeting, Friday afternoon, 30 May 1919, folder Correspondence, 1919, box 766, AHA Records.

153.　A potential danger in such an emphasis, as Bohan has argued, is that a focus on national history in education may promote a bias toward nationalism and isolationism. See Bohan, "Digging Trenches."

154.　On the history of the NCSS, see Murry R. Nelson, "The Early Years: 1921–1937," *Social Education* 59, no. 7 (1995): 399–407; Robert Orrill and Linn Shapiro, "Forum Essay: From Bold Beginnings to an Uncertain Future: The Discipline of History and History Education," *The American Historical Review* 10, no. 3 (June 2005): 727–51; Ben A. Smith, J. Jesse Palmer, and Stephen T. Correia, "Social Studies and the Birth of NCSS: 1783–1921," *Social Education* 59, no. 7 (1995): 393–98; Stephen J. Thornton, "NCSS: The Early Years," in *NCSS in Retrospect*, ed. O. L. Davis Jr., 1–7 (Washington, DC: National Council for the

Social Studies, 1996); Louis M. Vanaria, "The National Council for the Social Studies" (PhD diss., Columbia University, 1958).

155.   "Temporary Constitution," folder 8, box 7, subseries 4B, NCSS Records.

156.   Thornton, "NCSS: The Early Years."

157.   "A National Council for the Social Studies," *The Historical Outlook* 12, no. 4 (1921): 144. Quoted in Murry Nelson, "Directionless from Birth: The National Council for the Social Studies, 1921–1937," ERIC Document, ED 391706 (November 1995), 3.

158.   John Jarolimek, "NCSS and Elementary School Studies," in Davis Jr., *NCSS in Retrospect*, 103–10.

159.   Thornton, "NCSS: The Early Years."

160.   Keith Barton examined some of the 625 surveys of individual school districts conducted between 1911 and 1928 by U.S. educators (including Franklin Bobbitt, Ellwood P. Cubberley, Charles H. Judd, Abraham Flexner, Alexander J. Inglis, and George Strayer). Barton argues for the importance of looking beyond traditional accounts of social studies history to examining committee recommendations and teaching in schools more closely. See Keith Barton, "Classroom Practice in the Formative Years of Social Studies" (paper presented at the annual meeting of the American Educational Research Association, April 10, 2006, San Francisco, CA). One of the 625 surveys was conducted in the Grand Rapids Public Schools. See *School Survey Grand Rapids Michigan* (Grand Rapids, MI: White Printing Company, 1916). No survey of teaching in the Detroit Public Schools for these years exists.

161.   *School Survey Grand Rapids Michigan* (Grand Rapids, MI: White Printing Company, 1916), 177.

162.   *School Survey Grand Rapids Michigan*, 177.

163.   *School Survey Grand Rapids Michigan*, 181.

164.   Detroit Board of Education, *Annual Report of the Superintendent 1914–1915* (Detroit: Detroit Board of Education, 1915), 32.

165.   Detroit Board of Education, *Annual Report of the Superintendent 1914–1915*, 33–35.

166.   Leah A. Spencer, "Developing Worthy Social Attitudes and Ideals," *Modern Education* 4, no. 1 (October 1931): 14, 44–46.

167.   Detroit Board of Education, *Course of Study in Geography* (Detroit: Detroit Board of Education, 1917), 4.

168.   Detroit Board of Education, *Course of Study in Geography*, 486.

169.   Arthur Dondineau, "Social Sciences and the Teaching of Citizenship," *The Detroit Journal of Education* 2, no. 3 (February 1922): 23–28.

170.   Dondineau, "Social Sciences and the Teaching of Citizenship," 25.

171.   Dondineau, "Social Sciences and the Teaching of Citizenship," 7.

172.   Dondineau, "Social Sciences and the Teaching of Citizenship," 7.

173.   Detroit Board of Education, *Annual Report of the Superintendent 1922–23* (Detroit: Detroit Board of Education, 1923), 5.

174. Detroit Board of Education, *Annual Report of the Superintendent 1922–23*, 6.
175. Henry Harap, "The Objectives of the Social Studies in the Elementary Grades," *The Journal of Educational Method* 6 (October 1926): 58.

Chapter 3. "Neither Fish nor Fowl": Social Studies in the Interwar Years

1. Martin Carnoy and Henry Levin, *Schooling and Work in the Democratic States* (Stanford, CA: Stanford University Press, 1985); Ira Katznelson and Margaret Weir, *Schooling for All: Class, Race, and the Decline of the Democratic Ideal* (New York: Basic Books, 1985). Both books argue that the Great Depression had a profound effect on education. See also Mirel, *The Rise and Fall*, 132–34; Ravitch, *Left Back*, 238–83.

2. Larry Cuban, while acknowledging there were more changes at the elementary level than at the secondary level, also argues there was more continuity than change in teaching practices from the 1920s to the 1950s. Cuban, *How Teachers Taught*, 61. Also see David Tyack, Robert Lowe, and Elisabeth Hansot, *Public Schools in Hard Times: The Great Depression and Recent Years* (Cambridge, MA: Harvard University Press, 1984), 189.

3. W. G. Kimmel to Edgar B. Wesley, 31 July 1933, folder 3, box 18, subseries 4B, NCSS Records.

4. Elmina R. Lucke, "The Social-Studies Curriculum in Lincoln School of Teachers College," in National Council for the Social Studies, *Fourth Yearbook: The Social Studies Curriculum*, 134–54 (Philadelphia: McKinley Publishing Company, 1934).

5. Louis M. Vanaria, "Social Education: The Mission of a Professional Journal," *Social Education* 34, no. 7 (1970): 782–86, 795.

6. Vanaria, "The National Council for the Social Studies," 6.

7. Hertzberg, *Social Studies Reform*, 39; Nelson, "Directionless from Birth," 5.

8. Nelson, "Directionless from Birth," 17.

9. Quoted in Nelson, "Directionless from Birth," 3.

10. "Social Education Asks—What Was One of Your Most Interesting or Significant Experiences During Your Year as President of the National Council for the Social Studies? Responses of Twenty-Five Former Presidents of NCSS," *Social Education* 34 (November 1970): 802–12, 868.

11. American Historical Association, *Annual Report of the American Historical Association for the Year 1923* (Washington, DC: American Historical Association, 1924), 38.

12. Hertzberg, *Social Studies Reform*, 37.

13. Nelson, "Directionless from Birth," 3.

14. Edgar Dawson, "An Organization to Promote the Social Studies," *The Historical Outlook* 12, no. 8 (1921): 300–331.

15. Vanaria, "The National Council for the Social Studies," 7.

16. Novick, *That Noble Dream*, 190.

17. For overviews of the Commission, see Gary B. Nash, Charlotte A. Crabtree, and Ross E. Dunn, *History on Trial: Culture Wars and the Teaching of the Past*

(New York: A. A. Knopf, 1997), 25–52; Joseph Watras, *Philosophic Conflicts in American Education, 1893–2000* (Boston: Pearson/Allyn and Bacon, 2004), 93–101; Watras, "Historians and Social Studies Educators."

18. See Novick, *That Noble Dream*, 190–91; Diane Ravitch, "From History to Social Studies," in *Challenges to the Humanities*, ed. Chester E. Finn Jr., Diane Ravitch, and P. Holley Roberts, 80–95 (New York: Holmes and Meier, 1985); Watras, *Philosophic Conflicts*, 93–95.

19. Kliebard, *The Struggle*, 242.

20. Charles Beard, *A Charter for the Social Studies in Schools* (New York: Charles Scribner's Sons, 1932), 20–21.

21. American Historical Association Commission on the Social Studies in the Schools and August C. Krey, *Conclusions and Recommendations of the Commission* (New York: Charles Scribner's Sons, 1934), 7.

22. Beard, *A Charter for the Social Sciences*, 18.

23. Beard, *A Charter for the Social Sciences*, 20–21.

24. Charles Beard, "The Problems of Objectives," n.d., folder Investigation of History and Other Social Sciences in the Schools, box 769, AHA Records.

25. American Historical Association and Krey, *Conclusions and Recommendations*, 55.

26. Link, "The American Historical Association."

27. Jenness, *Making Sense of Social Studies*, 108.

28. The reviews are cited in the following document: "Published Reviews of An Introduction to the History of the Social Sciences in the Schools," folder An Introduction to the History of the Social Sciences in Schools, B, box 770, AHA Records.

29. American Historical Association and Krey, *Conclusions and Recommendations*, 55.

30. Watras, *Philosophic Conflicts*, 96.

31. Beardsley Ruhl to A. C. Krey, 15 December 1932, folder Beard's Charter, box 789, AHA Records.

32. Ernest Horn, "Reasons for Not Signing the Summary Volume," 31 March 1934, folder Volume on Findings A, box 779, AHA Records.

33. Bessie L. Pierce to A. C. Krey, 18 December 1934, folder Volume on Findings C, box 780, AHA Records.

34. Kliebard, *The Struggle*, 242; Novick, *That Noble Dream*, 191.

35. A. C. Krey, *A Regional Program for the Social Studies* (New York: Macmillan Company, 1938), 63.

36. "Building America," folder 5, box 9, subseries 4, NCSS Records. In the mid-1940s, the *Building America* series, like the AHA Commission on the Social Studies, was accused of having communist sympathies. The series was discontinued in 1948.

37. "Report of the Meeting of the Advisory Council of the Civics Research Institute," 27 February 1934, folder Civics Research Institute, 1934–1936, box 15, subseries 4D, NCSS Records.

38. "Report of the Meeting of the Advisory Council of the Civics Research Institute."

39. Beard, *A Charter for the Social Sciences in Schools,* 97.

40. "A Project for the Improvement of the Curriculum in the Social Studies," folder 1, box 19, subseries 4B, NCSS Records.

41. See Anne-Lise Halvorsen, "'Don't Know Much about History': *The New York Times* 1943 Survey of U.S. History and the Controversy it Generated," *Teachers College Record* 118, no. 1 (2012): 1–32.

42. Thornton, "NCSS: The Early Years," 5.

43. Dawson, "Manuscript on the History of the National Council for the Social Studies."

44. James A. Michener, ed., *The Future of the Social Studies: Proposals for an Experimental Social Studies Curriculum,* Curriculum Series, No. 1 (Cambridge, MA: The National Council for the Social Studies, 1939).

45. Ruth West, "Foreword," in Michener, *The Future of the Social Studies,* iii–iv.

46. Michener, "The Problem of Social Studies," in Michener, *The Future of the Social Studies,* 2 (emphasis in the original).

47. Vanaria, "Social Education."

48. Vanaria, "Social Education," 795.

49. A leading social studies educator of the time, Ralph Preston, described fusion as follows: "Fusion goes beyond the cross fertilization of academic fields...It unites and harmonizes the child's motor activities, spiritual insights, intellectual discoveries, and creative impulses." This interpretation of the fusion curriculum suggests that educators see social studies as an all-inclusive subject. See Ralph C. Preston, "Units Employing Fusion" in *Social Education of Young Children: Kindergarten-Primary Grades,* ed. Mary Willcockson, 125–29 (Washington, DC: National Council for the Social Studies, 1956).

50. Dorothy McClure Fraser, "The Organization of the Elementary-School Social Studies Curriculum," in *Social Studies in the Elementary School: The Fifty-sixth Yearbook for the National Society for the Study of Education Part II,* ed. Nelson B. Henry, 129–62 (Chicago: The University of Chicago Press, 1957), 130. Fraser cited a study from the early 1950s that found that around one-third of upper elementary teachers used the fusion curriculum. Also see Robert V. Duffey, "A Study of the Reported Practices of 538 Temple University Graduates and Students in their Teaching of Social Studies in the Elementary School (PhD diss., Temple University, 1954).

51. Howard E. Wilson, "The Fusion of Social Studies in the Junior High School: A Critical Analysis," in the National Council for the Social Studies, *Some Aspects of the Social Sciences in the Schools,* 118–31 (Philadelphia: McKinley Publishing Company, 1931).

52. Wilson, "The Fusion of Social Studies," 130–31.

53. Wilson, "The Fusion of Social Studies," 121.

54. Judd, "Needed Revisions in Social-Science Instruction," 9–10.

55. Fraser, "The Organization of the Elementary-School."

56. Edgar B. Wesley, *Teaching the Social Studies,* 2nd ed. (Boston: D. C. Heath and Company, 1942). The first edition of this book was published in 1937.

57. National Education Association, *The Social Studies Curriculum, Fourteenth Yearbook, Department of Superintendence* (Washington, DC: National Education Association, 1936).

58. Daniel Tanner and Laurel Tanner, *History of the School Curriculum* (New York: Macmillan Publishing Company, 1990), 287.

59. Jarolimek, "NCSS and Elementary School Social Studies," 104.

60. Howard Wilson to Bessie Pierce, 5 December 1934, folder Meetings, 1934–35, box 1, series 8A, NCSS Records.

61. Sarah Clayton Burrow and Corinne A. Seeds, "Teaching Social Studies in the Primary Grades: Community Living through an Ongoing Interest in Airplanes," in *The Social Studies in the Elementary School*, ed. William E. Young, 157–99 (Washington, DC: National Council for the Social Studies, 1941).

62. Burrow and Seeds, "Teaching Social Studies in the Primary Grades," 168–71.

63. C. C. Barnes, ed., *The Contribution of Research to the Teaching of the Social Studies* (Cambridge, MA: The National Council for the Social Studies, 1937), v.

64. Mary Kelty, *Learning and Teaching History in the Middle Grades* (Boston: Ginn & Company, 1936), 6.

65. Reese, *America's Public Schools*, 175.

66. Detroit Board of Education, *Annual Report of the Superintendent 1928–1929* (Detroit: Detroit Board of Education, 1929), 42.

67. Pflieger, "Social Studies."

68. Pflieger, "Social Studies," 488.

69. Pflieger, "Social Studies," 488.

70. Pflieger, "Social Studies," 489.

71. Pflieger, "Social Studies," 365.

72. Detroit Board of Education, *The Superintendent's Annual Report for the 93rd Year of the Detroit Public Schools, Part 1* (Detroit: Detroit Board of Education, 1937), 19.

73. Detroit Board of Education, *Annual Report of the Superintendent 1939–1940, Part 2* (Detroit: Detroit Board of Education, 1940), 6.

74. Detroit Board of Education, *Annual Report of the Superintendent 1939–40*, 10.

75. Detroit Board of Education, *Annual Report of the Superintendent 1937–38* (Detroit: Detroit Board of Education, 1938), 17.

76. Spencer, "Developing Worthy Social Attitudes."

77. The GRPS did not document its curriculum in the detail that the DPS did. This overview of the GRPS social studies curriculum suggests that some school districts continued to highlight historical content in the early grades.

78. Grand Rapids Board of Education, *Annual Report of the Superintendent 1930–32* (Grand Rapids, MI: Grand Rapids Board of Education, 1932), 37.

79. Grand Rapids Board of Education, *Annual Report of the Superintendent, 1932–34* (Grand Rapids, MI: Grand Rapids Board of Education, 1934), 19.

80. Grand Rapids Board of Education, *Annual Report of the Superintendent, 1934–35* (Grand Rapids, MI: Grand Rapids Board of Education, 1935), 14–15.

81. Board of Education of the City School District of the City of Cleveland, *Report of the Superintendent of Schools, 1935-36* (Cleveland, OH: Board of Education of

the City School District of the City of Cleveland, 1936), 29.

82. Board of Education of the City School District of the City of Cleveland, _Report of the Superintendent of Schools, 1939–40_ (Cleveland, OH: Board of Education of the City School District of the City of Cleveland, 1940), 131.

83. Board of Education of the City School District of the City of Cleveland, _Report of the Superintendent of Schools, 1939–40_, 133.

84. Board of Education of the City School District of the City of Cleveland, _Report of the Superintendent of Schools, 1939–40_, 132.

85. Robert E. Keohane and Howard C. Hill, "The Social Studies Curriculum in the University of Chicago Laboratory Schools," in the National Council for the Social Studies, _The Social Studies Curriculum_, 176–193 (Philadelphia: McKinley Publishing Company, 1934).

86. The only Cardinal Principle not referenced was "Command of Fundamental Processes" (i.e., writing, reading, oral and written expression, and mathematics). This omission makes sense because these processes were generally taught in reading and mathematics lessons. See C. C. Ball, "Social Studies in the Schools of San Antonio," in the National Council for the Social Studies, _The Social Studies Curriculum_, 115–28 (Philadelphia: McKinley Publishing Company, 1934).

87. Ball, "Social Studies in the Schools of San Antonio," 116.

88. Novick, _That Noble Dream_, 192.

89. Hayes is quoted in Novick, _That Noble Dream_, 192.

90. Diane Ravitch, "Tot Sociology."

Chapter 4. "Romance or Reality": Paul Robert Hanna and the Expanding Communities Approach

1. Educators have used various terms for this approach: for example, expanding environments, expanding horizons, and widening horizons. Throughout this book, I use Hanna's term: expanding communities.

2. Brophy, "The De Facto National Curriculum"; Naylor and Diem, _Elementary and Middle School Social Studies_.

3. For example, see Jere Brophy, Janet Alleman, and Anne-Lise Halvorsen, _Powerful Social Studies for Elementary Students_, 3rd ed. (Belmont, CA: Wadswoth Cengage Learning, 2012); Michigan Department of Education, _Grade Level Content Expectations: Social Studies_ (Lansing, MI: Michigan Department of Education, 2007); Teachers' Curriculum Institute, _Social Studies Alive!_ (Palo Alto, CA: Teachers' Curriculum Institute, 2003). For a concise discussion of the debates about elementary social studies, see Brophy and Alleman, "A Reconceptualized Rationale"; Jere Brophy and Bruce VanSledright, _Teaching and Learning History in Elementary Schools_ (New York: Teachers College Press, 1997), 1–10.

4. See Stallones, _Paul Robert Hanna_, 164.

5. Leriche, "The Expanding Environments."

6. Paul R. Hanna, "Social Education for Childhood," _Childhood Education_ 14 (October 1937): 74–77.

7. Evans, *The Social Studies Wars*, 50–52.

8. Martin Gill, "Paul R. Hanna: The Evolution of an Elementary Social Studies Textbook Series" (PhD diss., Northwestern University, 1974), 78.

9. For discussions of Hanna's contributions, see Gill, "Paul R. Hanna"; Jared Stallones, "Paul Hanna and 'Expanding Communities,'" *International Journal of Social Education* 18, no. 2 (2003–2004): 33–43; Stallones, *Paul Robert Hanna*; Jared Stallones, "Paul Hanna: The Early Years," in *The Life and Times of Paul and Jean Hanna*, ed. Thomas L. Dynneson, 1–13 (Washington, DC: National Council for the Social Studies, 2002).

10. Stallones, *Paul Robert Hanna*, 11–18; Paul R. Hanna, interview by Martin Gill, 5 September 1973.

11. Hanna, interview by Martin Gill, 103.

12. Hanna, interview by Martin Gill, 69.

13. George Counts, *Dare the School Build a New Social Order?* (New York: The John Day Co., 1932), 55.

14. "Hold Schools Fail to Teach Realities; Educators Charge Neglect of Current Social Needs in Training of Youth," *The New York Times*, November 20, 1932.

15. Hanna, interview by Martin Gill, 7.

16. See Cuban, *How Teachers Taught*, 67–83.

17. Lincoln School Teachers College, *Curriculum Making in an Elementary School* (Boston: Ginn & Company, 1927).

18. Lincoln School Teachers College, *Curriculum Making*, 70–72.

19. Lincoln School Teachers College, *Curriculum Making*, 60.

20. Lincoln School Teachers College, *Curriculum Making*, 131–44.

21. Hanna, interview by Martin Gill.

22. Hanna, interview by Martin Gill, 11.

23. Stallones, *Paul Robert Hanna*, 40–46.

24. Paul R. Hanna, "The Analysis of Children's Interests," folder Results and Questions 1 and 2, box 234, Paul Robert Hanna Papers, 1920–1997, Hoover Institution, Stanford, CA (hereafter cited as Hanna Papers); Paul R. Hanna, "Interests Questionnaire," folder Results and Questions 1 and 2, box 233, Hanna Papers; Paul R. Hanna, "Brief Description of Two Units of Work with Some Underlying Theory," folder 13, box 192, Hanna Papers.

25. Alice Carey, Paul R. Hanna, and J. L. Meriam, *Partial Catalog: Units of Work Activities, Projects, Themes, Etc.* (New York: Bureau of Publications, Teachers College, 1932), folder 7, box 149, Hanna Papers.

26. Hanna, interview by Martin Gill, 7.

27. Hanna, "Romance or Reality."

28. Hanna, "Romance or Reality," 322.

29. Hanna, "Romance or Reality."

30. Stallones, *Paul Robert Hanna*, 175.

31. Hanna, "Romance or Reality," 320 (emphasis in the original).

32. Hanna, "Romance or Reality." See Stallones, *Paul Robert Hanna*, 217–25, for an analysis of Hanna's role in the 1938 Progressive Education Association Con-

ference that attempted to reach a consensus between advocates of child-centered education and advocates of social reconstructionism.

33. Paul R. Hanna, "Building Toward a World Community," speech to the American Council on Education (1942), folder 12, box 98, Hanna Papers.

34. Hanna, interview by Martin Gill, 36.

35. Paul R. Hanna, "Needed Changes in Elementary Curriculum," n.d., folder 10, box 104, Hanna Papers; Paul R. Hanna, "We Teach Both Subject Matter and Children—An Indispensable Blend for a Sound Elementary School Curriculum," *NEA Journal* (May 1954): 273–75.

36. See Mary Louise Seguel, *The Curriculum Field: Its Formative Years* (New York: Teachers College Press, 1966); Stallones, *Paul Robert Hanna*.

37. For a discussion of Hanna's work in Virginia, see Gill, "Paul R. Hanna"; Hanna, interview by Martin Gill; Stallones, "Paul Hanna"; Stallones, *Paul Robert Hanna*. According to Hanna's account, he played a significant role in writing the core social studies curriculum. He talked about the curriculum development from the perspective of "I" rather than "we." Other accounts describe greater collaboration between Hanna and his colleagues (and identify Caswell as the leader). In fact, Hanna was not listed as an author of the curriculum documents. My discussion, in addition to Hanna's account, relies on four additional sources: Lynn M. Burlbaw, "Hollis Leland Caswell's Contributions to the Development of the Curriculum Field" (PhD diss., University of Texas, 1989); Angela Fraley, *Schooling and Innovation: The Rhetoric and the Reality* (New York: Tyler Gibson Publishers, 1981); David Hicks and Stephanie van Hover, "'A Magnificent Adventure': Negotiating and Structuring Curricular Change in Virginia," in *Education and the Great Depression*, ed. E. Thomas Ewing and David Hicks, 263–92 (New York: Peter Lang, 2006); Seguel, *The Curriculum Field*, 139–56.

38. Hicks and van Hover, "'A Magnificent Adventure.'"

39. Hanna, interview by Martin Gill, 8.

40. Wesley Mitchell, ed., *Recent Social Trends in the United States: Report of the President's Research Committee on Social Trends* (New York: Whittlesey House, 1934).

41. Mitchell, *Recent Social Trends*, xiii.

42. Paul R. Hanna, "Social Studies in the New Virginia Curriculum," *Progressive Education* 11 (January 1934): 129–34.

43. Hanna, "Social Studies in the New Virginia Curriculum," 132.

44. Hanna, "Social Studies in the New Virginia Curriculum," 132.

45. Stallones, "Paul Hanna: The Early Years."

46. Hanna, interview by Martin Gill, 8 (emphasis added).

47. I found no data on specific course requirements at institutions that offered teacher education. However, one national survey found that teachers were poorly prepared to teach content from the social sciences. See Earle U. Rugg, Wesley E. Peik, Frank K. Foster, Walton C. John, and Robert B. Raup, *National Survey of the Education of Teachers*, Vol. 3 (Washington, DC: U.S. Department of the Interior, 1933), 107.

48. Hanna's curriculum structure around the basic human activities had deep roots in education theory. For example, decades earlier Herbert Spencer classified the facets of human existence into five categories: (1) life and health; (2) earning a living; (3) rearing a family; (4) citizenship; and (5) leisure. In some ways, Hanna's activities resembled the *Cardinal Principles* endorsed by the CRSE, and more specifically, the fourteen topics recommended by the CRSE's Committee on Social Studies in their 1915 report (e.g., health; protection of life and property; recreation; education; and so forth). See National Education Association, *The Teaching of Community Civics*.

49. Hollis L. Caswell and Doak S. Campbell, *Curriculum Development* (New York: American Book Company, 1935).

50. Hicks and van Hover, "'A Magnificent Adventure,'" 279; Leriche, "The Expanding Environments." Stallones explains that Hanna used this sequence that is based on children's experiences rather than on their developmental stages. See Stallones, *Paul Robert Hanna,* 164–65.

51. Harold Rugg and Louise Krueger, "The Social Studies in the Elementary School—A Tentative Course of Study," n.d. Quoted in Gill, "Paul R. Hanna," 37.

52. Hanna used others' ideas about communities in his books. Hanna, interview by Martin Gill, 96. In the early 1920s, theorists in social studies education often assumed people belonged to multiple communities at the same time. For example, in his 1924 book on curriculum, Franklin Bobbitt, a Professor of Educational Administration at the University of Chicago, wrote: "The citizen appears to be a member of many groups. He is a member of a family group. As a vocatioist, [sic] he is a member of the labor union. In his religion, he is a member of a church organization.... As a human being, he belongs to the world-group called humanity." Franklin Bobbitt, *How to Make a Curriculum* (Boston: Houghton Mifflin Company, 1924), 98.

53. Paul R. Hanna, "Design for a Social Studies Program," in *Focus on the Social Studies: A Report from the 1965 DESP Annual Meeting,* ed. Department of Elementary School Principals, National Education Association, 28–45 (Washington, DC: National Education Association, 1965).

54. Hanna, "Design for a Social Studies Program."

55. Paul R. Hanna, "Society-Child-Curriculum," in *Assuring Quality for the Social Studies in Our Schools,* ed. Paul R. Hanna, 2–29 (Stanford, CA: Hoover Institution Press, 1987).

56. Hanna, "Society-Child-Curriculum," 11.

57. Hanna, interview by Martin Gill, 6.

58. State Board of Education, *Tentative Course of Study for Virginia Elementary Schools – Grades I—VII* (Richmond, VA: State Board of Education, 1934).

59. State Board of Education, *Tentative Course of Study.*

60. State Board of Education, *Tentative Course of Study,* 16–17.

61. Hanna, "Romance or Reality," 322.

62. State Board of Education, *Tentative Course of Study,* 25.

63. Hollis L. Caswell, interview by Angela E. Fraley, 1978. Quoted in Fraley, *Schooling and Innovation.*

64. Caswell and Campbell, *Curriculum Development*, 184.

65. Hanna, "Romance or Reality," 322.

66. For discussions of intercultural education, see Rachel Davis DuBois, *All This and Something More: Pioneering in Intercultural Education* (Bryn Mawr, PA: Dorrance & Company, Inc., 1984), 62–98; Nicholas V. Montalto, *A History of the Intercultural Educational Movement, 1924–1941* (New York: Garland Press, 1982); Yoon Pak, "If There Is a Better Intercultural Plan in any School System in America, I Do Not Know Where It Is," *Urban Education* 37, no. 5 (2002): 588–609.

67. There were also some college professors who criticized the entire program (not just social studies) for its movement away from the traditional disciplines. They were concerned that as a result of this educational program, elementary students would not be prepared for either a skilled trade or higher education. See Hicks and van Hover, "'A Magnificent Adventure,'" 284–85.

68. Hicks and van Hover, "'A Magnificent Adventure,'" 287.

69. Gill, "Paul R. Hanna," 58.

70. Gill, "Paul R. Hanna," 76.

71. Hanna, interview by Martin Gill, 69.

72. Hanna created an identity as a scholar and a highly respected teacher at Stanford University. In his thirty-two years at Stanford University (1935–67), he established the Stanford International Development Education Center (SIDEC) and helped found the Paul and Jean Hanna Archival Collection on the Role of Education in Twentieth-Century Society at the Hoover Institution. See Stallones, *Paul Robert Hanna*, for discussions of Hanna's many projects.

73. Gill, "Paul R. Hanna," 71.

74. Gill, "Paul R. Hanna," 72.

75. See Gill, "Paul R. Hanna" for an extensive discussion of the history of Hanna's textbooks and of his complicated relationship with Scott, Foresman and Company's management, particularly with his editor, Harry Johnston. Hanna accused Johnston of stealing ideas from his (Hanna's) social studies texts to use in the publisher's reading series.

76. Gill, "Paul R. Hanna," 90.

77. Gill, "Paul R. Hanna," 92.

78. Stallones, *Paul Robert Hanna*, 169–70.

79. Gill, "Paul R. Hanna," 102.

80. Hanna, interview by Martin Gill, 53.

81. Paul R. Hanna, Genevieve Anderson, and William S. Gray, *David's Friends at School* (Chicago: Scott, Foresman and Company, 1936); Paul R. Hanna, Genevieve Anderson, and William S. Gray, *Peter's Family* (Chicago: Scott, Foresman and Company, 1935); Paul R. Hanna, Genevieve Anderson, and William S. Gray, *Susan's Neighbors* (Chicago: Scott, Foresman and Company, 1937).

82. See Evans, *This Happened in America*, for an analysis of Rugg's textbooks.

83. Hanna, interview by Martin Gill, 3.

84. Rugg and Krueger wrote a social studies textbook series for grades three through six: Harold Rugg and Louise Krueger, *Man and His Changing Society: The Rugg Social Science Series. Elementary School Course Vol. 1–8* (Boston: Ginn & Company, 1936–38). The titles of the books are: *The First Book of the Earth; Nature Peoples; Communities of Men; Peoples and Countries; The Building of America; Man at Work: His Industries; Man at Work: His Arts and Crafts;* and *The Story of Civilization.* These books were successful but not nearly as successful as Hanna's books (or as Rugg's junior high school textbooks). See Evans, *This Happened in America,* 96.

85. Harry Johnston to Paul R. Hanna, 6 March 1936, folder 8, box 98, Hanna Papers. Rugg's textbooks incorporated teacher responses to some extent in the transition from pamphlets to texts. See Evans, *This Happened in America.*

86. Harold Rugg and Louise Krueger, *Communities of Men* (Boston: Ginn & Company, 1936).

87. Harold Rugg and Louise Krueger, *The First Book of the Earth* (Boston: Ginn & Company, 1936), v.

88. Evans, *This Happened in America,* 95–96.

89. Hanna, interview by Martin Gill, 120.

90. Gill, "Paul R. Hanna," 103.

91. There were other arguments about intellectual property rights and about the marketing strategy. See Gill, "Paul R. Hanna" for a discussion of these arguments.

92. Zerna Sharp to Paul R. Hanna, 28 March 1935, folder 7, box 97, Hanna Papers.

93. Paul R. Hanna to Harry Johnston, 4 October 1935, folder 7, box 97, Hanna Papers.

94. Paul R. Hanna to Zerna Sharp, 9 April 1935, folder 7, box 97, Hanna Papers. Probably the emphasis on Christmas was a response to the editors' wish that the textbooks fit the holidays curriculum in existing curricular approaches.

95. Paul R. Hanna to Zerna Sharp, 4 September 1935, folder 7, box 97, Hanna Papers.

96. Paul R. Hanna to Willis Scott, 16 March 1936, folder 8, box 98, Hanna Papers.

97. Paul R. Hanna to Harry Johnston, 4 October 1935, folder 7, box 97, Hanna Papers.

98. Hanna, "Design for a Social Studies Program."

99. Hanna, Anderson, and Gray, *Peter's Family.*

100. Hanna, Anderson, and Gray, *Peter's Family,* 95.

101. Stallones, *Paul Robert Hanna,* 174.

102. Paul R. Hanna, Genevieve Anderson, and William S. Gray, *Centerville* (Chicago: Scott, Foresman and Company, 1938).

103. E.T. McSwain, "Centerville," 1 October 1938, folder 10, box 98, Hanna Papers.

104. McSwain, "Centerville."

105. McSwain, "Centerville."

106. Hanna, Anderson, and Gray, *Centerville.*

107.   "Child's Middletown," *Time* 32, no. 14, October 3, 1938, 42.

108.   Hanna largely escaped these attacks from journalists and educators. His *Building America* series, which was criticized, was the exception.

109.   See folder 10, box 98, Hanna Papers, for the correspondence between school-children and Hanna.

110.   Gill, "Paul R. Hanna," 144.

111.   Hanna, interview by Martin Gill.

112.   Paul R. Hanna, Genevieve Anderson Hoyt, and William S. Gray, *At Home* (Chicago: Scott, Foresman and Company, 1956); Paul R. Hanna, Genevieve Anderson Hoyt, and William S. Gray, *At School* (Chicago: Scott, Foresman and Company, 1957); Paul R. Hanna, Genevieve Anderson Hoyt, and Clyde F. Kohn, *In City, Town, and Country* (Chicago: Scott, Foresman and Company, 1959); Paul R. Hanna, Clyde F. Kohn, and Robert A. Lively, *In All Our States* (Chicago: Scott, Foresman and Company, 1956); Paul R. Hanna, Clyde F. Kohn, and Robert A. Lively, *In the Americas* (Chicago: Scott, Foresman and Company, 1956); Paul R. Hanna, *Beyond the Americas* (Chicago: Scott, Foresman and Company, 1956).

113.   Gill, "Paul R. Hanna," 148.

114.   Stallones, *Paul Robert Hanna*, 185.

115.   Gill, "Paul R. Hanna," 109.

116.   Hanna, interview by Martin Gill, 31.

117.   Hanna, interview by Martin Gill, 31.

118.   Ravitch, *Left Back*.

119.   Paul R. Hanna, *Without Machinery* (Chicago: Scott, Foresman and Company, 1939).

120.   Paul R. Hanna to Zerna Sharp, 27 July 1936, folder 8, box 98, Hanna Papers.

121.   Paul R. Hanna, I. James Quillen, and Gladys L. Potter, *Ten Communities* (Chicago: Scott, Foresman and Company, 1940), 504.

122.   Hanna, interview by Martin Gill, 36.

123.   Gill, "Paul R. Hanna," 128, 110.

124.   Stallones, *Paul Robert Hanna*, 287.

125.   Stallones, *Paul Robert Hanna*.

126.   Stallones, *Paul Robert Hanna*, 249–90. Stallones discusses Hanna's many international education projects.

127.   Stallones, *Paul Robert Hanna*, 294.

128.   Thomas D. Snyder, ed., *120 Years of American Education: A Statistical Portrait* (Washington, DC: U.S. Department of Education, Office of Educational Research and Improvement, 1993), 16.

129.   Hanna, interview by Martin Gill, 8. Hanna noted that despite his efforts to make this curriculum accessible, teachers still struggled with the everyday life content.

130.   James W. Fraser, *Preparing America's Teachers: A History* (New York: Teachers College Press, 2007), 180–83.

131.   Cuban, *How Teachers Taught*, 102–3.

132. See Carole Kismaric, *Growing Up with Dick and Jane* (San Francisco: Collins, 1996).

133. For particularly stinging criticisms of the expanding communities approach, see Diane Ravitch, "Tot Sociology"; Frazee and Ayers, "Garbage In, Garbage Out." In general, these scholars prefer a history-oriented approach to social studies. Specifically, they criticize the expanding communities approach.

134. Hanna, interview by Martin Gill.

135. Dewey, *The Child and the Curriculum*.

136. Ravitch, "Tot Sociology"; Frazee and Ayers, "Garbage In, Garbage Out."

137. Stallones, *Paul Robert Hanna*, 186–89.

138. Isaac L. Kandel, *The Cult of Uncertainty* (New York: The Macmillan Company, 1943).

139. Richard Gross, interview by Jared Stallones, 9 August 1998. Cited in Stallones, *Paul Robert Hanna*, 189.

140. Stallones, *Paul Robert Hanna*, 188.

141. Stallones, *Paul Robert Hanna*, 100–111.

142. Evans, *This Happened in America*.

143. See Robert E. Newman Jr., "History of a Civic Education Project Implementing the Social Problems Technique of Instruction" (PhD diss., Stanford University, 1961).

144. Pak, "If There Is a Better Intercultural Education Plan."

145. Hanna, "Design for a Social Studies Program."

146. Hanna, "Design for a Social Studies Program," 30.

147. John R. Lee, *Teaching Social Studies in the Elementary School* (New York: Free Press, 1974).

Chapter 5. "A Revolution Is Needed": Social Studies in the Hot and Cold War Eras

1. Irving Morrissett, "The Needs of the Future and the Constraints of the Past," in *The Social Studies: Eightieth Yearbook of the National Society for the Study of Education, Part II*, ed. Howard D. Mehlinger and O. L. Davis Jr., 36–59 (Chicago: The University of Chicago Press, 1981), 55.

2. Edgar B. Wesley, *Teaching Social Studies in Elementary Schools* (Boston: D. C. Heath, 1946), 49.

3. Wesley, *Teaching Social Studies*.

4. Fraser, "The Organization of the Elementary-School."

5. Wesley, *Teaching Social Studies*, 232.

6. Wesley, *Teaching Social Studies*, 475.

7. Ralph Preston, *Teaching Social Studies in the Elementary School* (New York: Rinehart & Company, Inc., 1950), 65. This was the first of six editions.

8. Preston, *Teaching Social Studies*, 66–69.

9. Preston, *Teaching Social Studies*, 59.

10. C. C. Barnes, "Detroit's 12-Year Widening-Area Plan for Social Studies," *Clearing*

House 14, no. 2 (October 1939): 94–97.

11.   Barnes, "Detroit's 12-Year," 96.

12.   Barnes, "Detroit's 12-Year," 94.

13.   Elmer F. Pflieger and Grace L. Weston, *Emotional Adjustment: A Key to Good Citizenship* (Detroit: Wayne University Press, 1953).

14.   National Council for the Social Studies, *The Social Studies Mobilize for Victory* (Washington, DC: National Council for the Social Studies, 1943).

15.   "Resolutions Adopted by the National Council for the Social Studies at the Twenty-Fifth Annual Meeting in Milwaukee, November 22–24, 1945," folder 1, box 1, series 2D, NCSS Records.

16.   The National Council for the Social Studies, *The Social Studies Look Beyond the War: A Statement of Postwar Policy Prepared by an Advisory Commission and Adopted by the National Council for the Social Studies* (Washington, DC: The National Council for the Social Studies, 1944). See also "Advisory Commission on Postwar Policy," folder 72, box 4, series 7, NCSS Records.

17.   The National Council for the Social Studies, *The Social Studies Look,* 19.

18.   The National Council for the Social Studies, *The Social Studies Look,* 19–20.

19.   See Hilda Taba and William Van Til, eds., *Democratic Human Relations: Promising Practices in Intergroup and Intercultural Education in the Social Studies, Sixteenth Yearbook of the National Council for the Social Studies* (Washington, DC: National Council for the Social Studies, 1945); Montalto, *A History of the Intercultural Educational Movement.*

20.   The Committee for the Sixteenth Yearbook for the National Council for the Social Studies, "Some Remarks in Conclusion," in Taba and Van Til, *Democratic Human Relations,* 337–53.

21.   Helen Trager and Marian Radke, "Early Childhood Airs Its Views," *Educational Leadership* 5, no. 1 (October 1947): 16–24.

22.   William E. Vickery and Stewart G. Cole, *Intercultural Education in American Schools: Proposed Objectives and Methods* (New York: Harper, 1943).

23.   There was an exception in the Detroit Public Schools. See Administrative Committee on Intercultural Education, *Promising Practices in Intergroup Education* (Detroit: Detroit Board of Education, 1947); Detroit Board of Education, *Building One Nation Indivisible: A Bulletin on Intercultural Education for the Detroit Public Schools* (Detroit: Detroit Board of Education, 1944), 37–43.

24.   See Cherry A. McGee Banks, "The Intergroup Education Movement," in *Multicultural Education, Transformative Knowledge, and Action,* ed. James A. Banks, 251–77 (New York: Teachers College Press, 1996); Zoe Burkholder, *Color in the Classroom: How Americans Taught Race, 1900–1954* (Oxford, U.K.: Oxford University Press, 2011); Michael R. Olneck, "The Recurring Dream: Symbolism and Ideology in Intercultural and Multicultural Education," *American Journal of Education,* 98, no. 2 (February, 1990): 147–74; Daniel Perlstein, "American Dilemmas: Education, Social Science, and the Limits of Liberalism," in *Research in Politics and Society: The Global Color Line: Racial and Ethnic Inequality and Struggle from a Global Perspective,* ed. Gwenn Moore and J. Allen Whitt, 357–79

(Stamford, CT: JAI Press, 1999); Diana Selig, *Americans All: The Cultural Gifts Movement* (Cambridge, MA: Harvard University Press, 2008), 277.

25. Banks, "The Intergroup Education Movement."

26. Anne-Lise Halvorsen and Jeffrey Mirel, "Intercultural Education in Detroit, 1943–1954," *Paedagogica Historica* (forthcoming).

27. Anne-Lise Halvorsen and Jeffrey E. Mirel, "Educating Citizens: Social Problems Meet Progressive Education in Detroit, 1930–52," in *Clio at the Table: A Conference on the Uses of History to Inform and Improve Education Policy*, ed. Kenneth Wong and Richard Rothman, 9–36 (New York: Peter Lang, 2009).

28. Detroit Board of Education, *Detroit Board of Education Proceedings, 1944–45* (Detroit: Detroit Board of Education, 1945), 207–8. The 2007 figure is calculated using the U.S. Bureau of Labor Statistics Inflation Calculator, which can be found at http://www.bls.gov/cpi/.

29. Detroit Board of Education, *Progress Report: The Citizenship Education Study of the Detroit Public Schools and Wayne University* (Detroit: Detroit Board of Education, 1947), 6.

30. Stanley E. Dimond, *Schools and the Development of Good Citizens* (Detroit: Wayne University Press, 1953), 1–8.

31. National Council for the Social Studies and Howard R. Anderson, *Teaching Critical Thinking in the Social Studies* (Washington, DC: National Council for the Social Studies, 1942).

32. Detroit Board of Education, *Problem Solving* (Detroit: Detroit Board of Education, 1948).

33. Pflieger and Weston, *Emotional Adjustment*, 65.

34. Arnold R. Meier, Florence Damon Cleary, and Alice M. Davis, *A Curriculum for Citizenship: A Total School Approach to Citizenship Education* (Detroit: Detroit Board of Education and Wayne University Press, 1952), viii.

35. Pflieger and Weston, *Emotional Adjustment*, 37–39.

36. Angus and Mirel, *The Failed Promise*, 80–82.

37. Evans, *The Social Studies Wars*, 104–105.

38. Helen Heffernan, "Social Studies in Relation to the Total Elementary-School Program," in *Social Studies in the Elementary School Program*, ed. Wilhelmina Hill, 128 (Washington, DC: U.S. Department of Health, Education, 1960) (emphasis added).

39. Helen McCracken Carpenter, ed., *Skills in Social Studies* (Washington, DC: National Council for the Social Studies, 1953). Also see Helen McCracken Carpenter to Merrill Hartshorn, January 23, 1952, box 3, folder 36, series 7, NCSS Records.

40. See Wilhelmina Hill, ed., *Selected Resource Units: Elementary Social Studies, Kindergarten-Grade Six* (Washington, DC: National Council for the Social Studies, 1961).

41. Angus and Mirel, *The Failed Promise*, 119.

42. Wesley, *Teaching Social Studies*, 20.

43. Paul R. Hanna, "Education for Survival," n.d., folder 8, box 36, Hanna Papers.

44. Ralph C. Preston, "The Yearbook's Proposals in Relation to Certain Realities Facing the Elementary School," in *Social Studies in the Elementary Schools: The Fifty-Sixth Yearbook for the National Society of the Study of Education*, ed. Nelson B. Henry, 306–14 (Chicago: The University of Chicago Press, 1957).

45. Preston, "The Yearbook's Proposals," 308.

46. Mortimer Smith, *And Madly Teach: A Layman Looks at Public School Education* (Chicago: H. Regnery Co., 1949).

47. Arthur Bestor, *Educational Wastelands: The Retreat from Learning in Our Schools* (Urbana, IL: The University of Illinois Press, 1953).

48. See Evans, *The Hope for American School Reform*, 15–34, for a discussion of Bestor's criticism of social studies.

49. Bestor, *Educational Wastelands*, 55. See Evans, *The Hope for American School Reform*, 15–21; John L. Rudolph, *Scientists in the Classroom: The Cold War Reconstruction of American Science Education* (New York: Palgrave Macmillan, 2002), 29.

50. Allan Nevins, "American History for Americans," *The New York Times Magazine*, May 2, 1942.

51. See Evans, *The Hope for American School Reform*, 150–54; Rudolph, *Scientists in the Classroom*.

52. Evans, *The Hope for American School Reform*, 69.

53. Jerome Bruner, *The Process of Education* (Cambridge, MA: Harvard University Press, 1960).

54. Bruner, *The Process of Education*, 31.

55. Bruner, *The Process of Education*, 19.

56. Bruner, *The Process of Education*, 33.

57. On the new social studies, see Evans, *The Hope for American School Reform*; Evans, *The Social Studies Wars*, 122–48; Barbara Slater Stern, ed., *The New Social Studies: People, Projects, and Perspectives* (Charlotte, NC: Information Age Publishing, 2010).

58. Evans, *The Hope for American School Reform*, 165.

59. Ronald W. Evans, "National Security Trumps Social Progress: The Era of the New Social Studies in Retrospect," in Stern, *The New Social Studies*, 1–37.

60. "Announcement for Project Social Studies," *Social Education*, 26 (1962): 300.

61. Evans, *The Social Studies Wars*, 127.

62. Edwin P. Fenton and John M. Good, "Project Social Studies: A Progress Report," *Social Education* 29, no. 4 (1965): 206–8.

63. See Evans, *The Hope for American School Reform*, 216.

64. Evans, *The Tragedy of American School Reform*, 203.

65. Evans, *The Social Studies Wars*, 129.

66. Edwin Fenton, *The New Social Studies* (New York: Holt, Rinehart, and Winston, 1967).

67. For a history and analysis of MACOS, see Evans, *The Tragedy of American School Reform*, 99–147; Evans, *The Hope for American School Reform*, 153–57; Evans, *The Social Studies Wars*, 142–44.

68. Charles Laird, *Through These Eyes* (Watertown, MA: Documentary Educational

Resources, 2003), DVD, http://www.nfb.ca/film/through_these_eyes/.

69. Peter B. Dow, *Schoolhouse Politics: Lessons from the Sputnik Era* (Cambridge, MA: Harvard University Press, 1991). Dow was the MACOS Project Director.

70. Jerome Bruner, "The Emergence of Man: An Elementary Course of Study" (undated working draft), 1. Cited in Dow, *Schoolhouse Politics*, 80. The materials used the word man rather than human.

71. Dow, *Schoolhouse Politics*, 80.

72. Barbara B. Herzstein, interview by Anita Mischler, 14 March 1970. Cited in Dow, *Schoolhouse Politics*, 153.

73. Laird, "Through These Eyes."

74. Dow, *Schoolhouse Politics*, 135.

75. Chara Haeussler Bohan and Patricia Randolph, "The Social Studies Curriculum in Atlanta Public Schools during the Desegregation Era," *Theory and Research in Social Education* 37, no. 4 (2009): 543–69.

76. G. Sidney Lester, David J. Bond, and Gary A. Knox, *A Social Studies Curriculum for the Modern World: The Marin Social Studies Project* (Corte Madera, CA: Marin Social Studies Project, 1971), 6. Cited in Dow, *Schoolhouse Politics*, 135.

77. Dow, *Schoolhouse Politics*, 150–51; Evans, *The Tragedy of American School Reform*, 114–47. Evans argues the attacks on MACOS were part of the larger controversy on academic freedom.

78. Dow, *Schoolhouse Politics*, 210.

79. "History in the Schools: Report of the Study Committee, Organization of American Historians," 4–5, folder Executive Committee Meetings, Minutes and Reports 1966–7, no. 5 2007–213/337, NCSS Records.

80. Irving Morrissett, ed., *Concepts and Structure in the New Social Science Curricula* (New York: Holt, Rinehart and Winston, 1967).

81. Lawrence Senesh, *Our Working World* (Chicago: Science Research Associates, 1964); Lawrence Senesh, *Our Working World: Cities at Work* (Chicago: Science Research Associates, 1967); Lawrence Senesh, *Our Working World: Families: Problems Book* (Chicago: Science Research Associates, 1973).

82. Gill, "Paul R. Hanna," 151.

83. Richard Gross, "The Status of the Social Studies in the Public Schools of the United States: Facts and Impressions of a National Survey" (paper presented at the Annual Meeting of the National Council for the Social Studies (Washington, DC, November 4–7, 1976), 24.

84. Rosemary Ann Blanchard, Lawrence Senesh, and Sheryll Patterson-Black, "The Organic Social Studies Curriculum and the 1994 NCSS Standards: A Model for Linking the Community and the World," *The Social Studies* 90, no. 2 (1999): 63–67.

85. "History in the Schools: Report of the Study Committee, Organization of American Historians," 4–5.

86. "History in the Schools: Report of the Study Committee, Organization of American Historians."

87. "Political Science Course Content Improvement Project for Elementary and Secondary Schools," n.d., folder NSF Summer Programs and Printed Materials

1961–62, 2007–213 313, NCSS Records.

88. Gill, "Paul R. Hanna," 74.

89. Hanna, interview by Martin Gill, 34.

90. Hanna, interview by Martin Gill, 35.

91. "Curriculum Planning in American Schools: The Social Studies," November, 1958, folder 37, box 3, series 7, NCSS Records.

92. "Curriculum Planning in American Schools," 21.

93. Louis J. Herbert and William Murphy, eds., *Structure in the Social Studies* (Washington, DC: National Council for the Social Studies, 1968).

94. Charles R. Keller, "Needed: Revolution in the Social Studies," in Herbert and Murphy, *Structure in the Social Studies*, 1–8.

95. Ralph W. Cordier, "Preface," in Herbert and Murphy, *Structure in the Social Studies*, v.

96. Paul R. Hanna, "Revising the Social Studies," in Herbert and Murphy, *Structure in the Social Studies*, 27. In the 1960s, Hanna included the disciplines in his model of the expanding communities. See Chapter 4.

97. Paul Hanna, "Revising the Social Studies."

98. Evans, *The Tragedy of American School Reform*, 44; Evans, *The Social Studies Wars*, 136.

99. See Evans, *The Tragedy of American School Reform*, 44–46, for a description of the 1971 NCSS Guidelines. Gary Manson, Gerald Marker, Anna Ochoa, and Jan Tucker were task force members.

100. National Council for the Social Studies, *Social Studies Curriculum Guidelines: Position Statement* (Washington, DC: National Council for the Social Studies, 1971), 6 (emphasis in the original).

101. National Council for the Social Studies, *Social Studies Curriculum Guidelines*, 7.

102. National Council for the Social Studies, *Social Studies Curriculum Guidelines*, 17.

103. National Council for the Social Studies, *Social Studies Curriculum Guidelines*, 25.

104. National Council for the Social Studies, *Social Studies Curriculum Guidelines*, 15.

105. Gerald W. Marker to Shirley Engle, October 8, 1970, folder: Executive Committee Meetings 1970 11/22–25/70, 8, 2007–213 337, NCSS Records.

106. National Council for the Social Studies, *Social Studies Curriculum Guidelines*, 9.

107. Evans, *The Tragedy of American School Reform*, 44–45.

108. Lee, *Teaching Social Studies*.

109. Lee, *Teaching Social Studies*, 8.

110. Lee, *Teaching Social Studies*, 9.

111. John Jarolimek and Huber M. Walsh, *Readings for Social Studies in Elementary Education*, 3rd ed. (New York: Macmillan, 1974).

112. Anna Ochoa and Gary A. Manson, "Social Issues, Social Action, and the Social Studies," in Jarolimek and Walsh, *Readings for Social Studies in Elementary Education*, 425–31.

113. Donald W. Oliver and James P. Shaver, *Teaching Public Issues in the High School* (Boston: Houghton Mifflin, 1966). Also see Chara Haussler Bohan and Joseph R. Feinberg, "The Contributions of Donald Oliver, Fred Newmann, and James

Shaver to the Harvard Social Studies Project," in Stern, *The New Social Studies*, 111–32; Evans, *The Hope for American School Reform*, 157–61.

114.   Ochoa and Manson, "Social Issues," 427.

115.   Ochoa and Manson, "Social Issues," 430.

116.   Ochoa and Manson, "Social Issues," 428.

117.   Bruner, *The Process of Education*, 20.

118.   See Jane Bernard-Powers, "Composing Her Life: Hilda Taba and Social Studies History," in Crocco and Davis, *Bending the Future to Their Will*, 185–206; Jack R. Fraenkel, "Hilda Taba's Contributions to Social Studies Education," *Social Education* 56, no. 3 (1992): 172–78.

119.   Fraenkel, "Hilda Taba's Contributions," 172.

120.   Hilda Taba, *Teacher's Handbook for Elementary Social Studies* (Palo Alto, CA: Addison-Wesley, 1967).

121.   Fraenkel, "Hilda Taba's Contributions," 177.

122.   Gross, "The Status of the Social Studies in the Public Schools," 24.

123.   Walter Parker, *Social Studies in Elementary Education*, 14th ed. (Boston: Allyn & Bacon, 2011).

124.   Brophy, Alleman, and Halvorsen, *Powerful Social Studies*.

125.   Oliver and Shaver, *Teaching Public Issues*; Louis E. Raths, Merrill Harmin, and Sidney B. Simon, *Values and Teaching: Working with Values in the Classroom* (Columbus, OH: C. E. Merrill Books, 1966).

126.   Sidney B. Simon, Leland W. Howe, and Howard Kirschenbaum, *Values Clarification: A Handbook of Practical Strategies for Teachers and Students* (New York: Hart, 1972).

127.   Charles Silberman, *Crisis in the Classroom: The Remaking of American Education* (New York: Random House, 1970). For accounts of open education, see Evans, *The Tragedy of American School Reform*, 60–64; Diane Ravitch, *The Troubled Crusade: American Education 1945–1980* (New York: Basic Books, 1983), 239–51.

128.   Roland S. Barth, *Open Education and the American School* (New York: Agathon Press, 1972).

129.   Evelyn Berger and Bonnie A. Winters, *Social Studies in the Open Classroom: A Practical Guide* (New York: Teachers College, 1973), 5. See also Shirley H. Engle and Wilma S. Longstreet, *A Design for Social Education in the Open Curriculum* (New York: Harper and Row, 1972); Vito Perrone and Lowell Thompson, "Social Studies in the Open Classroom," *Social Education* 36, no. 4 (April 1972): 460–64.

130.   Theodor Schuctat, *Informal Education: 'Open Classroom' Provokes Change, Controversy* (Arlington, VA: National School Public Relations Association, 1972), 4.

131.   Evans, *The Tragedy of American School Reform*, 29.

132.   James A. Banks, "Multicultural Education: Historical Development, Dimensions, and Practice," in *Handbook of Research on Multicultural Education*, ed. James A. Banks and Cherry McGee Banks, 3–24 (New York: Macmillan Publishing, 1995).

133.   "Overview of the 1974 Ethnic Heritage Program," folder Correspondence

Information Re: Meetings Advisory Council 1975–76, 2007–213 57, NCSS Records.

134. Center for Ethnic Studies, "Kindergarten Social Studies Unit," 2007–213 362, NCSS Records.

135. "Social Studies Curriculum Materials 1969, 48th Annual Meeting, National Council for the Social Studies," folder Annual Meeting 1968, Miscellaneous Printed Materials, 2007–213 222, NCSS Records.

136. Department of Social Studies, Detroit Public Schools, "Bibliography on Afro-American History and Culture," *Social Education* 33, no. 4 (April 1969): 447–61.

137. Mirel, *The Rise and Fall*, 306–7.

138. See James A. Banks, "Teaching Ethnic Studies: Concepts and Strategies," *National Council for the Social Studies 43rd Yearbook* (Washington, DC: National Council for the Social Studies, 1973).

139. Carlos E. Cortes, Geneva Gay, Rocard L. Garcia, and Anna S. Ochoa were also on the Task Force. See National Council for the Social Studies, *Curriculum Guidelines for Multiethnic Education: Position Statement* (Arlington, VA: National Council for the Social Studies, 1976).

140. National Council for the Social Studies, *Curriculum Guidelines*, 9.

141. For example, the third edition of Dorothy Skeel's popular social studies methods textbook had expanded coverage of cultural pluralism and a new curricular unit on Africa. Dorothy J. Skeel, *The Challenge of Teaching Social Studies in the Elementary School*, 3rd ed. (Pacific Palisades, CA: Goodyear, 1979).

142. Ravitch, "A Brief History of Social Studies."

143. John Jarolimek, "The Social Studies: An Overview," in *The Social Studies: Eightieth Yearbook for the National Society for the Study of Education*, ed. Howard D. Mehlinger and O. L. Davis Jr., 3–18 (Chicago: The University of Chicago Press, 1981).

144. Preston, *Teaching Social Studies*. Based on informal school district surveys in Montana and California, Richard Gross reported that more than 70 percent of K–4 teachers taught little or no social studies "in the current back to basics mania." Elementary teachers in two Colorado districts taught social studies on average one hour a week. Gross, "The Status of the Social Studies," 9.

145. Keller, "Needed: Revolution in the Social Studies."

146. National Commission on Social Studies in the Schools, *Charting a Course: Social Studies for the 21st Century* (Washington, DC: National Commission on Social Studies in the Schools, 1989), v–vi.

147. Jarolimek, "The Social Studies: An Overview."

Chapter 6. Social Studies at Risk: The Eras of Educational Excellence and Accountability

1. For example, see Evans, *The Social Studies Wars*, 166–68; Linda Symcox, *Whose History? The Struggle for National Standards in American Classrooms* (New York: Teachers College Press, 2002). After the U.S. Senate rejected the standards in a 99–1 vote, the standards were revised.

2. Evans, *The Tragedy of American School Reform*, 160–63; Hertzberg, *Social Studies Reform*; Stephen J. Thornton and Keith C. Barton, "Can History Stand Alone? Drawbacks and Blind Spots of a 'Disciplinary' Curriculum," *Teachers College Record* 112, no. 9 (2010): 2471–95.

3. National Commission on Excellence in Education, *A Nation at Risk: The Imperative for Educational Reform: A Report to the Nation and the Secretary of Education, United States Department of Education* (Washington, DC: National Commission on Excellence in Education, 1983).

4. National Commission on Excellence in Education, *A Nation at Risk*, 9.

5. See Lawrence C. Stedman and Marshall S. Smith, "Weak Arguments, Poor Data, Simplistic Recommendations," in *The Great School Debate: Which Way for American Education?* ed. Beatrice Gross and Ronald Gross, 83–105 (New York: Simon and Schuster, 1985); Daniel Tanner, "A Nation 'Truly' at Risk," *Phi Delta Kappan* 75, no. 4 (1993): 288–97; Maris A. Vinovskis, *From A Nation at Risk to No Child Left Behind* (New York: Teachers College Press, 2009), 16–17.

6. Ben Brodinsky, "Back to the Basics: The Movement and Its Meaning," *Phi Delta Kappan* 58, no. 7 (March 1977): 522.

7. William J. Bennett, *First Lessons: A Report on Elementary Education in America* (Washington, DC: U.S. Department of Education, 1986), 1, 29.

8. Bennett, *First Lessons*, 30.

9. Bennett, *First Lessons*, 29.

10. Bennett, *First Lessons*, 31.

11. John I. Goodlad, *A Place Called School* (New York: McGraw Hill, 1984), 210.

12. Goodlad, *A Place Called School*, 213.

13. Kieran Egan, "Social Studies and the Erosion of Education," *Curriculum Inquiry* 13, no. 2 (1983): 195–214.

14. Egan, "Social Studies," 195–214.

15. Ravitch, "Tot Sociology."

16. Thornton and Barton, "Can History Stand Alone?"

17. See Hertzberg, *Social Studies Reform*; Social Science Education Consortium, and Project SPAN, *The Current State of Social Studies: A Report of Project SPAN* (Boulder, CO: Social Science Education Consortium, 1982); Social Science Education Consortium, and Project SPAN, *The Future of Social Studies: A Report and Summary of Project SPAN* (Boulder, CO: Social Science Education Consortium, 1982); Douglas P. Superka and Sharryl Hawke, *Social Roles: A Focus for Social Studies in the 1980s* (Boulder, CO: Social Science Education Consortium, 1982). The SSEC, working independently from the NCSS, played a key role in disseminating materials about the new social studies in the 1960s.

18. Social Science Education Consortium, and Project SPAN, *The Current State of Social Studies*, 84.

19. Social Science Education Consortium, and Project SPAN, *The Future of Social Studies*, 54–57.

20. National Commission on Social Studies in the Schools, *Charting a Course: Social Studies for the 21st Century* (Washington, DC: National Commission on Social

Studies in the Schools, 1989).

21. National Commission on Social Studies in the Schools, *Charting a Course*, 7.

22. National Commission on Social Studies in the Schools, *Charting a Course*, 25.

23. National Commission on Social Studies in the Schools, *Charting a Course*, 25.

24. National Commission on Social Studies in the Schools, *Charting a Course*, 25.

25. National Council for the Social Studies, "Social Studies for Early Childhood and Elementary School Children: Preparing for the 21st Century," *Social Education* 53, no. 1 (1989): 14–23.

26. National Council for the Social Studies, "Social Studies for Early Childhood," 15.

27. Diane Ravitch, "The Search for Order and the Rejection of Conformity: Standards in American Education," in *Learning from the Past: What History Teaches Us about School Reform*, ed. Diane Ravitch and Maris A. Vinovskis, 167–90 (Baltimore: The Johns Hopkins University Press, 1995).

28. Diane Ravitch, *National Standards in American Education: A Citizen's Guide* (Washington, DC: Brookings Institution Press, 1995); Vinovskis, *From A Nation at Risk*, 125.

29. National Council on Education Standards and Testing, *Raising Standards for American Education* (Washington, DC: U.S. Government Printing Office, 1992).

30. Vinovskis, *From A Nation at Risk*, 125.

31. Gary B. Nash, Charlotte Crabtree, and Ross E. Dunn, *History on Trial: Culture Wars and the Teaching of the Past* (New York: A. A. Knopf, 1997), 157; Ravitch, *National Standards in American Education*; Vinovskis, *From A Nation at Risk*, 32–55, 124–28.

32. Stanley M. Elam and Alec M. Gallup, "The 21st Annual Phi Delta Kappa/ Gallup Poll of the Public's Attitude Toward the Public Schools," *Phi Delta Kappan* 71, no. 1 (September 1989): 41–54.

33. Vinovskis, *From A Nation at Risk*, 53, 125.

34. *Goals 2000: Educate America Act of 1994*, Public Law 103–227, 103rd Cong., (March 31, 1994) (emphasis added).

35. In December 2001, the U.S. Congress eliminated funding for Goals 2000. However, many of the Goals 2000 initiatives appeared in NCLB, enacted in 2002.

36. Center for Civic Education, *National Standards for Civics and Government* (Calabasas, CA: Center For Civic Education, 1994); National Center for History in the Schools, *National Standards for History, Basic Edition* (Los Angeles: University of California, 1996); National Council for Geographic Education, *Geography for Life: National Geography Standards* (Washington, DC: National Geography Research and Exploration, 1994); National Council on Economic Education, *Voluntary National Content Standards in Economics* (New York: National Council on Economic Education, 1997); National Council on Economic Education, *Voluntary National Content Standards in Economics*, 2nd ed. (New York: National Council on Economic Education, 2010).

37. National Center for History in the Schools, *National Standards for History*, 4.

38. Center for Civic Education, *National Standards for Civics and Government*, 15.

39. National Council on Economic Education, *Voluntary National Content Standards*, 11.
40. National Council for Geographic Education, *Geography for Life*.
41. National Center for History in the Schools, *National Standards for History*, 4.
42. National Center for History in the Schools, *National Standards for History*, 14–16.
43. National Center for History in the Schools, *National Standards for History*.
44. See Evans, *The Social Studies Wars*, 166–68; Nash, Crabtree, and Dunn, *History on Trial*; Symcox, *Whose History?*
45. National Council for the Social Studies, *Curriculum Standards for Social Studies: Expectations of Excellence* (Washington, DC: National Council for the Social Studies, 1994); National Council for the Social Studies, *National Curriculum Standards for Social Studies: A Framework for Teaching, Learning, and Assessment.* (Silver Spring, MD: National Council for the Social Studies, 2010).
46. National Council for the Social Studies, *National Curriculum Standards for Social Studies*.
47. National Council for the Social Studies, "A Vision of Powerful Teaching and Learning in the Social Studies: Building Social Understanding and Civic Efficacy," *Social Education*, 57, no. 5 (1993): 213–22.
48. Fred Newmann, "Qualities of Thoughtful Social Studies Classes: An Empirical Profile," *Journal of Curriculum Studies* 22 (1990): 443–61.
49. National Council for the Social Studies, "A Vision of Powerful Teaching and Learning in the Social Studies: Building Effective Citizens," *Social Education* 72, no. 5 (2008): 277–80.
50. National Council for the Social Studies, *Powerful and Authentic Social Studies* (Washington, DC: National Council for the Social Studies, 2000).
51. Michigan Department of Education, *Grade Level Content Expectations*, 7.
52. Michigan Department of Education, *Grade Level Content Expectations*, 2.
53. California was one of the first states to produce a set of learning expectations for social studies. California State Board of Education, *History-Social Science Framework for California Public Schools* (Sacramento, CA: California Department of Education, 1988).
54. California State Board of Education, *History-Social Science Content Standards for California Public Schools* (Sacramento, CA: California Department of Education, 2005); Virginia Department of Education, *History and Social Science Standards of Learning for Virginia Public Schools* (Richmond, VA: Virginia Department of Education, 2008), v. See also Stephanie van Hover, David Hicks, Jeremy Stoddard, and Melissa Lisanti, "From a Roar to a Murmur: Virginia's History & Social Science Standards, 1995–2009," *Theory and Research in Social Education* 38, no. 1 (2010): 80–113.
55. Massachusetts Department of Education, *Massachusetts History and Social Science Curriculum Framework* (Malden, MA: Massachusetts Department of Education, 2003), 5.
56. Massachusetts Department of Education, *Massachusetts History and Social Science*, 16.
57. *No Child Left Behind Act of 2001*; Vinovskis, *From A Nation at Risk*, 172.
58. Fitchett and Heafner, "A National Perspective," 119; Phillip J. VanFossen,

"'Reading and Math Take So Much of the Time...': An Overview of Social Studies Instruction in Elementary Classrooms in Indiana," *Theory and Research in Social Education* 33, no. 3 (2005): 376–403; Kenneth E. Vogler, Timothy Lintner, George B. Lipscomb, Herman Knopf, Tina L. Heafner, and Tracy C. Rock, "Getting off the Back Burner: Impact of Testing Elementary Social Studies as Part of a State-Mandated Accountability Program," *Journal of Social Studies Research* 31, no. 2 (2007): 20–34.

59.   National Council for the Social Studies, "Powerful and Purposeful Teaching."

60.   Jere Brophy, *Teaching (Educational Practices Series No. 1)* (Geneva: International Bureau of Education, 1999).

61.   Jere Brophy, "Classroom Organization and Management," *Elementary School Journal* 83 (1983): 265–85.

62.   Eric M. Camburn and Seong Won Han, "Two Decades of Generalizable Evidence on U.S. Instruction from National Surveys," *Teachers College Record* 113, no. 3 (2011): 561–610; Jennifer McMurren, *Choices, Changes, and Challenges: Curriculum and Instruction in the NCLB Era* (Washington, DC: Center on Education Policy, 2007): 1, 7; National Center for Education Statistics, *The Nation's Report Card: Civics 2010 (NCES 2011–466)* (Washington, DC: Institute of Education Sciences, U.S. Department of Education, 2011); National Center for Education Statistics, *The Nation's Report Card: U.S. History 2010 (NCES 2011–468)* (Washington, DC: Institute of Education Sciences, U.S. Department of Education, 2011).

63.   *No Child Left Behind Act of 2001*, Subpart 3, Civic Education.

64.   Joellen Killion, "What Works in the Middle: Results-Based Staff Development," http://www.learningforward.org/midbook/index.cfm.

65.   Rick Shenkman, "O.A.H. 2009: Sam Wineburg Dares to Ask If the Teaching American History Program Is a Boondoggle," *History News Network*, April 19, 2009, http://hnn.us/articles/76806.html.

66.   *No Child Left Behind Act of 2001*, Sec. 2351.1. See Fitchett and Heafner, "A National Perspective," 119.

67.   Fitchett and Heafner, "A National Perspective."

68.   National Council for the Social Studies, *National Curriculum Standards for Social Studies*, 12.

69.   National Governors Association Center for Best Practices, Council of Chief State School Officers, *Common Core State Standards for English Language Arts & Literacy in History/Social Studies, Science, and Technical Subjects* (Washington, DC: National Governors Association Center for Best Practices, Council of Chief State School Officers, 2010).

70.   S. G. Grant, Kathy Swan, and John Lee, "Lurching Toward Coherence: An Episodic History of Curriculum and Standards Development in Social Studies" (paper presented at the annual meeting of the American Educational Research Association, Vancouver Canada, April 15, 2012), 14–15.

71.   Council of Chief State Officers, "Social Studies Assessment, Curriculum, and Instruction (SSACI), http://www.ccsso.org/Resources/Programs/Social_Studies _Assessment_Curriculum_and_Instruction_%28SSACI%29.html; Kathy Swan,

telephone conversation with author, June 28, 2012.

72. Grant, Swan, and Lee, "Lurching Toward Coherence," 14–15.

73. Kathy Swan, telephone conversation with author, June 28, 2012.

74. Grant, Swan, and Lee, "Lurching Toward Coherence."

75. Swan, e-mail message to author, June 28, 2012.

76. Brophy, "The De Facto National Curriculum."

77. Kieran Egan, "What Children Know Best," *Social Education* 43, no. 2 (1979): 130–34.

78. Frazee and Ayers, "Garbage In, Garbage Out."

79. National Council for the Social Studies, "Powerful and Purposeful Teaching and Learning in Elementary School Social Studies," *Social Education* 73, no. 5 (2009): 252–54.

80. Janet Alleman and Jere Brophy, *Social Studies Excursions, K–3. Book One: Powerful Units on Food, Clothing, and Shelter* (Portsmouth, NH: Heinemann, 2001); Janet Alleman and Jere Brophy, *Social Studies Excursions, K–3. Book Two: Powerful Units on Communication, Transportation, and Family Living* (Portsmouth, NH: Heinemann, 2002); Janet Alleman and Jere Brophy, *Social Studies Excursions, K–3. Book Three: Powerful Units on Childhood, Money, and Government* (Portsmouth, NH: Heinemann, 2003).

81. Brophy and Alleman have written extensively about cultural universals. For example, see Jere Brophy and Jan Alleman, *Children's Thinking about Cultural Universals* (Mahwah, NJ: Erlbaum, 2005); Brophy and Alleman, "Early Elementary Social Studies," in Levstik and Tyson, *Handbook of Research*, 33–49; Jere Brophy and Janet Alleman, "Primary-Grade Students' Knowledge and Thinking About Families," *Journal of Social Studies Research* 29, no. 1 (2005): 18–22; Jere Brophy and Janet Alleman, "Primary Grade Students' Knowledge and Thinking about Transportation," *Theory and Research in Social Education* 33, no. 2 (2005): 218–43; Jere Brophy, Janet Alleman, and Carolyn O'Mahony, "Primary-Grade Students' Knowledge and Thinking about Food Production and the Origins of Common Foods," *Theory and Research in Social Education* 31, no. 1 (2003): 9–39.

82. Brophy and Alleman, "A Reconceptualized Rationale."

83. Margit McGuire and Bronwyn Cole, "Using Narrative to Enhance Learning through Storypath," in *Making a Difference: Revitalizing Elementary Social Studies* NCSS Bulletin 109, ed. Margit McGuire and Bronwyn Cole, 25–37 (Silver Spring, MD: National Council for the Social Studies, 2010).

84. McGuire and Cole, "Using Narrative to Enhance Learning," 37.

85. Marilyn Boyle-Baise, Leana McClain, and Sarah Montgomery, "Living One's Civics," in McGuire and Cole, *Making a Difference*, 37–49; Marilynne Boyle-Baise and Jack Zevin, *Young Citizens of the World: Teaching Elementary Social Studies through Civic Engagement* (New York: Routledge, 2009).

86. Boyle-Baise, McClain, and Montgomery, "Living One's Civics"; Arthur W. Dunn, *The Social Studies in Secondary Education: Report of the Committee on Social Studies of the Commission on the Reorganization of Secondary Education* (Washington, DC: National Education Association, 1916).

87. Rahima Wade, "Beyond Expanding Horizons: New Curriculum Directions for Elementary Social Studies," *The Elementary School Journal* 103, no. 2 (2002), 115–30. Rahima Wade, ed., *Community Action Rooted in History: The CiviConnections Model of Service-Learning* (Silver Spring, MD: National Council for the Social Studies, 2007).

88. National Service-Learning Cooperative, *Essential Elements of Service-Learning* (St. Paul, MN: National Youth Leadership Council, 1998).

89. Hirsch Jr., *Cultural Literacy.*

90. Core Knowledge Foundation, *Core Knowledge Sequence: Content Guidelines for Grades K–8* (Charlottesville, VA: Core Knowledge Foundation, 1999).

91. Anna M. Phillips, "Nonfiction Curriculum Enhanced Reading Skills, Study Finds," *The New York Times*, March 11, 2012.

92. Lisa Delpit, *Other People's Children: Cultural Conflict in the Classroom* (New York: New Press, 1995).

93. Fred Newmann, "Another View of Cultural Literacy: Go for Depth," *Social Education* 52, no. 6 (1988): 432, 434–36, 438.

94. Brophy and Alleman, "A Reconceptualized Rationale."

95. E. D. Hirsch Jr., Joseph F. Kett, and James S. Trefil, *The Dictionary of Cultural Literacy* (Boston: Houghton Mifflin, 1993); E. D. Hirsch Jr., Joseph F. Kett, and James S. Trefil, *The New Dictionary of Cultural Literacy* (Boston: Houghton Mifflin, 2002).

96. Marilyn L. Kourilsky, *KinderEconomy+: A Multidisciplinary Learning Society for Primary Grades* (New York: Joint Council on Economic Education, 1992).

97. Marilyn Kourilsky and Michael Ballard-Campbell, "Mini-Society: An Individualized Social Studies Program for Children of Low, Middle, and High Ability," *Social Studies* 75, no. 5 (1984): 224–28; Ellen Ortiz and Marilyn Kourilsky, "The Mini-Society and Mathematical Reasoning: An Explanatory Study," *Social Studies Review* 24, no. 2 (1985): 37–45.

98. Paulo Freire, *Pedagogy of the Oppressed* (New York: Seabury Press, 1970).

99. See Bill Bigelow, *A People's History for the Classroom* (Milwaukee, WI: Rethinking Schools, 2008); Bigelow, Christensen, Karp, Miner, and Peterson, *Rethinking Our Classrooms*; Bigelow and Peterson, *Rethinking Columbus.*

100. Wade, *Social Studies for Social Justice.*

101. Wade, *Social Studies for Social Justice*, 33.

102. National Commission on Social Studies in the Schools, *Charting a Course*, vi.

103. Keith C. Barton, "Introduction," in Barton, *Research Methods in Social Studies Education*, 1–10.

104. Keith C. Barton and Linda Levstik, "'Back When God Was Around and Everything': Elementary Children's Understanding of Historical Time," *American Educational Research Journal* 33, no. 2 (1996): 419–54.

105. Bruce VanSledright, *In Search of America's Past: Learning to Read History in Elementary School* (New York: Teachers College Press, 2002).

106. Alleman and Brophy, *Children's Thinking about Cultural Universals.*

107. Brophy and Alleman, "Early Elementary Social Studies." For research on

teachers' use of social studies programs, see Richard Prawat, Jere Brophy, and Susan McMahon, *Experts' Views on the Elementary Social Studies Curriculum: Visions of the Ideal and Critique of Current Practice, Series No. 14-A* (East Lansing, MI: The Center for the Learning and Teaching of Elementary Subjects, Institute for Research on Teaching, 1990).

108. The Iowa Tests of Basic Skills and the TerraNova include assessments of elementary social studies, but the assessments are not generally aligned with state content expectations.

109. National Council for the Social Studies, "Social Studies for Early Childhood." The position was adopted by NCSS in 1998 and published in 1999.

110. There is a "general knowledge and science" assessment for grades K–1 that includes some social studies content, but there are no social studies achievement scores in the third, fifth, and eighth grades when tests in reading, mathematics, and science are administered. For more information, see National Center for Education Statistics, *User's Guide to the Longitudinal Kindergarten–First Grade Public-Use Data File NCES 2002–149* (Washington, DC: National Center for Education Statistics, 2002).

111. Jarolimek, "The Social Studies."

Conclusion. Opportunities for Twenty-First-Century Elementary Social Studies

1. United States Bureau of Education, *The Social Studies in Secondary Education*, 9.

2. National Council for the Social Studies, *Social Studies Curriculum Guidelines*, 7.

3. National Council for the Social Studies, *Curriculum Standards for Social Studies;* National Council for the Social Studies, *National Curriculum Standards for Social Studies.*

4. Eric M. Camburn and Seong W. Han, "Two Decades of Generalizable Evidence on U.S. Instruction from National Surveys," *Teachers College Record* 113, no. 3 (2011): 561–610; Jack Jennings and Diane S. Rentner, "Ten Big Effects of the No Child Left Behind Act on Public Schools," *Phi Delta Kappan* 88, no. 1 (2006): 110–13.

5. National Center for Education Statistics, *The Nation's Report Card: Civics 2010 (NCES2011–466)* (Washington, DC: Institute of Education Sciences, U.S. Department of Education, 2011). National Center for Education Statistics, *The Nation's Report Card U.S. History 2010 (NCES 2011–468)* (Washington, DC: Institute of Education Sciences, U.S. Department of Education, 2011).

6. Meira Levinson, "The Civic Empowerment Gap: Defining the Problem and Locating Solutions," in *Handbook of Research on Civic Engagement,* ed. Lonnie Sherrod, Judith Torney-Purta, and Constance A. Flanagan, 331–61 (Hoboken, NJ: John Wiley & Sons, 2010).

7. Michener, *The Future of the Social Studies.*

8. Nelson, "Directionless from Birth."

9. Bestor, *Educational Wastelands*, 28.

10. Kliebard, *The Struggle*, 245.

11. See Stephen Thornton, *Teaching Social Studies that Matters: Curriculum for Active Learning* (New York: Teachers College Press, 2005); Brophy and Alleman, "Early Elementary Social Studies."

12. Thornton, *Teaching Social Studies that Matters.*

13. Brophy and Alleman, "Early Elementary Social Studies," 36.

14. National Governors Association Center for Best Practices, Council of Chief State School Officers, *Common Core State Standards for English Language Arts.*

15. Anne-Lise Halvorsen, Nell K. Duke, Kristy A. Brugar, Meghan K. Block, Stephanie L. Strachan, Meghan B. Berka, and Jason M. Brown, "Narrowing the Achievement Gap in Second-Grade Social Studies and Content Area Literacy: The Promise of a Project-Based Approach," *Theory and Research in Social Education* 40, no. 2 (2012): 198–229.

16. Marilynne Boyle-Baise, Ming-Chu Hsu, Shaun Johnson, Stephanie C. Serriere, and Dorshell Stewart, "Putting Reading First: Teaching Social Studies in the Elementary Classroom," *Theory and Research in Social Education* 36, no. 3 (2008): 233–55.

17. Janet Alleman and Jere Brophy, "Effective Integration of Social Studies and Literacy," in McGuire and Cole, *Making a Difference,* 51–66.

18. Alleman and Brophy, "Effective Integration."

Index

HISTORY OF SCHOOLS & SCHOOLING

THIS SERIES EXPLORES THE HISTORY OF SCHOOLS AND SCHOOLING in the United States and other countries. Books in this series examine the historical development of schools and educational processes, with special emphasis on issues of educational policy, curriculum and pedagogy, as well as issues relating to race, class, gender, and ethnicity. Special emphasis will be placed on the lessons to be learned from the past for contemporary educational reform and policy. Although the series will publish books related to education in the broadest societal and cultural context, it especially seeks books on the history of specific schools and on the lives of educational leaders and school founders.

For additional information about this series or for the submission of manuscripts, please contact the general editors:

Alan R. Sadovnik
Rutgers University-Newark
Education Dept.
155 Conklin Hall
175 University Avenue
Newark, NJ 07102

Susan F. Semel
The City College of New York, CUNY
138th Street and Convent Avenue
NAC 5/208
New York, NY 10031

To order other books in this series, please contact our Customer Service Department:

800-770-LANG (within the U.S.)
212-647-7706 (outside the U.S.)
212-647-7707 FAX

Or browse online by series at:

www.peterlang.com